The Naked Clansmen
on
Mull & Iona

1700-1860

Ian McPhee

Matador
9 Priory Business Park,
Wistow Road, Kibworth Beauchamp,
Leicestershire. LE8 0RX
Tel: 0116 279 2299
Email: books@troubador.co.uk
Web: www.troubador.co.uk/matador
Twitter: @matadorbooks

ISBN 978 1838591 489

British Library Cataloguing in Publication Data.
A catalogue record for this book is available from the British Library.

Printed and bound by CPI Group (UK) Ltd, Croydon, CR0 4YY

Matador is an imprint of Troubador Publishing Ltd

Cover Image:
A view from Beinn Chladan, which overlooks what used to be the Braighcreich
crofting community on Mull. It shows three stone ruins at the eastern end, the largest
of which was once home to a crofting family. The remnants of a barn and a byre can
be seen to the right of the former home. Between the ruins and the coastal headland,
darker patches of ground can be seen, that form part of a large peat field.

In memory of the
families who suffered
during the Highland potato famine

Contents

List of Illustrations

Abbreviations and Measurements

A&BC	Argyll and Bute Council
b.	Born
c.	Circa, meaning about
HIES	Highland and Island Emigration Society
NRS	National Records of Scotland
NLS	National Library of Scotland
NSA	New Statistical Account of Scotland
OPR	Old Parochial Register
OSA	Old Statistical Account of Scotland
PLIC	Poor Law Inquiry Commission
RAHS	Royal Australian Historical Society Journal and Proceedings
ROMHC	Ross of Mull Historical Centre

Measurements

1 inch (in)	=	2.54 centimetres (cm) or 25.4 millimetres (mm)
1 foot (ft)	=	30.48 centimetres
1 cubic foot	=	7.4805 gallons
1 yard (yd)	=	0.914 metre (m)
1 chain	=	66 feet, 22 yards or 100 links
1 mile (ml)	=	1.609 kilometres (km)
1 fathom	=	6 feet or 1.829 metres
1 acre (ac)	=	0.405 hectares (ha)
1 acre	=	10 square chains
1 acre	=	4 roods
1 rood	=	40 perches or ¼ acre
1 square mile	=	2.59 square kilometres (sq km)
1 square mile	=	640 acres
1 ounce (oz)	=	28 grams (g)
16 ounces (oz)	=	1 pound (lb)
1 pound (lb)	=	0.454 kilograms (kg)
1 ton (t)	~	1 tonne (t)
1 boll	~	6 bushels; of meal about 140 lbs (63.5 kg)
1 shilling (s)	=	12 pence (d)
1 pound (£)	=	20 shillings (s)

Glossary and Explanations

Acre	a Scotch acre is a little larger than 1¼ English acres
Athol-brose	mixture of whisky and honey
Bailie	magistrate or court officer
Bannock	thick round flat cake usually made from oatmeal
Barn	a building to store hay, grain or farm supplies
Bere	four-rowed barley
Boll	dry measure of varying capacity according to product and locality
Bothy	common cottage for farm workers
Bowman	share farming tenant working for a tacksman
Brae	a hill, hilly upland, slope or brow
Brose	oatmeal plus boiling water or milk and a little salt (porridge)
Burn	stream
Byre	a building to house cattle
Car	horse-drawn wheel-less sled with 2 poles, dragged over ground
Chamberlain	business manager for the nobility; similar to an accountant
Charter	a grant of land made by the Crown or a feudal superior
Clachan	a small cluster of houses
Corn	in Scotland meant oats, in England generally meant grain
Cottar	a landless farm labourer
Covenanters	Presbyterianism supporters and those against arbitrary royal authority
Creel	wicker basket, also a peat basket often carried on the back
Croft	a small farm, often on marginal land, primarily for cultivation
Decreet	final judgement or decree from a court of law
Dirk	a short dagger carried by a Highlander
Dun	low hill or hill fort
Dyke	wall
Factor	an agent who managed property for a proprietor
Fale-dyke	wall built of sods
Fencibles	men, aged 16-60, capable of being called upon to join a home militia
Firth	a wide inlet of the sea or an estuary
Flit	to move from one location to another
Garron	small inferior work horse
Girnal	chest for holding meal or grain
Glebe	a ministers farm or land provided to him over and above his stipend
Grass-mail	rent for pasture
Heritable	able to be inherited
Heritor	a landowner; also one liable for the upkeep of a parish church

Indian meal	maize
Jacobites	supporters of exiled King James VII of Scotland and his heirs
Kail	colewort, also broth made of colewort and vegetables
Kirk	Presbyterian church and informal name for Church of Scotland
Laird	landed proprietor
Loch	lake
Lowlands	non Gaelic area, S.E. of a line from Dumbarton to Stonehaven
Machair	land between the sea and land proper; sandy soil, poor crop land
Mail-land	land unit of about 3 soums i.e. grazing for 3 cows or 15 sheep
Manse	home provided for a parish minister
March dyke	boundary wall between neighbouring farms
Martinmas	St. Martin's Day, 11th November
Meal	flour made from grain such as oats or barley
Merk	Scottish coin; 2/3 of a Scots pound or 13 and 1/3 pence Sterling
Merkland	land where a sovereign or proprietor received duty of one merk
Muileach	a native of the Isle of Mull
Mull	a promontory
Parish	a religious division within a county with own church and minister
Parochial	pertaining to a parish
Quern	a small hand operated stone grinding mill
Quoad sacra	a parish that only functions for religious matters
Ross	point of land jutting out into the sea
Runrig	where alternate ridges of a field are worked by different tenants
Shieling	temporary dwellings for those tending summer grazing areas
Soum	unit of grazing land sufficient to keep 1 cow or horse or 5 sheep
Stirk	a year old bullock
Sheriff	judicial and administrative officer
Sheriff Substitute	deputy sheriff
Tack	lease
Tacksman	a person of note with a lease over land or a gentleman farmer
Targe	a circular Scottish shield
Thirl	to bind a tenant by lease to grind his grain at a certain mill
Traigh	strand or flat piece of land bordering a body of water or shoreline
Vassal	tenant holding land under a lord or superior
Whig	a covenanter; a Presbyterian or dissenter from Church of Scotland
Whitsunday	White Sunday or Pentecost Sunday, the 7th Sunday after Easter

Acknowledgements

Some of the material provided in *The Naked Clansmen on Mull & Iona 1700-1860*, was provided by the Ross of Mull Historical Centre at Bunessan on Mull. The staff at the Centre do their utmost to assist all those interested in the history of their area. At the other end of the island, the Mull Museum has also been another source of information.

Mull residents Tim and Linda Dawson have helped me on numerous occasions over the years with local issues and information. At the most appropriate time of the year, Tim was able to take the photo that has been used for the cover of this book.

In Edinburgh, staff at both the National Records Office and National Library provided helpful assistance in locating important historical information for this book. Heraldic artist and calligrapher in the Court of the Lord Lyon, David Allan SUA, FSA, gave invaluable advice. Historian Bruce Bishop FSA, ASGRA, sourced documents from various archives that proved to be invaluable. Not only did Bruce locate those documents when I was unable to, he provided an interpretation without which they would have been almost meaningless. Bruce's contributions enhanced this publication significantly.

In 2006 I made a visit to the Argyll and Bute Council's archives at Lochgilphead to conduct research. Since that time, the archives have been transformed into a well organised resource. Librarian Jackie Davenport helped me retrieve some obscure but relevant information about the Argyll Estates from council records.

I am grateful to numerous authors for the wonderful books that have provided information about the Highlands and islands of Scotland. In particular, authors John MacCormick, E. Mairi MacArthur, Jo Currie, Charles Maclean and J Stewart Cameron, who have written books about Mull and Iona.

In Australia, graphic artist Steve Tortosa made a major contribution helping me overcome numerous text formatting problems with the InDesign computer programme used to write and publish this book. At short notice, Steve was always obliging and made himself available to help solve whatever problem was encountered. He also played a part in assisting me develop, present and improve numerous images in the book.

As she did in my first book, graphic artist Anna Blacka created the format of the book. Anna applied her considerable expertise to many images that appear in the following pages, assisted with proof-reading, indexing, and also prepared the book for publication. Others I am thankful to for assisting in my endeavour include Helen Pfann for identifying a number of improvements and for reviewing the book, Marilynne Dearn for several illustrations and mapping expert Jeff Madsen.

Finally, I am indebted to members of my immediate family, whose constructive criticism and suggestions on how to improve the text contributed immensely to a much better publication.

Preface

History is not only relevant to the dead, but to the living and the yet unborn.

In so many ways both Mull and Iona were, and still are, extraordinary places. My first visit to the islands was in 2003. Apart from the landscape, I was struck at the time by the large number of stone ruins that littered Mull which had once been the homes of local inhabitants during the 'Highland Clearances'. That term is used to denote the period between 1785 and 1860 during which thousands of tenants were displaced and evicted from Highland and island land in Scotland.

At the time of my visit, the Ross of Mull Historical Centre was operating from a small portable cabin on the side of the road leading out of Bunessan to Fionnphort. Conditions were cramped, but there was an infectious enthusiasm for all aspects pertaining to the history of the local area. One of those I was fortunate enough to meet and learn from at the Centre, was local historian Attie (Alasdair) MacKechnie.

Two years before my visit, the Centre had been awarded Heritage Lottery funding for a project called "Discover the Ross". Its aim was to establish walking trails and guide books for areas of historical and wildlife significance. After identifying a personal interest in the Braighcreich crofting community, it was my good fortune to participate with one of the Centre's staff to lay out concrete way markers down the length of the walking trail past the former crofts in that community. That participation fuelled my interest in the history of Mull and Iona during the Highland Clearances.

It soon became apparent that there was a paucity of information about many aspects of the crofting townships and the ordinary people who lived in them during the Clearances. It was not unusual for the aristocracy and the landed gentry of Scotland to leave behind a written record of their lives from court cases, land transactions and general correspondence for historians to follow. Relatively little was ever recorded about the lives of the ordinary people. Unfortunately, many gaps in the history of crofting communities like those on Mull and Iona remain.

Seeking historical information in Scotland is fraught with difficulties. Many documents suffer from their age, not to mention being hard to decipher. Records are scattered in national institutions, local council archives, church records and in private archives. Access is sometimes an insurmountable barrier. For those reasons, it was impossible to avoid relying on a number of secondary sources for some information.

Over the years I have been researching in Scotland, I have been dismayed how poorly some records are maintained and stored. Worse than dealing with poorly maintained or archived material, is finding that a source that had previously been accessed and noted by other writers, is no longer available, having been either lost, stolen or misplaced.

Unfortunately that was a situation I came across on more than one occasion during my search of official records.

The Duke of Argyll's files at Inveraray hold a bountiful quantity of information related to the past management of the vast Argyll Estates. Apart from restricted access and a lack of archiving, these files remain largely unpublished. The most significant publication to date has been the Argyll Estate Instructions Mull Morvern Tiree 1771-1805, by E. R. Creegan, published in 1964. It is a pity so much valuable historical information of such significance has not been made accessible to all.

Anyone researching and writing about Scottish history during the 1700s and 1800s will come across a great variation in the spelling of both place names and personal names. That can create a dilemma - which form of spelling to use and how to index those variations. I have endeavoured to be as consistent as possible throughout the text but some inconsistency has been unavoidable.

A great deal of the information contained in the following pages is applicable to other districts throughout the Highlands and islands of Scotland. Mull and Iona are microcosms of those areas. As such, the information pertaining to those two islands can give readers an insight into many aspects of Gaelic life and culture prior to the Improvement Era and to that during the Highland Clearances.

For reasons of practicality, personal interest and other limitations, this book concentrates on the Duke of Argyll's Estates on Mull and Iona. Fortunately, some aspects of life in those areas, especially during the 1800s, has been documented more so than many other places. The Argyll Estates were originally spread right across Mull, but after large areas were sold off, ended up occupying mainly the large Ross district of the island. For that reason and those mentioned previously, the Ross of Mull and to a lesser extent, the small island of Iona are central to this book.

I have been fortunate to have the opportunity to write about many of the issues that have intrigued me about life during the Highland Clearances on Mull and Iona. They include historical information about the management of the Argyll Estates, croft establishment, the effects of overpopulation, upheaval in the Presbyterian Church, the 1846 potato famine, famine relief, crofter evictions, the fishing industry, the demise of the small crofting communities and emigration.

To the best of my knowledge, some of the information presented in this book related to the famine years on Mull has not been published before. As such, in a small way, it can hopefully add to the available store of information about that era on the Duke of Argyll's Estate on Mull.

The Naked Clansmen on Mull & Iona 1700-1860 contains some genealogical material pertinent to the author. That information is used mainly to help emphasise the relevance of some historical occurrences, and highlight issues in some of the old records. Utilising that material also provides a continuous thread for this story about the Highland Clearances and helps humanise what occurred during that controversial period.

The clansmen and clanswomen who form the core of this true story are typical of those who suffered when the clan system declined and came to an end. This publication gives a basic description of the Highland way of life prior to the era of improvement, which ended their traditional way of living. It then follows the transition of people who were displaced by the introduction of Lowland sheep and agricultural land reform in the Highlands. Many of those people ended up in communities as either crofters or cottars. The lives of crofters and cottars is explained and viewed through the life and times of families who lived in a community at Creich on the Isle of Mull. I have sought to portray what has been discovered about them and their community in the historical context of the times.

People from the crofting communities on Mull and Iona, like thousands of other Highland Scots, were marginalised as a result of isolation, poverty and famine. Eventually many were evicted from their homes. Their plight, and what was done to prevent them from starving to death during the potato famine years, is explained in detail. To extricate themselves from grinding poverty and the necessity for famine relief, some were able to emigrate to places like Canada, USA, Australia and New Zealand unaided, while others could only do so with assistance. The role emigration played in their salvation is an important part of the Highland story in Scotland.

Producing any book about history is challenging. In my case, it has also been a rewarding privilege. I have learnt a great deal and been able to answer numerous questions that have never been explained satisfactorily or answered at all in many of the Scottish history books I have read. In writing this book, I have tried to strike a balance between complexity, detail and simplicity, to produce a holistic, easy to read story that redresses those shortcomings while exploring past Highland life in a meaningful way. That approach has been taken for both those with some knowledge of Scottish history, and those unacquainted with Gaelic life and culture.

Is history not only relevant to the dead, but to the living and the yet unborn, as paraphrased in the quote from Edmund Bourke (1729-1797) at the start of the Preface? I think it is. After years of research, it has been my endeavour to share with readers what I believe is an interesting, informative, historical account about people from Mull and Iona who are representative of their contemporaries throughout the Highlands and Islands of Scotland.

Ian McPhee
July 2019

1

Background History

The islands of Mull and Iona are part of the Inner Hebrides group of islands situated close to the Scottish mainland. They are subdistricts of Argyll.[1] Iona has a land area of only about 355 acres (877 ha), while Mull is a substantial island with a land area of almost 225,000 acres (90,900 ha). Mull is hilly with Ben Mor being the highest peak at 3,170 feet (966 m).[2] Like some other islands in the Hebrides, Mull has a high annual rainfall which averages 70 inches (1,778 mm) with comparatively mild winter temperatures.

The climate on Scotland's west coast is ameliorated by one of the world's strongest currents known as the Gulf Stream. A warm ocean current that originates near Mexico, it flows north, past the east coast of the U.S.A. From there it crosses the Atlantic and mixes with colder oxygen rich Arctic waters around Norway, where it is known as the North Atlantic Drift. Ocean currents then flow south from Norway around the west coast of Scotland where their average temperature is about 8° Celsius.

Despite an extensive coastline and numerous sea lochs penetrating Mull, the island has limited protection for shipping. Scottish writer Martin Martin[3] nominated only three safe anchorages after visiting the island about 1695: "The bay of Duart on the east side, and to the north of the castle of that name, is reckoned a safe anchoring-place, and frequented by strangers. Lochby on the opposite west side, is but an indifferent harbour..."[4]

The sea and seashore were generous to the early residents of Mull and Iona, as they abounded with numerous types of aquatic life, including herring, cod, salmon, ling, mackerel, rockfish, sea perch and various types of flat fish like sole and flounder. Shellfish such as oysters, clams, cockles and mussels were plentiful around the coast, while crustaceans including crabs and lobsters could also be procured. Although abundant, seafood supplemented the Highlanders' diet rather than being the staple component.

Martin Martin stated Mull had "no wood here, except a few coppices on the coast." In those mostly coastal stands of native trees grew birch, hazel, rowan and holly. Woodlands may have been limited, but Martin noted an "abundance of wild fowl in the hills and valleys; and among 'em the black cock, heath-hen, tarmagan, and very fine hawks: the sea-coast affords all such fowl as are to be had in the Western Isles."[5] The most prominent animals living on Mull were deer and foxes.

Being part of Argyll, Mull and Iona were populated by people who were once part of a Gaelic kingdom on Scotland's west coast called Dalriada. Long before Scotland became a nation, descendants of those Gaelic speaking people developed into separate groups

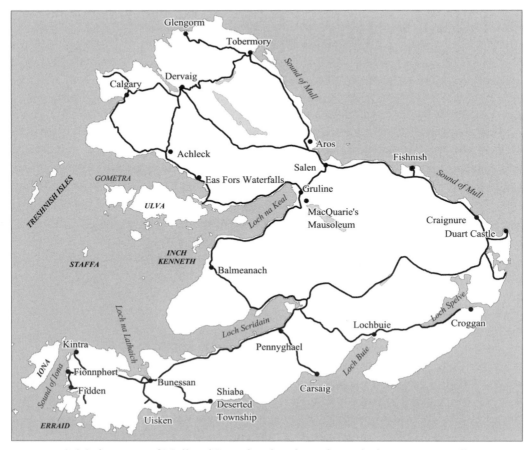

1. Modern map of Mull and Iona showing the main roads that traverse Mull.

called clans. The clan was originally a biological group, and the people who belonged to a particular clan were blood relatives, sharing a common ancestry and usually living in close proximity or sharing a defined locality.

While clans may have originally started as biological groups, they did not stay that way. Clans evolved and developed to be quite different and somewhat removed from their beginnings. By the time surnames came into use during the latter part of the Middle Ages, clans were not necessarily made up of people related solely by blood. Essentially they became a group of people who supported a particular leader. Many small family groups adopted the surname of more powerful clans under whose protection they lived while others were absorbed into stronger rival clans.

The Gaelic Kingdom in the Western Isles was raided by Scandinavians from Norway (Norse or Vikings) during the eighth and ninth centuries. From about the ninth century, they controlled and settled in the area for over 300 years.[6] They left their mark in the people they mixed with and the names of places where they lived. There is a strong Norse influence on islands like Colonsay and Islay, but relatively few Norse place names on Mull, which would indicate they may not have had a significant presence on the island.

When the Norwegians relinquished control of the Western Isles in 1266, it left a vacuum that eventually saw Clan Donald (the MacDonalds) emerge as the strongest clan in the region. With the grudging acceptance of the Crown, they ruled the Western Isles between 1353-1493 under the title Lordship of the Isles. It was a period of comparative peace and stability among the clans in the region.

Abolition of the Isle Lordship in 1493 precipitated change and instability in the Western Isles. The Crown took over responsibility for issuing 'charters' (a form of land ownership) which had been granted previously by the "Lord of the Isles".[7] While the MacDonalds lost their legal authority, they remained a force to be reckoned with in the Western Isles and coveted a return to their former status.

Early Christianity and Clan MacLean

Separated from Mull by a sliver of water a little over one mile (2 km) wide, Iona has a different narrative to that of its much larger neighbour. It has a unique and special place in Scottish history. Credit for that distinctness can be traced back to St. Columba, who travelled from Ireland and founded a monastery on Iona in 563 AD.

Columba and the monks on Iona were responsible for spreading and promoting Christianity in many parts of Scotland. Destruction of the monastery and murder of monks during Viking raids in the eighth and ninth centuries, did not stop the monastic outpost on Iona prospering to become a pre-eminent religious centre. Owned by the Roman Catholic Church, it grew to become a jewel in the crown of Christianity in Scotland. A stone monastery was built for the order of St. Augustine in 1074, which was rebuilt again in 1203 for the Benedictine Order. During the Reformation (1517-1648), the church was forced to close the monastery (which became a ruin) and cede ownership of Iona to the Crown. Competing clans thereafter jockeyed to control and occupy the island. One of those was Clan MacLean.

For centuries Mull was occupied and dominated by Clan MacLean. It was one of the most powerful clans in the Western Isles. Like other large clans, it developed into a number of significant landowning branches. When the Lordship of the Isles was abolished, the clan had four independent branches: the MacLeans of Duart, the house of the chief, the MacLeans of Lochbui, the oldest cadet branch, the MacLeans of Coll and the MacLeans of Ardgour. The Clan's seat of power was Duart Castle.

Factors such as clan warfare, clan allegiance to the Crown, marriage alliances, the quality of a clan's leadership and luck determined a clan's fortune. Throughout the era of the clan system, some clans prospered, some fell and some disappeared altogether.

Clan MacLean continued its dominance of Mull throughout the 1500s. By century's end, the whole island was under charter to them and their vassals the MacKinnons and MacQuaries. The lion's share was controlled by the MacLeans of Duart.

Battle of Port Bheathain

Visible from the southern shores of Mull is the island of Colonsay, home since time immemorial to the MacDuffies.[8] It was one of the smaller clans in the region. While their island home was not far from that of the MacLeans, the MacDuffies had always been allied to the powerful MacDonalds of Islay.

The MacDonalds of Islay often fought with the MacLeans of Mull, and thus so did the MacDuffies. For that reason, despite Mull and Colonsay being close to one another, there has never been a significant number of MacDuffies on Mull. Of course, as the two islands are within sight of each other, it was inevitable during peaceful periods that some MacDuffie families would become established on such a large island as Mull.

In the 1500s and early 1600s, members of the MacDuffie Clan clashed on numerous occasions with the MacLeans of Duart. Many of those skirmishes went unrecorded and the majority were of little historical importance. Such battles became part of clan folklore. Not being found in ordinary history books, it is interesting to examine one of the more memorable of those conflicts.

A ferocious battle between the MacLeans of Mull and the MacDuffies of Colonsay took place on the Ross of Mull in the days when interclan strife was rife. Details of the event were passed down through the generations orally by local Mull residents.[9] For that reason, the date of the incident is unknown, although it was probably in the 1500s.

The story of the battle began in Glen More on Mull, where MacGillivary of Glen Caineal was murdered while hunting by a MacLean of Duart clansman. MacGillivary was a supporter of the Clan MacLean Chief (MacLean of Duart) and held in high regard by him. Fearing for his life after the deed, the perpetrator fled to Colonsay where he sought protection from the Chief of Clan MacDuffie.

MacLean of Duart demanded the fugitive's head or his return to Mull to be tried for his crimes. The men of Colonsay soon after killed him, decapitated him and sent the head back to Mull where it was dumped ashore on the Ross of Mull. While satisfying the demand, a slender piece of twig that had been passed through the eye-holes of the head to act as a handle, was viewed as an indignity to the dead clansman. The insult inflamed a simmering feud between the Chief of MacLeans and the Chief of the MacDuffies.

Following the incident, scores of well armed MacDuffie clansmen, intent on stealing some of MacLeans' cattle on Mull, set sail from Colonsay. Their boats were soon spotted by a lookout at Dun a' Gheard, a hill fort perched 100 feet (30 m) above sea level on a steep-sided rocky spur, about a mile (1.6 km) south west of the Kilviceuen parish church. Alerted to the raid, the MacLeans had time to muster a large force of men to meet them.

The MacDuffies landed in a snug little bay with a sandy foreshore called Port Bheathain, where they encamped overnight. On the day of the battle, the MacLeans sent part of their small army to meet the intruders, while the rest waited behind a hill, ready to ambush the attackers. The MacDuffies, seeing a seemingly inferior force of MacLeans advancing towards them, charged and engaged in battle. As had been planned, the MacLeans soon withdrew with the MacDuffies giving chase. On a pre-arranged signal, the MacLeans, lying in wait out of sight, rose up and joined the battle, attacking from the sides and rear.

Trapped, outnumbered and unable to resist the assault, the MacDuffies fought a retreat back to shore where they found their boats high and dry. As they dragged them into the water and tried to man the oars, more MacDuffie clansmen were slaughtered. Tradition has it that large numbers of arms and fingers were cut off during the escape, and when the boats returned to Colonsay, bucketfuls of thumbs were taken out of them.

Port Bheathain is often referred to as the Bay of Thumbs. Apparently the main battle took place away from the coast in a glen between Loch Assapol and the township of Shiaba. Many bodies were buried close to where they fell and burial mounds could be seen until recent times. New tree plantations have apparently obscured the location of the mounds. (NB Some believe that Eachuin, the MacLean chief who led his clan at the Battle of Flodden in 1513 was the chief during the Battle of Port Bheathain).

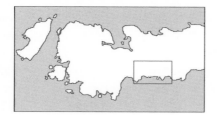

2. The southern side of the Ross of Mull.

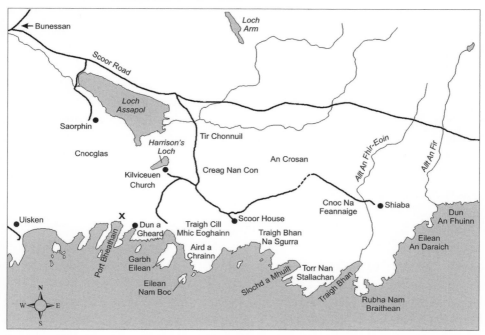

3. Map showing the location of Port Bheathain on the Ross of Mull where the MacLeans of Duart savaged a retreating force of MacDuffies. The place is marked with an x on the map.

The MacLean - MacDonald Feud

It was during the 1500s that one of the most notorious feuds in the Isles erupted. It began about 1560 with a dispute between the MacDonalds of Islay and MacLeans of Duart over the right to a peninsula of Crown land on Islay known as the Rhinns. The MacLeans claimed it was theirs, while the MacDonald Clan maintained they had a longstanding right to it.

Each of the protagonists raided one another's property during the feud. At one point, the MacDonalds laid waste to the Ross of Mull. It was also during that conflict, part of which corresponded with the Reformation, that in 1576 the Crown confirmed ownership of Iona and the Ross of Mull by the MacLeans of Duart, who had received a charter to it 15 years beforehand.

After years of conflict, Sir Lachlan MacLean, the head of his clan, sought to extend his claim on Islay beyond the Rhinns. In pursuit of his objective, he landed on the island at Loch Gruineart with a force of about 800 men in August 1598 to take Islay by force. In the ensuing bloody Battle of Traigh Ghruinneart, the Macleans were beaten convincingly by a smaller force of MacDonalds. About 280 MacLeans were killed including 200 ordinary clansmen, 80 gentlemen and their leader Sir Lachlan MacLean.[10]

This momentous battle saw a settlement of the feud whereby the Crown recognised the MacDonalds as the legitimate tenants of the Rhinns on Islay. It is fair to say both clans were weakened by the years of constant warfare and their standing with the Crown diminished. Having been the most powerful clan in the Western Isles for hundreds of years, the supremacy of the MacDonalds was over and from the end of the 1500s the Clan's power and influence declined.

Settlement of the dispute for the MacLeans of Duart saw their continued ownership of Iona and substantial estates on Mull throughout much of the 1600s. Unfortunately for the clan, it seems inept leadership from the MacLeans of Duart early in the century caused them to fall into financial difficulties. A failure by the clan's 17th chief Lachlan MacLean to pay outstanding debts he had incurred, eventually led to his imprisonment in Edinburgh's debtors' gaol. In 1633, Archibald Campbell (later the Marquis of Argyll), helped secure his release by buying up his debts in return for possession of Duart land on Mull. The land was then leased back to Lachlan MacLean.[11]

The Campbell Takeover of Mull and Iona

Demise of the MacDonalds saw the rise of the Campbell Clan in both political influence and military might. Campbell support of the Protestant faith during the Reformation contrasted sharply with clans in the Western Isles like the MacDonalds who supported Catholicism. Following the Reformation, Iona and land at the western end of Mull originally owned by the Catholic Church ended up in Campbell hands.

A protracted Civil War known also as the War of the Three Kingdoms engulfed England, Scotland and Wales between 1642 and 1651. The conflict was between King Charles I

(1625-1649) together with high church Royalists who opposed Parliamentarians with fundamental religious beliefs. The war was a multi-faceted conflict, the complexities of which are not possible to explore in detail here. The MacLeans and the Campbells took opposing sides in the dispute. The MacLeans backed the King and Royalists while the Campbells backed Parliamentary forces which became known as Covenanters.

During the Civil War years, the Campbells and MacLeans attacked each other's territory with abuses on both sides. In 1647, the Campbells, in conjunction with parliamentary forces, invaded Mull, where they rampaged over the island killing many defenseless locals and their livestock. To stop further bloodshed, Lachlan MacLean, besieged in Duart Castle, surrendered.

The Civil War entered a new phase when Scotland and England went to war against one another. A turning point came in July 1651 at the Battle of Inverkeithing on the north shore of the Firth of Forth, where Royalist forces backing Charles II (1649-1685) were defeated by an English parliamentary army. The MacLeans suffered a devastating loss at Inverkeithing. Sir Hector MacLean, the 19th clan chief, and nearly all the clansmen from Mull he was leading were killed. Before the year was over, an English army led by Oliver Cromwell went on to defeat the Scots.

The cost of the War and its aftermath saw the MacLeans of Duart deeper in debt, a situation the Campbells were able to exploit to their advantage. When Charles II regained his crown in 1660 and the monarchy was restored (The Restoration), the Marquis of Argyll was executed for treason and his estates forfeited. His heirs however, continued to pursue the MacLeans. Eventually regaining government favour, the Campbells were given approval in 1674 to invade Mull to recover outstanding dues and eject MacLean tenants from their land. The Campbell forces that subsequently invaded and plundered the island caused considerable damage including the hamstringing of cattle for sport, which ended only after the MacLeans surrendered.[12]

Conflict did not end with the Macleans' surrender. Warfare between the two clans erupted again in 1679 and again the Campbells' prevailed.[13] By 1691 the Campbells of Argyll had used legal, financial and military means to assert their dominance and secure much of MacLean of Duart's land on Mull (including the Ross of Mull), Iona, Tiree and Morvern. From that point, their ownership of those areas was never successfully challenged or reclaimed by the MacLeans. By the reign of King William III (1689-1702), the Campbells had become the largest landowners on Mull.[14]

Unlike the era when the MacDonald's controlled Mull, the Campbells of Argyll secured firm control over their land by resettling their own clansmen and supporters on the island. Among those were the Campbells of Dunstaffnage who held Castle Dunstaffnage about three miles (5 km) north of Oban at the entrance to Loch Etive. The Campbells of Argyll leased three large areas on Mull to them, namely, northern Aros, south-east Torosay and the Ross of Mull which included Iona. While the ordinary people who lived there had to heed their new owners' wishes, they remained loyal to the chief of their own clan.

Writing over a century later in what was to become known as the Old Statistical Account, the Reverend Dugald Campbell, a minister on Mull, commented on the calamitous Civil War years and also a dark period of famine and pestilence during the reign of King William. He stated, "The destructive rage with which the civil war years were carried on in the time of Charles the first, and a famine and pestilence, in the time of King William, almost depopulated the whole parish. In the reign of the latter Prince, people were dying for want upon the high road, buried where they breathed their last, as the few surviving relations had neither the strength nor means to carry them to the common burying places... King William's days are still remembered with horror."[15]

The famine years described by Rev. Dugald Campbell, are known as the "Seven Ill Years", the "Ill Years" or "King William's Ill Years".[16] It is believed volcanic activity in Iceland may have caused a spike in the cold weather of the "Little Ice Age", an extended period of climatic cooling between the Middle Ages and the 20th Century, which led to widespread grain crop failures from 1695 to 1699. Those failures, proceeded by several poor harvests, resulted in a disastrous national famine and starvation in Scotland. It has been estimated Scotland lost between 5 and 15 per cent of its population from an increased death rate, lower birth rate and emigration (to Ulster) as a result of the famine.[17] In parts of the Highlands, the population loss was greater than 20 per cent.

People and Parishes

Written accounts about life anywhere on Mull or Iona prior to the 19th Century are few and far between. Observations were recorded only occasionally by outsiders. After a stay on Mull in 1688, the governor of the Isle of Man described the people he saw:

> "... the men to be large-bodied, stout, subtle, active, patient of cold and hunger... bound their appetites by their necessities, and their happiness consists, not in having much, but in coveting little. The women seem to have the same sentiments with the men;... The usual outward habit of both sexes is the plaid; the women's much finer, the colours more lively, and the squares larger than the men's,... This serves them for a vail and covers both head and body. The men wear theirs after another manner,... it is loose and flowing,... Their thighs are bare, with brawny muscles... what is covered is only adapted to necessity - a thin brogue on the foot, a short buskin of various colours on the leg, tied above the calf with a striped pair of garters..." [18]

On his visit to the island in the 1690s, Martin stated Aros Castle was a ruin and the existence of only two parish churches on Mull. He noted the inhabitants were "all Protestants, except two or three, who are Roman Catholicks; they observe the festivals of Christmas, Easter, Good Friday, and St. Michael's.[19] They speak the Irish language generally, but those of best rank speak English; they wear the same habit as the rest of the islanders."[20]

Areas throughout Scotland were divided into parish districts that were recognised as such by both the church and the government of the day. The parish minister was not only a servant of the church but also of the estate owner, whose largesse he relied upon. In the hierarchy of the local community, a parish minister was commonly second in importance only to the estate owner or landholder.

In the days of traditional clan life, Mull had a number of parishes. These were Tobermory, Kilninian, Kilmore, Salen, Torosay, Kinlochspelve, Kilfinichen and Kilviceuen. Eventually they were reduced or amalgamated to form three, each with its own minister: Kilninian and Kilmore in the north, Torosay in the middle and Kilfinichen and Kilviceuen, occupying two western arms and also the island of Iona.

The clansmen living on Mull and Iona who are part of this narrative, have been recorded as living in the Parish of Kilfinichen and Kilviceuen. The parish was divided into four geographical subdistricts: the Island of Iona which used to be known by the Gaelic term Icolmkill, meaning cell or cemetery; Ross, a Gaelic word meaning a point of land jutting out into the sea; Brolass signifying a grey or rugged ridge and Airdmeanach, to the north and east of Loch Scridain which joins Brolass at the head of the Loch.

Kilfinichen and Kilviceuen were originally two separate parishes that united to be served by the one minister. Their names originate from two places of public worship; one in the district of Airdmeanach called Kilfinichen; the other in the district of Ross called Kilviceuen. The western arm that was once the parish of Kilviceuen encompasses both Brolass and the Ross of Mull. For generations the boundary between the two areas was ill-defined and of little significance to local communities near it.

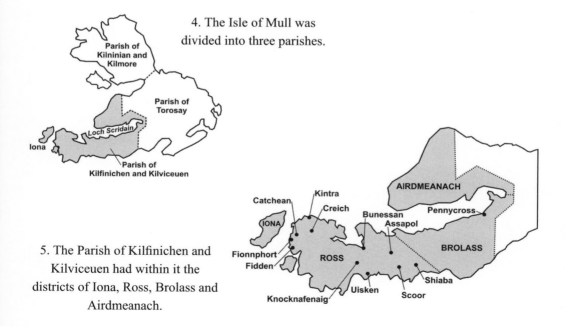

4. The Isle of Mull was divided into three parishes.

5. The Parish of Kilfinichen and Kilviceuen had within it the districts of Iona, Ross, Brolass and Airdmeanach.

It is certainly a mistake to think of the Ross district in terms of it being like the rest of Mull. There are many features that distinguish and differentiate it from other areas of the island. Surrounded by the sea on three sides and hemmed in on the east by the rugged hills of the adjoining district of Brolass, the Ross is like an island within an island. With only rough tracks and no roads until modern times, travelling overland to access other areas of the island was no easy task. Virtually all trade and travel with the outside world was by sea. Even the climate is a little different to other areas of the island.

The most basic form of transport in the Highlands was a small cart pulled by a single horse, and in more lavish circumstances, two horses. Such wheeled carts were impractical on Mull, as there were no roads or bridges prior to the 1800s, so people and animals used well-worn tracks to traverse the island. Crossing the island in 1773, a visitor wrote about the absence of roads: "We travelled diligently enough, but found the country, for road there was none, very difficult to pass".[21] It was not unusual for the hardy people of Mull to travel on rough tracks barefooted and bareheaded.

In 1764, Scottish minister and natural historian Rev. Dr. John Walker (1731–1803) toured the Hebrides and visited Mull, where he reported on numerous aspects of life on the island.[22] He stated the population of the the island was 5,325 with the Parish of Kilfinichen and Kilviceuen having 1,676 inhabitants. There were four places of public worship in the parish but astonishingly he noted "there is no Church at any of them."[23]

Rev. Dr. John Walker also detailed the adherence of Mull people to the Church of Scotland and the disadvantage children faced receiving an education. In a written report to one of the organisations who commissioned his tour he stated: "There are only eight or ten Persons in Mull who are Papists, and these are not Natives of the Country. Of all the inhabitants, only about 335 can understand... English, so that ministers are obliged... to deliver their Instructions in Gaelic. Though there is a legal parochial school in each of the three Parishes,... the Country is so extensive, and the inhabitants so much dispersed, that the greater part of the children, by their Situation, have no access to these Schools, and so grow up without ever being instructed in the English Language, or Principles of Religion."[24]

Walker's reference to a legal parochial school relates to a 1696 Act of Parliament, which mandated that every parish in Scotland had to have a school. The Act stated "in every paroch will be to the kirk and kingdom... a school founded and a schoolmaster appointed in everie paroch not already provided..."[25] English rather than Gaelic was to be used, a reflection of the anti-Gaelic sentiment among the ruling elite at that time.

Despite the primitive life on Mull, the people apparently were very healthy. There were few endemic diseases, and illnesses were often the result of local residents returning from mainland Scotland with an infection. In the early part of the 1700s smallpox was a significant killer on Mull and elsewhere, but this was overcome towards the end of the century by inoculation.[26]

In stark contrast to Iona and other areas of Mull, no one of note from the church, the aristocracy or ruling landowning class was ever domiciled on the Ross of Mull. For that reason there are no castles or even grand houses like elsewhere on the island. All the major branches of Clan MacLean that had dominated the island for centuries had their castles in more strategic places. For a different reason, there are no houses, and few if any house ruins that were once homes, built prior to the 1700s that in the past belonged to the common people apparent on the Ross of Mull.[27] That is because although some may have been built of stone, many were built primarily of timber, turf and thatch.

Generally speaking, until the end of the 1700s, people were self-sufficient, with only ever small amounts of money on hand to purchase basic necessities. They produced their own food, made their own clothes and built their own houses.

NOTES

1. Macinnes, A I, 1994, *Land Ownership, Land Use and Elite Enterprise in Scottish Gaeldom: from Clanship to Clearance in Argyllshire 1688-1858*, contained in Scottish Elites, edited by Devine, T M, p. 6.
2. Perott, D, 2001, *The Western Island Handbook*, p. 100.
3. Martin Martin was a Scottish writer who toured the islands circa 1695. He is best known for his work *A Description of the Western Islands of Scotland*, first published in 1703. Raised on the Isle of Skye, his observations are taken as incisive and accurate.
4. Martin, M, 1976, *A Description of the Western Islands of Scotland*, 2nd edn 1716, p. 251.
5. Ibid.
6. McDonald, R A, 2002, *The Kingdom of the Isles, Scotland's Western Seaboard c.1100 -c.1336*, p. 24.
7. Williams, R, 2000, *The Lords of the Isles,* p. 238.
8. The Battle of Port Bheathain was recorded in modern times using the clan name McPhee. In times past that clan name was also commonly expressed and recorded as MacDuffie which has been adopted for this account.
9. MacCormick, J, 1923, *The Island of Mull Its History, Scenes and Legends*, p. 161-164
10. McIan, R R, 1983, *The Clans of the Scottish Highlands*, p. 138.
11. Campbell, Alastair of Airds, 2002, *A History of Clan Campbell*, Vol 3 p. 15.
12. Campbell, Alastair of Airds, 2002, *A History of Clan Campbell*, Vol 3 p. 18.
13. Campbell, Alastair of Airds, 2002, *A History of Clan Campbell*, Vol 3 p. 22.
14. Currie, J, 2001, *Mull the Island and its People*, p. 13.
15. Statistical Account of Scotland, Number xii, *Parish of Kilfinichen & Kilviceuen*, p. 188.
16. Cullen, K J, 2010, *Famine in Scotland: The 'Ill Years' of the 1690s*, p. 14. The date range of the famine is generally accepted to be from 1695 to 1699. The term 'Seven Ill Years' is presumed to be a contemporary biblical reference to the seven years of famine in the Book of Genesis.
17. Cullen, K J, 2010, *Famine in Scotland: The 'Ill Years' of the 1690s*, p. 2 & 17.
18. MacCormick, J, 1923, *The Island of Mull Its History, Scenes and Legends*, p. 182

19. Saint Michael's day or Michaelmas was observed on 29th September. It was a popular celebration among Gaelic speakers until the 18th century.

20. Martin, M, 1976, *A Description of the Western Islands of Scotland*, 2nd edn 1716, p. 255.

21. Johnson, S and Boswel J, 1984, *A Journey to the Western Islands of Scotland and the Journal of a Tour to the Hebrides*, p. 135.

22. Following the Jacobite rebellion in 1745, a number of estates were forfeited to the Crown and administered by the Commissioners of the Annexed Estates. Walker received a commission from the Commissioners to tour the Hebrides which resulted in a 'Report on the Hebrides'. At the same time he was asked by the General Assembly of the Church of Scotland and the Society for the Propagation of Christian Knowledge (SPCK) to report on the state of religion and education in the Highlands.

23. Walker, J, and McKay, M M, 1980, *The Rev. Dr. John Walker's Report on the Hebrides of 1764 and 1771,* Edinburgh, J. Donald, p. 152.

24. Ibid.

25. NRS, *Supplementary Parliamentary Papers, Scroll Acts, Acta Parliamentarium Guliemi AD 1696, Act for Settling Schools*, Act No 26 The Acts of Parliament of Scotland Vol x 1696-1701 p. 62, PA7_15.

26. Statistical Account of Scotland, Number xii, *Parish of Kilfinichen & Kilviceuen,* p. 173.

27. Cameron, J S, 2013, *A History of the Ross of Mull,* p. 121.

2

Owners and Occupiers of Clan Land

In centuries long past, ordinary clansmen lived on their land unencumbered by leases or legal documentation. In the early years of the clan system, land was theirs by virtue of their occupation. The clan system did not have a land owning nobility and peasant class. A clan chief did not inherit land or estates, but inherited the right to represent his kinsmen or people to whom he was responsible.

Following the Norman Conquest of England in 1066, the feudal system was introduced to Scotland, whereby land was granted in return for military service or rent. It brought with it the ownership of land. From the Middle Ages, the Crown granted control over land to its influential supporters by issuing a legal instrument for it called a charter. Charters were a form of legal recognition to what had once been ancient rights in times past, over untitled land claimed or controlled by clan chiefs and overlords.[1]

Despite the adoption of the feudal system and issue of charters throughout Scotland, a clan chief's ability to acquire or control land, in large measure remained dependent on the number and the loyalty of his fellow clansmen who were prepared to fight for him.

During the 1500s and 1600s, rebellion against the Crown and clan warfare were rife and frequently dominated life in the Western Isles. It wasn't until the end of the 1600s, when internecine warfare had abated, that there was a begrudging adherence to the rule of law, and life in the Western Isles became more settled. By that time land ownership throughout the Highlands was also more clearly defined.

There still remained however, some areas of land (usually only suitable for grazing livestock) that had no defined ownership. As such, its use was freely available to those who had traditionally used it.[2] That situation came to an end in 1695, when the Scottish Parliament passed the Commonties Act. Except where the Crown had an interest, the Act allowed proprietors to apply for ownership of any untitled common land that existed next to their own properties without the need for payment. The Act states: "for preventing the disscords that arise about Commonties and for the more easie and expedit deciding thereof... Divisions are appoynted to be made of that part of the Commonty that is next adjacent to each heritors property".[3] The term 'common grazing' referred to in later pages of this book, is land owned by a proprietor apportioned for use by multiple tenants.

By the 1700s, clan chiefs were no longer just military chiefs at the apex of a clan. They were the legal owners of large tracts of land. Various members of a clan chief's extended family had also become part of a significant land owning aristocracy. Although

Argyllshire

6. At right, a map of Scotland with the shaded
area indicating the location of Argyllshire.

7. A map of Argyllshire. It is bounded in the north by Inverness Shire and other counties to
the east and south which form a minor part of the map (Glasgow and the mainland south of it
for example, are not part of Argyllshire). The darker shaded areas indicate the location of land
owned by the Argyll Estates relevant to this book.

on a smaller scale than their more wealthy superiors, they also owned significant areas of agricultural land. These two groups of people owned all the land.

Proprietors and the Argyll Estates

Land in the Highlands was divided among proprietors who were usually called heritors. The term heritor meant the landowner had a direct financial and managerial interest in the land he controlled.[4] The term 'laird' was also used to describe landowners and many today would be familiar with this description. The meaning of the word changed over the centuries. At various periods it was ascribed to a clan chief, owner of an estate, small landowners by virtue of Crown grant and so on.[5] In more recent times, it described a landowner or owner of a large stately house.

Proprietors of land in Scotland were fortunate to enjoy a system that gave them security of title that was also provided to any purchaser of their land. As one influential Highland landowner stated in the early 1800s, "In no country in Europe are the rights of proprietors so well defined, and so carefully protected, as in Scotland."[6]

Extensive areas of land that comprised many farms were called estates. In the main, clan chiefs and other significant landholders among the aristocracy were the owners of Highland estates.

Argyllshire, described in issues of the Slater's Directory during the 1850s as "Argyleshire, or, as it is frequently written Argyllshire, is a large county in the south-western extremity of the Highlands. What may be termed the continental part is bounded in the north by Invernesshire; on the east by that county, by Perthshire and Dumbartonshire; and on the south and west by bays and straights of the Atlantic Ocean. Its extreme length is one hundred and fifteen miles; its breadth averaging about thirty-three;... The mainland, including the peninsula of Kintyre, has been computed to contain 2,735 square miles; while the islands connected with it are supposed to comprise 1,063 more; whereby the whole extent of land in Argyleshire may be estimated at 3,800 square miles."[7]

The Argyll Estates were those large parcels of land owned by the chief of the strongest branch of the Campbell Clan. This particular Campbell family was an influential one, with a long history closely associated with the monarchs of Scotland and England. The Earldom of Argyll was conferred on one of its early members back in 1457. William III (1689-1702) further elevated the status of the family by promoting Archibald Campbell, 10th Earl of Arygll, to the rank of Duke. Hereditary chiefs of Clan Campbell have the Gaelic title MacCailean Mor, meaning Son of Great Colin, the name of an illustrious member of an early Campbell family.[8]

Over hundreds of years the Campbell family had profited handsomely from its close affiliation with various royal families. The Campbells were a powerful, prolific clan that by hook and by crook came to own huge areas of the western Highlands of Scotland, including a large part of Argyllshire on Scotland's west coast. At one point it was estimated the Campbells owned or controlled nearly a third of Scotland. As a group, this aristocratic family simply became known as the House of Argyll.

The areas, their location and the amount of land that made up the Argyll Estates varied over the years according to the fortunes, desires and abilities of the individual Campbell chief who inherited them. By the latter half of the 1700s the Argyll Estates included the island of Tiree, the island of Iona, large swathes of land on the Isle of Mull,[9] land on the mainland in the parish of Morven opposite Mull and land around Inveraray in the County of Argyll. Those estates were administered from a new mansion house built in a castle style at Inveraray in County Argyll, near Loch Fyne in the western Highlands. Clan chiefs no longer necessarily resided in large castles, as comfortable, two storey houses became the norm.

All large landholders had a substantial influence on the lives of those who lived or farmed land on Highland estates. Aristocratic owners such as the Duke of Argyll and the Duke of Sutherland were like monarchs and governments rolled into one. Tenants had to conform to their policies and dictates.

The Tacksman

Large farms and tracts of land were commonly leased to one of the chief's own relatives, fellow clansman or a person reliant on the proprietor. These men were 'tacksmen', because a lease was known as a tack.[10] Tacksmen in turn divided portions of those areas they did not wish to farm themselves among other rent paying tenants who supported their chief. They were commonly other clansmen or possibly relatives. In this way, clan chiefs were able to receive rents indirectly from large numbers of small tenants spread across extensive areas of land under their control.

No matter how long a farm lease, it was a common practice to renew them at Whitsunday. Whitsunday, which is short for White Sunday, is the 7th Sunday after Easter. Farm rents were sometimes paid at this point in the yearly calendar and also at Martinmas - St Martin's Day on 11th November.

Prior to the middle of the 1700s, tacksmen were commonly one of the clan chief's relatives and a numerous type of tenant on his estates. They were crucial members of any clan or an estate because they rallied the clansmen on behalf of the chief when military action was undertaken, and often became officers of any militia force. For most of the time when there was an absence of conflict, tacksmen were akin to gentlemen farmers. They leased land directly from the chief with a security of tenure often for periods of about twenty years. They lived a very agreeable life, often paying modest rents directly to their landlord, and were able to afford large numbers of servants to do the work.

By the latter half of the 1700s, the role tacksmen played recruiting clansmen for military action had become redundant.[11] Despite that, many maintained their privileged position on Highland estates. When famous British literary figure Samuel Johnson (1709-1784) toured the remote areas of the Highlands in 1773 with his companion James Boswell, he described them in the following terms: "Next in dignity to the laird is the tacksman; a large taker or leaseholder of land, of which he keeps part, as a domain, in his own hand, and lets part to under tenants... He holds a middle station, by which the highest and the lowest orders were connected. He paid rent and reverence to the laird, and received them from the tenants. This tenure still subsists, with its original operation, but not with the primitive stability."[12]

A tacksman's farm, as did any estate, employed and supported people with a wide diversity of occupations, including millers, mealers, workmen, grass-keepers, moor-herds, bowmen, merchants, brewers, shepherds, weavers, crafters, servants, tenant farmers and cottars.

Farm Workers

Mills of various descriptions were common features about the countryside. Whether they were sawmills, threshing mills, barley mills or oat mills, all were dependent on water and located near a reliable source. On Highland estates the miller was a key employee of the estate owner. He was responsible for milling grain produced on the estate by the small tenant farmers. The tenants were legally obliged or 'thirled' to use the landowner's mill and had to pay for the privilege.[13] In addition, each tenant gave the miller a small portion of the meal that was ground as payment for his services.

The backwardness of Mull and its people is brought home by an observer of the period who described the milling process on Mull as being extremely primitive compared to other places.[14] Mills set up to grind grain grown on the island were described as clumsy machines that were inefficient and left a considerable amount of waste. The old click mills that were apparently of Norse origin were still being used on Mull.

Click mills were dry stone buildings over or near a stream, that used a horizontal water wheel and two grinding stones to produce meal (fig. 9). The term 'click mill' comes from the projecting peg on the upper circular millstone which knocked the grain spout to give a steady trickle of grain into the hole in the centre of the stone.[15] The ground meal came out at the edge of the stone and was collected in the meal box (fig. 10).

Mealers were a type of subtenant who rented arable ground on which they grew a crop. The annual rent was an agreed amount of meal produced from the harvest. In addition to meal, they were required to supply half the horses. Mealers were also general workers on a tacksman's farm, and in return for their labour, their employer provided pasture for two or three cows and some sheep, as well as meal for them. Farm workmen were like mealers, who grew a crop and gave three-quarters of it to their employer. In addition to supplying the land, the employer also provided all the horses.

In England, hedges acted as fences, but in Scotland, if present, they were usually built of sod or stone. Whatever the form, they were an essential prerequisite for efficient farming practices. Unlike some more progressive areas in the Lowlands and in England, many estates in the Highlands were not fenced. This applied especially to places like Mull. On such open areas, grass-keepers were employed to care for the livestock. In

8. A click mill dating from the early 1800s at Dounby in the Orkneys.

9. Concept of the click mill used to grind grain.

10. The interior of the Dounby click mill. A small space, no bigger than a garden shed.

return for their labour they were provided with a house and land for a cow, a horse, some sheep and a crop. On the moors and hills, moor-herds carried out the same function under similar employment terms as the grass-keepers. A bowman was a tenant who was lent or supplied with farm equipment, seed and livestock by a tacksman and shared what was produced with him. A visitor to the Isle of Skye in the 1770s described a bowman as one "who takes care of the stock of cattle on a certain tract; and binds himself to give to the tacksman every year four stone of cheese, and two of butter, from each couple of milk cows. If there is any arable ground, he is provided with horses and a plough; and seed sufficient to sow it; and receives part of the crop, and some additional grass ground for two or three milk cows, for his trouble."[16] Sometimes the term was also applied to a ploughman or cattleman on a farm

The Small Tenant Farmer

Areas a tacksman or laird did not occupy or farm themselves were rented out to small tenants "without any lease at the will of the landlord, and subtenants who have small possessions of land let out to them from year to year, by the tacksmen and tenants."[17]

Subtenants, the most numerous tenants on many Highland estates during the 1600s and 1700s, paid a modest monetary rent together with some form of goods and service. They lived on the estates with their families in shared farming arrangements. Day labourers were employed as required, but they were few in number.

In the report on his tour through the Highlands in 1764, the Rev. Dr. John Walker vented his disapproval at the way land was sublet to small tenants on Mull, describing the practice as a relic of the old Feudal System. He noted the plight of subtenants in the following terms: "All the subtenants, which are the body of the people in the Highlands, are tenants at the will of the tacksmen, and are therefore his slaves... Their subjection also to the farmer on whose ground they live, leaves them no more time than what is barely sufficient for supporting themselves and families. The tacksman generally has one day of the week of the subtenants labour year round, which, with the spring and harvest work and other occasions, will amount to more than a third of his whole annual labour. He can therefore have neither time, nor ability to move one step out of the common road; or to attempt any improvement, which many would undoubtedly do were they but masters of their time and independent in their possessions."[18]

Rural communities lived on farms commonly called townships, where the land tenure was held under 'multiple tenancy'. The community as a whole rented the land rather than the individuals who lived there. Naturally some tenants within the community who worked more land than others, had to pay more. The townships were like farms that supported a number of self-sufficient families. Rent, partly in the form of grain or livestock, was paid to the estate owner who was a member of the landed gentry.

Farms or townships during the 1600s and 1700s had relatively small populations, commonly comprising between six and twenty-four families. Sometimes those families lived in one or more settlements. A few families living in a settlement with a cluster of small dwellings and rural buildings was known as a clachan.[19] Such clusters could be thought of as a farming village, but they were nothing like a village in the modern sense of the word.

While townships usually had access to the coast, they were generally located away from the shoreline, near fertile land suitable for cropping. Such communities were essentially self-sufficient and grew crops and raised livestock to feed and clothe themselves.

The Role of Cottars

The term cottar is an old one once used commonly throughout Scotland. In essence it meant a person who occupied a cottage on a few acres of land. The word cottar was derived from the word cottage. A cottar was a landless farm labourer who did not pay rent. In return for labour in the old traditional townships, cottars resided in the community where they could grow a few crops and raise some livestock for their own use. In return for that right, they provided their services to rent paying subtenants or a tacksman. On large communal farms they were an important source of seasonal labour. Cottars were often the sons and sons-in-law of farming tenants who, by tradition, willingly shared their land with them. In some cases a tenant supplied a patch of land and seed to a cottar, who in return, provided his labour to cultivate and sow the crop. The harvest was then shared between them.[20]

NOTES

1. Argyll, Duke of, 1887, *Scotland As It Was and As It Is*, 2nd edn, p. 38.
2. Argyll, Duke of, 1887, *Scotland As It Was and As It Is*, 2nd edn, p. 407.
3. NRS, Division of Commonties Act 1695.
4. Macinnes, A I, 1994, *Land Ownership, Land Use and Elite Enterprise in Scottish Gaeldom: from Clanship to Clearance in Argyllshire 1688-1858:* contained in Scottish Elites, 1994, edited by Devine, T M, p. 3.
5. McCrone, D, and Morris, A, 1994, *Lords and Heritages, The Transformation of the Great Lairds of Scotland:* contained in Scottish Elites, edited by Devine, T M, p. 171.
6. Sinclair, J, 'General Report of the Agricultural State and Political Circumstances of Scotland (Edinburgh 1814)', p.115-121 contained in A *History of the Highland Clearances, Agrarian Transformation and the Evictions 1746-1886*, 1982, Richards, E, p. 177.
7. NLS, Slaters Directory of Scotland, 1852, p. 225.
8. Campbell, Alastair of Airds, 2002, *A History of Clan Campbells*, Vol. 1, p. 50.
9. In 1700, the Campbells of Argyll owned land up and down the lenght of Mull including Brolass. They owned a greater area than any other proprietor, but that position changed over the years.
10. Argyll, Duke of, 1887, *Scotland As It Was and As It Is*, 2nd edn, p. 100.
11. Recruiting clansmen for military service ceased after the Battle of Culloden in 1746.

12. Johnson, S, and Boswell, J, 1984, *A Journey to the Western Islands of Scotland and the Journal of a Tour to the Hebrides*, p. 94-95.

13. Argyll, Duke of, 1887, *Scotland As It Was and As It Is*, 2nd edn p. 426.

14. Currie, J, 2001, *Mull the Island and its People*, p. 217. The observer referred to is surveyor Robert Reid, who visited Mull to assess Maclaine of Lochbuy's estate.

15. Information from the Dounby click mill, Dounby, Orkney.

16. Pennant, T, 1998, *A Tour in Scotland and Voyage to the Hebrides 1772*, p. 311.

17. Walker, J, and McKay, M M, 1980, *The Rev. Dr. John Walker's Report on the Hebrides of 1764 and 1771,* Edinburgh, Donald, J, p. 207.

18. Walker, J, and McKay, M M, 1980, *The Rev. Dr. John Walker's Report on the Hebrides of 1764 and 1771,* Edinburgh, Donald, J, p. 160.

19. Argyll, Duke of, 1887, *Scotland As It Was and As It Is*, 2nd edn, p. 260.

20. Devine, T M, 2004, *The Great Highland Famine* p. 8.

3

The Highland Way of Life in the 1700s

The reasons why ordinary clan families lived in a particular area or how people came to be tenants on Highland estates is unfortunately difficult and usually impossible to determine. There are few written records of the 1700s that identify under what circumstances a family occupied land.

Similarly, relatively few detailed accounts of the daily life and times of Scottish Highlanders were recorded by the people themselves to give us an accurate picture of the way they lived in centuries gone by. There is a heavy reliance on English scholars and writers such as Edmund Burt[1] and Samuel Johnson for this information, and some of those observers knew very little about Gaelic life. Anti Gaelic prejudice was also a factor in their writings.

Thankfully, despite the scant amount of relevant literature, it is possible to gain an understanding of how Highlanders lived a traditional lifestyle in a bygone era.

The Runrig Farming System

Tenants living in a clachan had basic facilities. In addition to houses for the people, there were byres for the animals and barns to store grain and farming equipment. The old communal townships nearly always had a winnowing barn and kiln. After grain crops were harvested they had to be threshed, which was usually done in a barn although sometimes also outside in the field. After threshing, a winnowing barn was used by the local farmers to separate the grain from the husk and straw. Opposite the barn doorway, a winnowing hole created a wind draft to separate the grain as it was tossed in the air. Near the winnowing barn, a small circular stone kiln was used for drying grain.

Around the houses and farm buildings were the infields that were under constant cultivation. Further away, divided by "rude and unsubstantial fences" were the outfields.[2] There crops could be rotated with grass or fallowed, and a cow kept to supply the household with milk. Beyond the outfield was a common grazing area.

The arable land around the township was farmed under a form of communal cultivation and crop rotation known as the 'runrig' system[3] (fig. 11). Under this farming method, fields were measured into strips that were sometimes up to 15 feet (5 m) in width. Horse drawn ploughs were then used to create large heaped mounds along the strips. In forming the ridges, furrows were also made which assisted drainage. The large ridges so formed were called 'rigs'. Seed was planted down their length to grow crops. Each tenant in the township commonly worked an equal number of strips across the field. Allocated strips were rotated and sometimes drawn by lot. Although it was a very fair system, it encouraged poor farming practices.

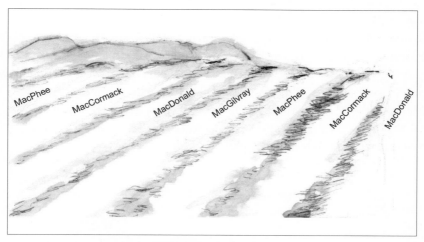

11. The runrig farming system.

Crops and Livestock

The main crops during this period were barley, oats and flax, with oats being the primary source of food for families in the Highlands and islands. Oats and barley were ground down to meal by householders using small, hand-operated rotary mills, or in crude click mills.

Flax was another hardy crop that grew well in the Highlands. After it was pulled from the ground and given some basic treatment, its fibre was spun into yarn that could be made into linen cloth. Linen production was a labour intensive cottage industry, where family members could produce a home grown product for a cash return. It was perhaps the most important industry in Scotland during the 1700s.[4] Women did the spinning and men wove the cloth on looms. Despite the merit of the end product it produced, flax as a crop was disliked because it depleted soil fertility and some aspects of its post harvest processing were unpleasant.

All rural households had a mixture of cows, horses, sheep, goats and fowls. Pigs were uncommon in the Highlands. The main reason for that was a lack of food scraps and other waste on Gaelic farms rather than a bias against the animal, although apparently in some areas there was a disdain for consuming pork and bacon.[5]

Sheep and cattle were the main farm animals. Just as cropping land was shared, so were grazing rights for livestock. Each tenant farmer was entitled to an equal number of cattle as determined by the carrying capacity of the land the community occupied. Each tenant had a measure of pastureland that would be capable of supporting a certain number of animals. The number of livestock which an area of land would support as determined by the landowner, was known as a soum or souming. Whether a farmer had a right to graze 5 animals or 10, they grazed in a common herd on communal pastureland, although owners could always recognise their own animals.

Cattle and other livestock went out to grazing areas prior to crops being planted in spring. Pastured in the hills for one or two months over summer, they were watched over carefully, often by women and younger family members. Families constructed their own rough stone huts known as shielings, so that those tending the herd would have shelter.[6] When pasture had been exhausted and the crops harvested, livestock would be brought back near the houses for the winter. Here they would forage as best they could around the houses, over the crop stubble and along the watercourses.

12. A woman milking a cow next to a shieling hut on the Isle of Lewis in the late 1800s.[7]

Highland sheep were a small, scrawny type of animal, white or grey in colour, that did not need to be shorn. They had straight horns and perhaps looked a bit like a soay breed of sheep today. Their fine, thin fleece was more like hair than wool. It was spun into a soft yarn used to make tartan cloth. Housed at night, the sheep had little cash value, but supplied families with wool and milk. From the early 1700s, coarse-wooled, black-faced sheep that were able to stay outdoors all year round gradually displaced them. As tough as nails, the Scottish Blackface thrived on heather covered hills. The original Highland breed of sheep is extinct.[8]

Black Highland cattle were valuable and had been used as an important commodity in lieu of cash since feudal times. By the 1700s they had developed into an essential part of the Highland's economy, being one of the few sources of cash. The economy based on cattle was commonly referred to as the 'black cattle economy'. The cattle were referred to as 'kyloes', from the Gaelic term Kyle meaning sea channel, as many of them were forced to swim across sea channels to reach mainland markets.

Cattle had to endure harsh winters when good feed was scarce, and as a result were often in poor condition at the end of that season. In most areas, the cattle were not consumed by the local people but either sold in their parish at a yearly market, or entrusted to a drover to sell on their behalf. Drovers were highly regarded in Highland communities. Cattle from all over northern and western Scotland were taken by drovers over well established drove roads to sell at cattle markets. The October cattle sale at Crieff in Perthshire was the biggest market until the 1770s when it was moved to Falkirk.

Highland Homes

Compared to lairds and country gentlemen, ordinary families lived in primitive accommodation. It was not uncommon for animals to share a portion of the house with the people. Houses varied considerably in quality and construction, but commonly had a rectangular shape with rounded corners.

The most basic houses in the Highlands were made using sod or peat and wood and without foundations. Sod refers to the 4 inches (10 cm) of topsoil which also contained plant leaves and roots. The plant fibres acted as a binding agent. House walls were made using posts with interlaced tree branches (called wattle) in a similar fashion to wickerwork. On the outside, the wooden walls were protected against the elements by a layer of sod, so that the sod acted like bricks. Timber was used as a frame for the roof. The roof frame was covered with thinner pieces of sod or peat called 'divots' that acted as tiles. The divots were then covered with thatch.

Houses were also commonly made of natural stone. The loose double stone walls packed with smaller stones were mostly not more than 6 feet (2 m) high. Although large trees were scarce, especially on many of the islands, house roofs had a framework of rough wood from local trees on which turf and thatch were placed.

The thatch was sometimes made from heath or barley that was pulled from the ground, roots and all, during periods of wet weather when other harvest work was not possible. Any suitable material was used as thatch - 'muran' or bent grass was particularly good, but bracken fern, bull rush and common rush were also used. To keep the thatch from being blown off, hand twisted ropes made of heather were placed lengthways across the roof to tie it down.

Whether made of sod or stone, the houses had no windows containing glass. Small openings for the admission of light, which could be filled with bricks of peat, sometimes acted as windows. Entrances only a few feet high did not have a door as such; boards

13. The Cottar's House
in the historic township
of Auchindrain.

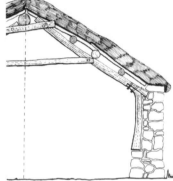

14. The diagram shows one of the methods
used to build thatched stone houses showing
'cruck frame' construction. In many areas
large trees were scarce, so roofing timbers
were valuable to any householder.[9]

15. The interior of an old style Highland home. One end has a crude partition where a bed is
located. The fire was central to every home.[10]

propped against the opening were used to keep the elements out. The uneven floors were earthen. In those primitive single-roomed houses, the fireplace was on a hearth of stones placed in the middle of the house. The absence of a chimney meant the smoke from the fire simply escaped through a small hole in the roof and any other openings in the building. The hole in the roof was not directly over the fire so that rain did not extinguish it. When heavy rain occurred, the hole was plugged with heather or fern.[11]

Building a thatched sod house was a comparatively simple and speedy process because not only did all the immediate family help in the construction, but the neighbours normally pitched in and helped as well. With the exception of timber, all the necessary materials were freely available and close at hand. Re-thatching a roof, which had to be done periodically, could be completed in a day or so. As one writer put it, a house built using sod "could be raised in a couple of days out of materials delved with the spade and cut by hatchet."[12]

Houses had few comforts. To provide light at night, people made their own candles from tallow derived from animal fat, and wicks of linen. In some cases oil was also extracted from a fish known as 'cuddies' (a type of codfish), for use in small iron lamps.[13] In the more remote areas, many of the poorest dwellings relied mainly on the fire.

In the crudest of dwellings, bedding may have been heather and blankets on the earthen floor, but usually straw filled sacks acted as mattresses. For others, simple timber bunks with straw sacks and blankets gave comfort when sleeping at night. There was a measure of privacy provided by a curtain or timber partition. Usually the parents and perhaps a baby might sleep in one bed, while all the children would sleep in one or two other beds.

Missing from any books researched by the author about people living in basic Highland homes is the issue of going to the lavatory. No mention has ever been found to shed light on such a crucial aspect of life for large families in small houses in a cold wet climate. Farm houses did not have a room for ablutions or a lavatory, and buildings away from the house with a pit or pan were not constructed. So what did people do? A newspaper article provided the answer.[14] People used an indoor chamber pot or some other container in the home, which was emptied on a dungheap. Against a wall of the house, the dungheap was close to the front door, usually on the downwind side, within throwing distance for the lady of the house. All the household kitchen waste also went on the dungheap. Like refuse from the cowshed, the dungheap ended up on the fields.

Peat and Black Houses

Coal was not available or affordable for many Highland communities. Island residents used peat dug from any nearby bog as a source of fuel for both cooking and heating. In its natural state peat has a moisture content of over 90% and, as such, required skillful handling before it was suitable to use as a dry fuel.

Individual tenants had peat cutting rights on common areas. Working to secure fuel for the family fire was hard, dirty work. It commonly involved standing in a black, gluey sludge to remove the wet peat from its natural location. Whether digging or stacking, workers were tormented by hordes of tiny, sandfly-like insects called midges. The female Highland midge (culicoides impunctatus) delivers a bite that causes discomfort to its victim.[15] Pesky midges harassed all those outdoors in the Highlands during summer.

Peat cutting was a communal activity usually carried out in April and May when the spring planting had been completed. After the top layer of turf that supported sedges and other greenery had been removed, individual slabs were cut from a trench about 12 inches (30 cm) deep and placed on the ground nearby. Here they were put in small piles to dry. A week or so later, the peat was turned over to dry out further. About six weeks after cutting, it was dry and ready to be stacked next to the house. Peat was stored meticulously beside households in stacks shaped like a pitched roof and covered with turf. They were not only covered with turf to prevent rain entering, but made so that rain caused minimal damage. There was much competition among individual households as to who had the best stack.[16]

Burning peat inside Highland cottages without chimneys produced some unusual effects. During prolonged periods of wet weather, smoke saturated roofs produced a thick black liquid that dripped on anyone unlucky enough to be beneath it. The smoke from the peat not only gave off a distinctive odour, but also left a dark discolouration on the interior. Those from more civilised areas of the country referred to the primitive dark dwellings as 'black houses'.

Clansmen lived simple lives. They conversed almost exclusively in their native Gaelic language. They built their own primitive homes on land owned by the aristocracy or landed gentry. They lived directly or indirectly from that land and commonly used black cattle as a commodity to earn hard currency.

16. A Highlander using a peat spade to cut peat in the late 1800s.[17]

The Family Diet

The primary food source for the family was oats. In England, cattle and horses lived on oats, whereas in Scotland it nourished the people. Harvested grain commonly had to be dried to prevent the growth of the plant fungus smut, and also before it could be milled to produce meal for human consumption. To do this, threshed grain or sheaves were dried in a township kiln that used warm air produced by a peat fire. After being ground down to meal, it could then be stored for future use.

Although wheat, oats and barley flour were available, bread requiring the presence of yeast or leaven was not baked. Instead, wholemeal scones and biscuits were commonplace. Whatever type of grain they had available was used to make them.[18]

Oats were cooked and eaten in various forms. Boiling water poured into a wooden bowl containing oatmeal with a little salt, followed by some milk, produced the main meal called 'brose'. Unlike porridge, the oatmeal for brose wasn't cooked, and therefore it didn't swell, thus providing a substantial meal capable of sustaining a hard day's work in the field. Oatmeal was also made into a thin porridge called 'gruel', and soured oatmeal that had been boiled made what was called 'sowans'. Large oatmeal scones called 'bannocks' were made in every household.[19] Oatmeal was also one of the main ingredients for haggis.

In addition to oats, 'bere' or barley also formed part of the diet. Once cleared of its husk in the barley mill, it was used in similar ways to oats. Barleymeal was made into porridge, as well as producing soft wholesome bannocks and biscuits. The grain was also boiled and eaten with meat as we would eat rice today. By the 1700s however, barley was used predominantly for brewing and distilling whisky rather than as a source of food.

The family diet was supplemented with fresh and smoked fish, milk, butter, cheese, eggs, poultry, some mutton and very occasionally beef. Kale or colewort, a member of the brassica genus of vegetables which includes cabbages and broccoli also formed part of the diet.[20] Households grew it in small enclosed kitchen gardens called kaleyards. In one respect, children living today would view mealtime in that era with some delight, because vegetables were not considered edible food in that bygone age. Even potatoes were not commonly consumed until the latter part of the 1700s.

Apart from water and milk, ale was the most common beverage consumed in the Highlands with every meal. Considering barley was so widely grown, it is hardly surprising it was brewed into an alcoholic drink.[21] When beer was brewed, the first brew was very strong, and this is what the men would drink. The residue of the mash was then rebrewed to make ordinary beer, which is what the women drank. Following this, whatever remained was brewed a third time to make small beer, a low alcoholic drink for the children. Ale was safer to drink than water or milk as any germs it may have contained were killed by the prolonged boiling of malt during the brewing process. It was also highly nutritious. By the middle of the 1700s barley was also routinely turned into whisky. Being strong, cheap and easy to produce, it became more popular than ale, and a drink synonymous with the Highlands.

17. Above, Highland women washing their clothes.[22]

18. At left, a woman using
a quern to grind grain.[23]

19. Highland women waulking the cloth. On the left in the picture, two
women can be seen grinding grain using a quern.[24]

The consumption of locally brewed ale, especially small ale, declined after the 1730s with the growing popularity of drinking tea.[25] In 1768, the minister of one parish, Rev. George Gordon complained, "The drinking of whisky instead of good ale is a miserable change, so likewise is the very general use of tea. These put together have been exceedingly hurtful both to health and morals. Hence too many become tipplers, neglect their business and go to ruin".[26]

Highland Women

Highland women had crucial roles in day to day life. Generally they participated in any activity that was being undertaken - from fishing to harvesting. In addition to cooking and other usual household duties, women also milked the cow.[27] For the work they performed and the hardship they endured, they were truly remarkable.

For some outdoor tasks, women commonly used a wickerwork basket known as a creel. Often made of willow or hazel, it had stout leather straps so that it could be used to carry loads of peat, seaweed and other items on a person's back.

When helping to bring in the harvest, women would often be heard singing Gaelic songs.[28] A daily task of the housewife was to grind the grain to be used for family meals. This was done in a small stone hand mill called a 'quern'. It was a monotonous and never ending job.

As mentioned previously, linen production was important during the 1700s. Women not only weeded the crop but used to spin the yarn that could then be made into household items such as bed-curtains and clothing for the family.

Other domestic duties were also basic. Laundry duties were done outside using soap made from tallow and ashes. Washing the family clothes and bedclothes was done in a peculiar manner. They were put in tubs on the ground containing water, and the women, rather than using their hands, used their feet to pummel them. With their skirts hitched up above their knees, it was a strange sight for any foreigner of the time.[29]

A social activity that brought a number of women together, was waulking the cloth. When a household received cloth from a weaver, it was commonly treated to shrink and soften it. This rather arduous task, was done in a most unusual way by a team of women. After initially being soaked in a mixture of water and human urine, a dozen or so neighbours would sit around a table and rub, squeeze and fold the moist fabric against a board. After that process, the cloth was placed on the ground and women sitting in two rows facing each other, would squeeze and work it against each other with their bare feet, hence the term waulking the cloth.[30] While working together, the women sang Gaelic songs, often with great gusto.

NOTES

1.   In the 1720s and 1730s, Edmund Burt wrote about many aspects of Highland life in 26 letters to a friend in London. They were first published in 1754.

2. Argyll, Duke of, 1887, *Scotland As It Was and As It Is*, 2nd edn, p. 391.
3. Skene, W F, 1886, *Celtic Scotland*, 2nd edn, vol. III, p. 378-80.
4. Macinnes, A I, 1994, *Land Ownership, Land Use and Elite Enterprise in Scottish Gaeldom: from Clanship to Clearance in Argyllshire 1688-1858*, contained in Scottish Elites, edited by Devine, T M, p. 15.
5. Burt, E, 1998, *Burt's Letters from the North of Scotland*, Letter VI, p. 65.
6. Argyll, Duke of, 1887, *Scotland As It Was and As It Is*, 2nd edn, p. 200-203.
7. Courtesy Edinburgh City Library.
8. Argyll, Duke of, 1887, *Scotland As It Was and As It Is*, 2nd edn, p. 330.
9. Anon, 1988, *Auchindrain, A Historic and Traditional Farming Community*, p. 20.
10. *London Illustrated News*, 15th January, 1853.
11. Johnson, S, and Boswell, J, 1984, *A Journey to the Western Islands of Scotland and the Journal of a Tour to the Hebrides*, p. 54.
12. Argyll, Duke of, 1887, *Scotland As It Was and As It Is*, 2nd edn, p. 249.
13. Johnson, S, and Boswell, J, 1984, *A Journey to the Western Islands of Scotland and the Journal of a Tour to the Hebrides*, p. 127.
14. *Inverness Courier*, 11th January, 1832.
15. Keay, J & J, 1994, *Encyclopaedia of Scotland*, p. 695.
16. Mull resident and local historian, Attie MacKechnie.
17. Courtesy National Museum, Edinburgh.
18. Johnson, S, and Boswell, J, 1984, *A Journey to the Western Islands of Scotland and the Journal of a Tour to the Hebrides*, p. 72.
19. Grant, I F, 2003, *Highland Folk Ways*, p. 296-7.
20. Martin, M, 1976, *A Description of the Western Islands of Scotland*, 2nd edn 1716, p. 201
21. Grant, I F, 2003, *Highland Folk Ways*, p. 303.
22. McIan, R R, 1900, *McIan's Highlanders at Home or Gaelic Gatherings*, p. 53.
23. George Washington Wilson Collection.
24. Pennant, T, 1998, *A Tour of Scotland*, London 1776: plate xxxiv, women at the quern and the luaghad with a view of Talyskir, p. 286.
25. Argyll, Duke of, 1887, *Scotland As It Was and As It Is*, 2nd edn, p. 308.
26. Statistical Account of Scotland Vol XVII, Parish of Mortlach, County of Banff.
27. Grant, I F, 2003, *Highland Folk Ways*, p. 198.
28. Burt, E, 1998, *Burt's Letters from the North of Scotland*, Letter XX, p. 213.
29. Burt, E, 1998, *Burt's Letters from the North of Scotland*, Letter III, p. 24.
30. Burt, E, 1998, *Burt's Letters from the North of Scotland*, Letter XX, p. 213.

4

Clan Rebellion and Demise

In 1685, James VII of Scotland also became King of England. James Stuart ruled as James VII of Scotland and James II of England. His support of Catholicism however led to the premature end of his reign in 1688. He was replaced by the Protestant Prince William of Orange, who ruled as William III with his wife Mary II as joint sovereigns. They were succeeded by Mary's sister Anne. It was during Queen Anne's reign that Scotland lost its sovereignty with the formation of the United Kingdom in 1707.

Queen Anne died in 1714 leaving no heirs. This led to the Elector of Hanover being invited to rule the United Kingdom as George I of England and Scotland. Many Scots, particularly those in the Highlands, resented the appointment, believing a descendant of James Stuart was the rightful heir to the throne.

Jacobites and Battle of Sherrifmuir

James VII's son, James Francis Stuart, made an attempt to regain his father's crown in 1715 and came to be known as the 'Old Pretender'. His supporters and sympathisers were known as Jacobites, derived from Jacobus, the Latin name for James.[1]

The rebellion that broke out in 1715 was timely for James Francis Stuart. Support for him was overwhelming in Scotland and there was resentment throughout the kingdom with laws that followed the Union of Crowns in 1707, not to mention the Hanovarian succession.

The Jacobite uprising was initiated and led by disgruntled nobleman John Erskine, 11th Earl of Mar. He was one of the key architects of the 1707 Act of Union and among Hanovarian King George I's ruling clique. Taking umbrage at a snub from the King, Mar went to Scotland where he met a number of Highland chiefs at the Braes of Mar (Braemar) in Aberdeenshire. It was there on 6th September 1715, he switched allegiance from George I when he raised the standard for James Francis Stuart.

Many Highland chiefs rallied to the cause of reinstating the Stuarts and called out their clansmen. Although the clan system was in decline at that point, clan loyalty was still strong. A chief was able to raise his own militia force because it was incumbent on the men of a clan to make themselves available to fight for and on behalf of their chief. Men between the age of 16 and 60, capable of military service in a militia, were known as fencibles or fencible men.

The powerful MacDonalds, the Camerons, the MacIntoshes and the MacLeans from

Mull were among Mar's strongest and most numerous supporters. Clansmen from the Inner Hebrides were marshalled on Mull at the head of Loch na Keal, and from there went to the mainland to fight for their cause.

Opposing the Jacobites was a government army led by John Campbell, the 2nd Duke of Argyll. As the Campbells and MacLeans were long standing enemies, it was hardly surprising they were up for a fight against each other. Over many years, the MacLeans, like other west Highland clans, had lost land and influence to the Campbells.

The government and Jacobite forces met near the town of Dunblane at Sherrifmuir on 13th November 1715. Despite the Jacobites outnumbering Argyll's men by four to one, poor leadership resulted in a failure to drive home their advantage. The battle was essentially a draw, after which both sides withdrew. The rebellion thus evaporated.

The Jacobites melted back to their homes, while James Francis Stuart eventually sailed back to France. As for John Erskine, 11th Earl of Mar, he also escaped to France, his estates and title being forfeited. True to his nickname of 'Bobbing John'[2] earned for his propensity of changing sides, Erskine abandoned the Jacobite cause, and later died in exile.

Retribution by the government was restrained, with some key rebels being executed and others imprisoned. One of those detained for treason was the notorious Rob Roy MacGregor (1671-1734) who escaped his captors with a price on his head.

Once again the Campbells were on the winning side with the government of the day. The 2nd Duke of Argyll was able to cement his control over land on Mull (Brolas and the Ross) and all of Iona. No doubt his influence with government had other benefits. The MacLeans from Mull were the biggest losers.

The 1716 Disarming

One significant aftermath of the 1715 rebellion was the disarming of all the rebels and others in areas of the Highlands that had supported the Jacobite cause. In order to prevent another insurrection, the United Kingdom Parliament passed a Disarming Act in November 1716, outlawing the bearing or owning of arms in defined areas of Scotland.

During the month of April 1716, James Campbell of Stonefield, Justice and Sheriff Depute of Argyll and his Deputy-Lieutenants, collected arms from men on the islands of Canna, Coll, Tiree and Mull. Weapons were also surrendered in the mainland areas of Morvern, Ardnamurchan and Sunart.

Today, historians and genealogists are fortunate that Stonefield's clerk kept a detailed list of all the men in the rebel areas. Every man in those areas, rebel or otherwise, had to hand in any weapon they possessed. He noted their name and the 'place of abode', whether or not they participated in the rebellion and what weapons were surrendered. There were five weapons listed - guns, swords, pistols, targets (normally spelt as targe, meaning circular shields) and dirks (daggers). It is impossible to say how effective the disarmament was, as some weapons were undoubtedly retained by their owners.

Despite Iona and the greater part of Mull being owned by the 2nd Duke of Argyll, the islands featured prominently in the disarmament. The names of 24 men were documented on Iona. On the Ross of Mull 107 men in 19 farms were recorded: 1 in Erraid, 11 in Fidden, 9 in Creich, 3 in Knockvologan, 2 in Pottie, 2 in Tireregan, 1 in Ardfenaig, 9 in Ardealanish, 7 in Knocknafenaig, 4 in Ardachy, 6 in Suidhe, 8 in Bunessan, 6 in Ardtun, 6 in Assapol, 8 in Ardchiavaig, 7 in Saorphin, 8 in Kilviceuen, 3 in Scoor and 6 in Shiaba.[3]

The figures for the Ross district of Mull indicate each of the townships or farms in that area had only a handful of families living in them. A census of the inhabitants on the Ross of Mull taken 63 years later in 1779, showed the average family at that time comprised about 4 people. If that average was applied back to the time of the 1716 Disarming, it would indicate the Ross had a population of 428. Considering some men may not have been recorded during The Disarming, it would be fair to conclude the population was possibly about 450 people.

On the Ross of Mull, Stonefield's clerk recorded two clan names that were uncommon on Mull and not associated with Iona. One was Cameron. The only Cameron name listed was that of John Cameron at Knocknafenaig, who was shown not to be a rebel or have a weapon. The other was McDuffie. Angus McDuffie lived at Kilviceuen (recorded as Kilvikewn), an ancient settlement site inhabited since 5,000 BC. Although McDuffie may have been born and raised on his clan homeland of Colonsay, the Disarming List indicates he was resident on Mull during the 1600s, where he may have settled due to marriage. Some of his and also Cameron's descendants are mentioned briefly in the following chapters. Those living at Knocknafenaig and Kilviceuen were listed as follows:[4]

Kilviceuen

Lachlan McLean of Gruline	a rebel sent in his gun
Archibald Mcffarlan	in the rebellion with his master Gruline
Donald McEan dui	a rebel no weapons handed in
Murdoch McIlvra	a rebel no weapons handed in
John McKoinich	not a rebel no weapons handed in
Donald McMillan	not a rebel no weapons handed in
Angus McDuffie	not a rebel handed in his dirk
John McLean	a rebel no weapons handed in

Knocknafenaig

John Cameron	not a rebel
John Beaton	a rebel had a sword and a gun
John McLean	sick
Hector McLean	not a rebel old and sick
Donald McLean	not a rebel
Neil McLean	not a rebel
Neil Beaton	not a rebel

The Forbes Report

In the early 1700s, John Campbell, the 2ⁿᵈ Duke of Argyll, grew increasingly dissatisfied with the poor financial returns he received from his estates on Mull. As mentioned previously, when the Campbells gained control of Iona and large parts of Mull, they secured their position by installing relatives on large areas of farmland at the expense of the MacLeans. Despite the majority of the tacksmen on his estates being Campbells, the 2ⁿᵈ Duke believed they were not offering satisfactory rents. Furthermore he believed they were extracting too many service dues from the many subtenants on his estates.

In 1737 the 2ⁿᵈ Duke of Argyll commissioned his friend, former eminent Scottish judge and Lord Advocate, Duncan Forbes of Culloden, to visit his Mull and Tiree Estates and report on their condition. Forbes, who could not speak Gaelic, was accompanied on the expedition by the Gaelic speaking Duke's chamberlain. A chamberlain was a business manager for the nobility, perhaps a bit like an accountant today.

The compelling report submitted by Duncan Forbes recommended that a greater return would be gained if farms were simply leased to the highest bidder rather than to the existing lease holder. It was also highly critical of tacksmen, stating they extracted too many free services such as peat cutting and help at harvest time from subtenants. Forbes recommended bypassing tacksmen and dealing directly with subtenants: "to deliver them from the tyranny of Tacksmen, to free them from the oppression of services and... encourage them to improve their farms by giving them... nineteen years by leases,... offering frankly for their farms such rent as fairly and honestly they could bear."[5]

The 2ⁿᵈ Duke of Argyll acted on the recommendations. A system of 'tenants at will' - tenancy at the will of the landowner came into existence which is to say, the Duke issued written leases directly to tenants. Nineteen year leases prohibiting subletting were introduced to encourage improvements to the land and smaller tenants were given the opportunity to bid for leases. Rather than pay any dues in the form of services, tenants were expected to pay a monetary rent directly to their landlord. A more stable income was also anticipated from former subtenants who would rent larger farms.

The new regime caused considerable upheaval on the Argyll Estates, as some leaseholders lost their traditional places in the community. Competitive bidding for leases dealt a blow to some tacksmen who were unable or unwilling to adjust to the new commercial realities of life. This applied particularly to a number of Campbells who could no longer count on clan loyalty or kinship to retain their positon.[6]

Small tenants continued on communal farms much as they had done prior to the new initiatives. A substantial increase in profits did not follow the introduction of the new measures. Factors such as bad seasons, poor farming techniques and low cattle prices had a significant part to play in how much rent a leaseholder could afford to pay his landlord. A higher price paid for a farm lease did not necessarily mean the new occupier could extract the greater return required to cover the higher rent. Not being overly successful, the new initiatives eventually fell by the wayside.

The Battle of Culloden

The Battle of Culloden was a defining moment in Highland history.

James Francis Stuart, the Old Pretender, who had failed in his attempt to regain the English throne in 1715, had a son called Charles Edward Stuart. His good looks and personality had given rise to his nickname of Bonnie Prince Charlie. Like his father, he also coveted the English throne.

Charles negotiated with England's old enemy the French to gain their assistance before deciding to make an attempt to defeat the English and retake the Crown for the Stuarts. With the backing of the French and with the support of many Scottish Highlanders, he was determined to engage the English in battle.

Bonnie Prince Charlie's campaign to seize the English throne began when he landed in the north of Scotland during 1745 and gained the support of numerous Highland clans. Among them was the powerful Cameron Clan, loyal to the Cameron Clan Chief known as Lochiel. The Campbell Clan was among those that opposed the Jacobite rebellion and sided with the established English monarchy.

Victorious in clashes against the English forces, Bonnie Prince Charlie and the Jacobite Army were able to march south to Derby, just 127 miles (204 km) from their goal of London. It was there the inexplicable decision to turn back was made. Possibly it was not knowing what had happened to the French forces that were supposed to assist them, as well as the lack of popular support that may have led to that decision. From there the rebel army retreated north to Scotland and the safety of the Highlands.

The Jacobite army however, was pursued by Royal troops under the command of the 25 year old Duke of Cumberland, who was the reigning King George II's brother. In April 1746, near the far north Scottish town of Inverness, Cumberland's forces finally caught up with those of Bonnie Prince Charlie. The ensuing battle on 16th April 1746 was a slaughter, with the clansmen no match against a superior force. The Battle of Culloden was a decisive victory for the British Government.

Following the victory, Cumberland and his men went on a rampage of violence and retribution against those who had participated in the rebellion. They scoured the countryside searching for fleeing clansmen and looted whatever they could take. In a campaign of cruel reprisal, men, women and children were killed and their homes burnt to the ground. In Argyllshire, 2,000 Campbell militiamen ruthlessly crushed any pockets of Jacobite resistance.[7]

The Battle, and mopping up operations afterwards saw 3,470 Jacobites and their sympathisers taken into custody. Some of those prisoners were beheaded, some were hung, drawn and quartered, some were exiled and 936 were sentenced to transportation to British Colonies.[8]

Fortunately the inhabitants on Mull were spared the carnage suffered in other places. Two reasons for that stand out. Firstly after the 1715 uprising, the MacLean chief had found sanctuary in France and was unable to call out his followers. Although some

20. David Morier's famous painting depicting the Battle of Culloden in 1746.[9]

21. The image above, titled The End of the 'Forty Five' Rebellion by W. B. Hole, depicts the retreat of defeated Highlanders following the Battle of Culloden.[10]

MacLeans fought with the Jacobites, others fought on the government side. Secondly, by 1745 large areas of Mull were under control of the Campbells who supported the government. Their dominance of Mull had grown with the decline of the MacLeans.

Culloden's Aftermath

The Highland chiefs paid a high price for their follies with the ambitious young Bonnie Prince Charlie. Their lands and estates were forfeited to the Crown. At least forty estates belonging to the supporters of the rebellion were seized. A number of estates were sold off, and a Board of Commissioners was established under the 1752 Annexing Act to administer those retained by the Crown. In the main, Commissioners on the Board were loyalist Scottish nobles. Money raised from the forfeited estates was to be spent:

> "... for the Purpose of civilising the Inhabitants upon the said Estates, and other Parts of the Highlands and Islands of Scotland, and promoting amongst them the Protestant religion, good Government, Industry and Manufactures, and the Principles of Duty and Loyalty to His Majesty, his Heirs and Successors and to no other use or purpose whatsoever..."[11]

A visitor to the Highlands 26 years after the battle was impressed by the benefits bestowed on Scotland, thanks to the money raised from the forfeited estates. He mentioned how schoolmasters had been stationed in remote areas, how poorer tenants were introduced to useful trades, how craftsmen were encouraged to settle on annexed estates, how linen and woollen manufacturers were established and how the Commissioners "have caused large tracts of barren and uncultivated grounds on different parts of estates to be enclosed, and planted with oaks, firs, and other trees..."[12]

The coup de grace - the final blow, was delivered to the Highland clans not by the sword but by the pen. The British Government used parliament to implement a number of Acts that repressed Gaelic culture and placed many restrictions on Gaelic people.

The 1747 Act of Proscription, known as the 'Black Act', prohibited clansmen, wearing their distinctive clothes, gathering together, and being taught Gaelic. Its objective was to destroy the clan system and undermine the cohesion of "these barbarous and disloyal savages."[13]

The 1747 Disarming Act was another attempt by the British Government at Westminster to disarm the rebellious Highlanders. Rigorously enforced by the government, it was more successful than the two previous Disarming Acts (1716 and 1725).

Concerned about the continued existence of Heritable Jurisdictions in Scotland that had been preserved with the Union of Scotland and England in 1707, the House of Lords requested a report on the different kinds of jurisdictions from the Court of Session in Scotland and a draft bill that parliament could adopt. At the time of the request, Duncan Forbes of Culloden was the Lord President of the Court (the highest in Scotland).

Forbes recommended their abolition, and his draft bill was largely adopted. Civil and criminal Heritable Jurisdictions were thus "abrogated, taken away, totally dissolved, and extinguished" with the 1747 Heritable Jurisdictions Act.[14]

The landowning clan chiefs and aristocrats who supported the Crown were adversely affected by the Heritable Jurisdictions Act. In Scotland, judicial powers were granted by the Crown and given only to significant landowners.[15] Those grants could be passed on from one family member to another, which meant magistrates and other judicial officers were heritable positions that could be held for life. Naturally this gave rise to cronyism and corruption. The office of sheriff played a crucial role in administering law and order in Scotland. Sheriffs handled everything from criminal justice and territorial disputes to tax collection.

The Heritable Jurisdictions Act abolished ancient Scottish hereditary sheriffdoms and other traditional jurisdictions, and forced Scottish landowners to accept the power of the English courts. It reformed a most uncoordinated legal system. It meant Scottish lords and clan chiefs lost much of the power they held over their subjects, although as landlords they had considerable rights under English law. It was one of the few positive outcomes of the Jacobite uprising. The clan system, based on Barons Courts and clan councils that formed the basis of Scottish law and local government, was made redundant.

NOTES

1.   Hume Brown, P, 1995, *Scotland A Concise History*, p. 291.
2.   Donnachie, I, and Hewitt, G, 2003, *Dictionary of Scottish History*, p. 388.
3.   Maclean-Bristol, N, 1998, *Inhabitants of the Inner Isles Morvern & Ardnarmuchan 1716*, District of Ross, p. 40-47.
4.   Maclean-Bristol, N, 1998, *Inhabitants of the Inner Isles Morvern & Ardnarmuchan 1716*, District of Ross, p. 41 and 46.
5.   Argyll, Duke of, 1887, *Scotland As It Was and As It Is*, 2nd edn, p. 258.
6.   Devine, T M, 1994, *Clanship to Crofters' War*, p. 16.
7.   Harrington, P, 1991, *Culloden 1746 the Highland Clans' Last Charge*, p. 86.
8.   Ibid.
9.   Grant, N, 1987, *Scottish Clans and Tartans*, An Incident in the Rebellion of 1745, p. 40.
10. Hole, W. B. 1882, *The Art Journal*, facing p. 65
11. Walker, J, and McKay, M M, 1980, *The Rev. Dr. John Walker's Report on the Hebrides of 1764 and 1771*, Edinburgh, Donald, J, p. 6.
12. Pennant, T, 1998, *A Tour in Scotland and Voyage to the Hebrides 1772*, p. 454.
13. Keay, J & J, 1994, *Encyclopaedia of Scotland*, p. 791.
14. Argyll, Duke of, 1887, *Scotland As It Was and As It Is*, 2nd edn, p. 274/5.
15. Argyll, Duke of, 1887, *Scotland As It Was and As It Is*, 2nd edn, p. 274.

5

Early Census and Highland Genealogy

Some years after the Battle of Culloden, more comprehensive records about ordinary Gaelic people began to appear. This chapter is concerned with two such records that were compiled in the late 1700s.

One was perhaps the earliest population census taken in Scotland, which has a particular relevance to genealogy. The other was a remarkable survey of all the parish counties in Scotland, which provides an insight into many cultural aspects of Highland life.

In 1770, John Campbell (1723-1806), succeeded his father John Campbell 4th Duke of Argyll, to become 5th Duke of Argyll, and take over responsibility for the Argyll Estates. Prior to his father's death, he had been known as the Marquess of Lorne, a courtesy title bestowed on the eldest son of an incumbent Duke of Argyll. He was a distinguished soldier who had fought against the Jacobites at the Battle of Falkirk Muir and at the Battle of Culloden. He was also a Member of Parliament for many years and in retirement was given the rank of Field Marshall.[1]

22. John Campbell, 5th Duke of Argyll[2]

1779 Census of the Argyll Estates

Unlike his predecessors who sought political achievement as a priority, the 5th Duke developed a keen interest in improving the huge areas of land under his control, with a clear view to increasing their productivity. When he took over the Argyll Estates, the runrig farming system dominated most areas. The 5th Duke sought to increase the output from his estate by replacing runrig farming on unfenced land with tenant farmers on enclosed farms of a moderate size. The large number of tenants removed from the areas they once occupied could then be redeployed to live and work on small fenced farms and in fishing villages. The reorganisation of the Estate was a huge undertaking, that required information and planning.

In pursuit of his goal, the 5th Duke instructed the chamberlains and overseers in each district on his Estate to undertake a census of the people who lived on his land. The districts included Central Argyll (Inveraray etc), Kintyre, Tiree, Roseneath and the combined areas of Mull, Iona and Morvern. Individual farms in each district were central to the list, which documented the names, ages, position in the family and occupations of the people living on them.

The census was completed towards the end of 1779. It became accessible to the general public when the details were edited from the original manuscript by historian Eric Cregeen and published as *Inhabitants of the Argyll Estate, 1779* by the Scottish Record Society in 1963.

It was estimated by Cregeen, that the Argyll Estate covered a massive area of 500 square miles in Argyll alone. As the census didn't include men and youths away at war or fishing, or the men and women engaged in seasonal work in the Lowlands when the census was taken, he estimated that a realistic population for the Estate was almost 15,000. The size of the average family was four.

Cregeen pointed out the census was compiled with a high degree of completeness and accuracy. When recording surnames, the Argyll Estate preferred Mc to Mac, and usually followed it with a capital letter. He commented on some of the shortcomings in the census. With different chamberlains involved, there was a lack of uniformity in the categories of information recorded. Also, the recorded age of inhabitants was unreliable, especially those of older people, which Cregeen stated was largely a matter of guess-work. The spelling of surnames varied greatly, even within the one family, and the names of females regrettably were not recorded. A male was deemed to be an adult when he attained the age of 16.

The census is of major significance because little or no documentation that recorded details about individual families of the common people in remote areas of the Highlands either existed, or has survived from the 1700s. Documentation generally improved in the 1800s as parish ministers recorded more births and marriages. The following table is how the basic population information for each of the 18 farms on the Ross of Mull was recorded for the 1779 Census.[3] Farm names are spelt as they were recorded.

Ross of Mull Farms	Men	Females	Male Children	Farm Total
Saorvein	16	30	18	64
Ardchivaig	11	20	9	40
Ardachy	6	20	8	34
Tirergan	11	23	6	40
Knockvilgan	11	23	15	49
Fidden	13	26	12	51
Pottie	6	9	8	23
Creich	12	11	3	26
Ardfinnaig	7	17	5	29
Sui	14	27	15	56
Bunnessan	16	37	13	66
Assaboll	12	33	10	55
Knocknafennaig	14	32	9	55
Ardelnish	14	45	18	77
Kilviccoin	13	27	17	57
Scoure	9	25	9	43
Sheabach	8	22	11	41
Artun	15	35	13	63
Total Inhabitants on the Ross of Mull				869

Patronymics and Highland Genealogy

Writing about the Scottish clans in the 1700s, Englishman Edmund Burt made the following observation about the Highlanders "They have a pride in their family, as almost every one is a genealogist."[4] It was an accurate observation considering a great deal of Gaelic history and genealogy was passed down orally,

Delving into the ancestry of any common Highlander is fraught with difficulties. For a start, Highland names were commonly based on patronymics, which is to say, the use of a Christian name derived from a father or male ancestor. Unlike a surname, such names were not permanent and changed with each succeeding generation.[5] Also, it did not identify from which clan the owner of the name came from. Gaelic speakers usually had the addition of the prefix Mhic or Mac meaning 'son of' to help clarify descent. A good example is MacDonald meaning son of Donald. Over time, the prefix Mhic was sometimes expressed as vic and Mac was often abbreviated to Mc. For women, the prefix was Nic, an abbreviation of Nighean, meaning daughter, and was used in a similar way to Mac.[6]

Patronymic names were replaced by surnames. Many Highlanders with a patronymic name simply adopted their clan name as a surname,[7] while others who lived under the protection of a stronger clan adopted its name. It was not unusual for tenants either voluntarily or through coercion, to take the name of their landlord. Names were also sometimes dropped and another assumed when a clansman undertook military action under a new chief, and thereafter joined some other clan.[8]

Problems of identification did not end with the general introduction of surnames during the 1700s.[9] As noted in the analysis of the 1779 census, the spelling of surnames in that era varied considerably. This applied especially when names were recorded by English speaking record keepers, writers, geographers, etc. who usually could not read or write Gaelic. They often recorded those names phonetically - they wrote them down as they sounded. As a consequence, Gaelic names were often recorded at different times and places with various spellings. Spelling in that early period was not fixed. For that reason, some clans today have many different names related to their Gaelic origins.

Christian names, occupations and the location of individual Highland families are valuable indicators in establishing a line of descent when comprehensive records are absent. The naming pattern described below, is one of the few ways that can help identify individual families. In some ways of course it can lead to confusion in the identification of individuals within families, because there can be several members of one generation with the same name in the same location.[10] Also a Christian name was used again if a child with that name died.

In the Highlands of Scotland, parents named their children after grandparents, themselves, their brothers and their sisters. Christian names were commonly given to offspring in a set order. Families had particular names that were passed on from generation to generation. Tradition generally, but not always, followed the pattern below:[11]

Son	Daughter
1st son after the paternal grandfather	1st daughter after the maternal grandmother
2nd son after the maternal grandfather	2nd daughter after the paternal grandmother
3rd son after his father	3rd daughter after her mother
4th son after the father's eldest brother	4th daughter after the mother's eldest sister
5th son after the mother's eldest brother	5th daughter after the father's eldest sister
6th son after the father's second brother	6th daughter after the mother's second sister
and so on	and so on

The McDuffies and Camerons of Knocknafenaig

As discovered when people were recorded on The Disarming List in 1716, the clan name McDuffie in its various forms was not common on the Ross of Mull. Sixty-three years after The Disarming, the 1779 census of the Argyll Estates verifies that to be the case. Despite an increase in the population, the census for the Ross of Mull lists only three households at two farms or localities where the clan name was recorded.

One location was Fidden, near the coast at the western end of Mull where a McDuffie family lived. The second location was Knocknafenaig, a fertile area among low hills, just over 1 mile (1.5 km) south of Bunessan. Two households with the clan name McDiffie were recorded as living there. There is absolutely no doubt the spelling of the name at the time it was recorded was taken down incorrectly. It should have been spelt as McDuffie. The head of each of the three households were brothers.

Forty-four year old Donald McDuffie was recorded living at Fidden with his two sons aged 14 and 11. It is more than likely his wife had died. He worked on the Estate as a bowman. Fifty-two year old Angus McDiffie, lived at Knocknafenaig with his wife, two daughters and two sons, aged four and one. His occupation was not listed. Forty year old John McDiffie also lived at Knocknafenaig where he resided with his wife, two daughters, his 92 year old father Neil and his mother. He worked on the Argyll Estate as a miller. Whether his father was actually 92 is impossible to verify.

It is interesting to note the continued presence of another uncommon Mull name at Knocknafenaig. Two Cameron families also resided there. They were descendants of the Cameron who was listed on the 1716 Disarming List at Knocknafenaig. John Cameron, 64, lived with his wife and two daughters. His 35 year old son, John Cameron junior, also lived there with his wife and three year old son. Cameron senior's daughter Catherine is not named on the 1779 census, but was recorded. She had married mill worker John McDiffie and was listed as his wife. Some of their children appear as members of another community later in this book.

How a Clan Name became a Surname

The surname McDuffie and variations similar to it, are derived from the Gaelic clan name of MacDhubhsith, "one of the oldest and most interesting Gaelic personal names we posssess."[12] When spoken in Gaelic, that name came out as Macduhe or Macdoohe. When expressed in English, it became Macduphie or MacDuffie. If the prefix Mac was omitted, it became Duphie or Duffie. The name MacDuffie was often abbreviated to MacPhee, McPhee, McPhie, MacFie or McFee.[13] As written records became more numerous, those names rather than MacDuffie were more commonly recorded.

The name McDuffie (or McDiffie) never appeared again on any early census or list of inhabitants of the Argyll Estates on the Ross of Mull. People with that name were later recorded with a spelling variation of McPhee. John McDiffie, the mill worker at Knocknafenaig, at some stage had his surname recorded as McPhie. That type of alteration of a surname was not an uncommon occurrence. A McDuffie family no longer resided at Kilviceuen, where it was recorded at the 1716 Disarming. It is possible the family relocated to Knocknafenaig as a result of marrying into the Cameron family that lived there.

Cameron, like McPhie, was a surname rarely found on Mull or Iona. The name became more common after the Jacobite defeat at Culloden, when several Cameron families who had supported the Jacobite cause moved from their clan area of Lochaber to Mull and Iona. After the McPhie Cameron marriage, both lived and worked on the Ross of Mull where they raised a family.

Towards the end of the 1700s, vaccination against smallpox and fewer deaths from famine thanks to the introduction of potatoes, gave rise to an increase in the size of families. The McPhie/Cameron family was typical. It had at least seven children whose baptism was recorded on the Ross of Mull.[14] Their first child, Flora, was born about 1773, followed by another daughter for which there is no record. Her birth (and possibly another child), was followed by Neil, Ann, Alexander, Malcolm, Catherine and Donald born circa 1794 (Appendix 2).

It was a common practice for parents to settle their children near them. Just how many, if any, of the McPhies' children were able to do that is impossible to say. As the post Culloden era progressed, families were unable to settle on the land as they once had.

Determining the fate of people who died in Scotland prior to 1855, is usually impossible. In the Highlands during those times, deaths were rarely recorded, although some were recorded in parish registers prior to that date. It was not until 1855 that the civil registration of births, deaths and marriages commenced in Scotland.[15]

The Statistical Account of Scotland

In 1791 parish ministers throughout Scotland were persuaded to furnish detailed census, statistical and descriptive information about their parishes to one of the leading advocates of Scottish agricultural improvement. His name was Sir John Sinclair (1754-1835). Sir John Sinclair of Ulbster, was a member of parliament for the county of Caithness and also a lay member of the Church of Scotland's General Assembly.

Sinclair's survey covered geography and topography, population, agricultural and industrial production and miscellaneous questions. It took him nearly 10 years to compile and publish what had been provided to him. Completed in 1799, the county by county survey was called the Statistical Account of Scotland.

As the parish minister for Iona and part of Mull, the Reverand Dugald Campbell (1746-1824) gathered and supplied the information for his parish of Kilfinichen and Kilviceuen. After moving from Lismore, he became the parish minister in 1780 and lived on a small farm beside the shore of Loch Assopol in the southern part of the Ross. After finding the ancient church chapel at Kilviceuen in ruins and with no manse, he built his own house next to the Loch, and preached outdoors on hillsides and in parishioners' homes.[16]

Reverend Dugald Campbell produced a detailed and descriptive 41 page report for the survey, which became known as the Old Statistical Account of Scotland (OSA).

Under the heading titled 'Animal and Vegetable Production', Rev. Dugald Campbell noted a significant change in farming and composition of farm animals in his parish. He noted in the past, farms had a mixture of animals including cows, horses, mares, sheep and goats. Goats, were now missing from the land having been banished from all property owned by the 5th Duke of Argyll.[17] Goats were banned because they competed with sheep and stripped the bark from trees. Highland sheep, with their fine wool and delicate flesh had been displaced by sheep with coarser wool from the Lowlands. The hills in the parish, once home to a mixture of animals had been converted into sheep walks.

A wonderful insight into life in the parish of Kilfinichen and Kilviceuen and the people who lived there was provided for posterity. As well as all the farmers, labourers and fishermen, Rev. Dugald Campbell stated there were: "6 broguemakers, 3 shoemakers and broguemakers, 2 boat carpenters, 1 wheelwright, 2 smiths, 3 millers, 6 peddlers who occasionally bought goods in the low country and sold them in the parish, and a great many weavers and tailors. There is only one boat in the parish that carries so much as 9 tons. There are no Jews, negroes, gipsies, foreigners, or persons born in England, Ireland, or the colonies. There are two surgeons, but without farms, their practice would not maintain them one-third of the year, There are six houses for retailing of spirits. There are no lawyers."[18]

Highlanders wore a distinctive type of footwear known as brogues. They were simple shoes without heels. Originally footwear such as this was made from untanned hides and worn with the fur on the inside. In years gone by they were made at home using home tanned leather. Sometimes holes were cut into them to allow water to escape. By the late 1700s broguemaking had become a recognised trade, and skilled craftsmen used tanned leather to make them, after which they were sold. Outlying communities in many of the islands did not have shops from which to purchase such goods. Supplies were purchased from peddlers who brought necessities into the area.

Rev. Campbell's parish was a relatively isolated area, inhabited predominantly by established families. He made several observations concerning the health of the local people and noted the fact that residents were generally long lived. Rev. Dugald Campbell also commented on the increase in the population of his parish:

> "The reason of the increase of population in this parish is common to it with the rest of the Hebrides. Few leave the country, if they can procure a house, which is easily built, with a spot of ground for crop, and a cow's grass. All marry young, and being healthy, their progeny is numerous. The parents also, that their children might settle in the country near them, often share their lands with them, whether male or female".
>
> There is another reason why population should increase upon the Duke of Argyll's property. From his estate, small tenants are never removed, while they behave properly. It is no secret in the country, that his Grace continued their farms to small tenants, at the former rent, though large augmentations were offered by gentlemen who were better able, and would pay their rents more punctually. From the same principle of humanity, it has also happened often, that his Grace, though with loss of rent, ordered farms to be divided into small portions, to accommodate numbers that would otherwise be destitute, and obliged, with weak and helpless families, to leave the country."[19]

Church ministers recorded marriages and baptisms in books called parochial (parish) registers. Later they became known as the 'Old Parish Registers' (OPR). The birth of a child was usually recorded when the child was baptised. If the child died beforehand, there was no record of the birth having occurred.

Rev. Dugald Campbell commenced a parish register soon after he settled into his new home near Loch Assopol in 1780. He reported on the problems his large parish posed when recording births, deaths and marriages on the Ross of Mull: "The incumbent is not sensible, that he missed registering either a marriage or baptism since the year 1782; but, considering the situation and extent of the parish, a few baptisms might be forgotten. This is the less to be wondered at, as parents often, in the more remote skirts, meet him with their infants at a distance from houses, where they were baptised, and where, in a rainy day, he could not mark the names in his memorandum book for the parish register. There are 13 burial places in the parish, at a great distance from the incumbent and from one another, so deaths are never recorded."[20]

NOTES

1. Campbell, Alastair of Airds, 2002, *A History of Clan Campbell*, Vol 3, p. 292.
2. Cregeen, E R, 1998, *Argyll Estate Instructions Mull, Morvern, Tiree 1771-1805*, image of John Campbell, 5th Duke of Argyll.
3. Cregeen, E R, 1963, *Inhabitants of the Argyll Estate 1779*, p. 71-82 .
4. Burt, E, 1998, *Burt's Letters from the North of Scotland*, Letter XIX, p. 200.
5. Black, G F, 2004, *The Surnames of Scotland*, p. xxiv & xxv.
6. MacPhee, E D, 1972, *The Mythology, Traditions & History of MacDhubhsith-MacDuffie Clan*, vol 1, part 1, p. 1.
7. Black, G F, 2004, *The Surnames of Scotland*, p. xxxvi.
8. Argyll, Duke of, 1887, *Scotland As It Was and As It Is*, 2nd edn, p. 480.
9. Davies, N, 2000, *The Isles A History*, p. 655.
10. Jonas, L, and Milner, P, 2002, *A Genealogist's Guide to Discovering Your Scottish Ancestors*, p. 23.
11. Ibid.
12. Black, G F, 2004, *The Surnames of Scotland*, p. 493.
13. MacPhee, E D, 1972, *The Mythology, Traditions & History of MacDhubhsith-MacDuffie Clan*, vol 1, part 1, p. iii.
14. Private research: Jillian King, Western Australia.
15. Jonas, L, and Milner, P, 2002, *A Genealogist's Guide to Discovering Your Scottish Ancestors*, p. 21.
16. Anon, *The Story of St. Ernan's Church, Creich, Isle of Mull, Centenary 1899-1999*, p.4.
17. Cregeen, E R, 1998, *Argyll Estate Instructions Mull, Morvern, Tiree 1771-1805*.
18. Statistical Account of Scotland, Number xii, *Parish of Kilfinichen & Kilviceuen*, p. 190-191.
19. Statistical Account of Scotland, Number xii, *Parish of Kilfinichen & Kilviceuen*, p.189.
20. Statistical Account of Scotland, Number xii, *Parish of Kilfinichen & Kilviceuen*, p. 190.

6

The Post Culloden 'Improvement' Era

A few years after the Battle of Culloden, there commenced a long period of unprecedented change throughout the Highlands. That change was to have a profound effect on the lives of ordinary clansmen.

The modernisation of agriculture between 1750 and 1850 was a period in Scottish history known as 'The Improvement'. The inhabitants of the Highland glens tended to resist change and cling to traditional farming ways. Those in the Lowlands, on the other hand, seemed to embrace change and the increased productivity that flowed from it.

Agricultural improvement coincided with industrialisation, road construction and the building of planned villages. In the Highlands, clan chiefs became landlords, sheep displaced black cattle, potatoes replaced oats as the main food source, farms were fenced, a kelp industry started, Highland regiments were raised, a fishing industry was established, emigration increased and small farms called crofts were made. That period coincided with an increasing population throughout the Highlands.

Landlordism

Following the Battle of Culloden, the nexus between the clan chief and the ordinary clansmen was broken. Traditionally clansmen were a valuable contributor to a clan chief's wealth and influence. A clan chief's power was measured against the number of clansmen who would fight for him, and it was through the efforts of those clansmen and their families that his land was developed and maintained. In return, clan families lived simple lives and paid minimal rent on what was their land by tradition.

Post-Culloden laws in Scotland meant the Highland chiefs were prohibited from recruiting clansmen to support their causes. Rather than custodians of clan land, clan chiefs became landlords who saw their property simply as an asset that could produce a monetary return. The higher the return the better.

After the Jacobite defeat in 1746, many large estate owners moved away from their holdings to live in cities such as Edinburgh and London. Instead of managing their properties wisely, it was common for such men to live a self-indulgent life style. Rather than build up their estates and improve their financial position, they funded their lives by spending the rent money from their estates. Some funded their extravagant mode of living by borrowing against assets.[1]

Debt engulfed many such estate owners. The old lairds who found themselves in this

49

position were forced to sell, if not all, then large portions of their holdings. Apart from squandering their children's inheritance and forfeiting their homes in the Highlands, they opened the door to many newcomers from the Lowlands and England. The newcomers' mantra was profit, and understandably few of them were interested in, or cared about, the clansmen or the old ways in the Highlands. Their aim was to take up large chunks of cheap agricultural land.

The ordinary clanspeople had given their loyalty and allegiance to their clan chiefs for hundreds of years but those notions were now anachronistic and obsolete. The people were increasingly a liability. The position of the clan and its people at that time was summed up perfectly by Englishman Samuel Johnson when he visited the Highlands in 1773 and made the following observation:

> "The clans retain little now of their original character, their ferocity of temper is softened, their military ardour is extinguished, their dignity of independence is depressed, their contempt of government subdued, and their reverence for their chiefs abated. Of what they had before the last conquest of their country, there remain only their language and their poverty. Their language is attacked on every side."[2]

Sheep and Shooting Rights

As noted previously, Highland farming was dominated by arable areas of unfenced land, with cattle as the main rural trading commodity and source of cash. The former chiefs, now landlords, discovered that sheep farming was the most profitable activity, and embraced this new enterprise. Farms used for the new wool growing enterprises were known as 'sheep walks'.

Prior to 1760 there were no sheep farms as such in the Highlands.[3] That changed when it became apparent black-faced Linton sheep could not only survive bitter Highland winters without being housed, but thrive. The product of selection by southern sheep breeders, Linton sheep could produce more meat per area than black cattle and thus were more profitable. During the last few decades of the 1700s, they spread from the south, into the main cattle producing areas of the Highlands, such as Perthshire, southern Argyll and Morvern.[4]

Sir John Sinclair of Ulbster, mentioned in connection to the Old Statistical Account of Scotland in the previous chapter, played a significant role in the spread of sheep into the Highlands. A notable improver, he carried out a trial in the far north of Scotland on his Langwell Estate in Caithness, with sheep that originated from the Cheviot Hills on the border between Scotland and England. Once known as the Long Hill sheep, they had been transformed into the Cheviot breed that produced a high yield of meat and wool.[5]

In 1792, Sinclair proved the Cheviot, although a breed not quite as tough as the black faced Linton, was not only hardy enough to withstand harsh conditions, but produced finer wool than Linton sheep for the emerging textile industry in England.[6]

In the face of strong opposition from native tenant farmers familiar with his plans, Sinclair promoted the introduction of Cheviot sheep into the Highlands, which he saw as an opportunity for his countrymen to improve their lot. He did not, however, foresee how those sheep would eventually lead to the displacement of so many of them.

From the 1790s onward, farmers from the Lowlands and Cheviot sheep advanced across the Highlands. As one writer has put it, in relation to the Highlands, "the new farmers themselves were as deliberate and artificial a creation as the quick-set hedge and the Cheviot sheep."[7]

The pastoral hills and valleys of the Highlands were seen as ideal areas in which to produce wool for the English wool trade. Lowland and English wool growers could pay landlords a much higher price for land used to produce wool than the indigenous tenant farmers growing oats and raising a few head of cattle. Viable sheep walks required a lot of land, but crucially, could be run with a minimal amount of permanent labour. Thus, land rented for sheep farming necessitated the removal of unwanted small tenants who commonly occupied the land. The old 'black cattle economy' was doomed.

The first to feel the full brunt of the new post-Culloden order were the tacksmen, the former chief's most prominent tenants. Some of the chief's more affluent kinsfolk who aspired to larger holdings, took up the new regime based on sheep, but many did not. There was no longer a role for those gentlemen farmers. Fortunately, many tacksmen had the financial means to emigrate to a better life in either Canada or the United States. They helped and encouraged many ordinary Highlanders to join them in what was the first of several phases between 1785 and 1860, the era known as the Highland Clearances.

In addition to sheep raising, many large estates earned an income by selling shooting rights to wealthy English individuals and syndicates. The charges for shooting were based on the grouse as a unit of value. Where a brace of birds was valued at say 5 shillings, larger game attracted a proportionately higher charge. English sporting shooters formed syndicates of 4 or 6, and rented the shooting rights over estates on a monthly basis.[8]

The new cultural and agricultural order in the Highlands required clearing the former clan chief's estates of now unprofitable and unwanted people. Naturally this was to take place over a prolonged period and in different ways. Eventually, however, displaced Highland families were forced to face a few limited options - move to the Scottish Lowlands, remain as tenants on small farms, or emigrate to other countries such as Canada and Australia.

No matter which course of action was undertaken, hardship was involved. The people in the Highlands were in an invidious position because they had no right of tenure over the land on which they lived or worked.[9] Few were masters of their own destiny. Moving to Glasgow or a rural part of Lowland Scotland could only be done if permanent work and a place to live could be found. Remaining in the Highlands and emigration were the favoured alternatives.

23. The Bunessan grain mill. The Duke of Argyll had it built in the 1700s. It was improved with a 14 foot (4.2 m) diameter waterwheel and enlarged with a second storey in the 1830s.[10]

Potatoes and Enclosure

The post-Culloden era heralded two new aspects of life on Mull and elsewhere in the Highlands. They were the introduction of potatoes and enclosure.

Oats, as the main crop and staple food source, had given way to the potato which had been introduced to South Uist from Ireland as early as 1743.[11] It gradually became the main food of people in the Highlands. There was considerable resistance to the acceptance of potatoes as a food, and it was only the example set by the parish ministers that saw it taken up by the local people. The Rev. Dugald Campbell reported that by the 1790s, potatoes had become the main source of food for the inhabitants of his parish.

This was an important development. In terms of food production, the potato grew a high yielding crop, able to support more people on a limited area compared to oats and barley. It was estimated that an acre of potatoes would support four times the number of people compared to the same area sown with oats.[12] Potatoes could also be grown on poorer areas where grain production was unsuitable.

The changes on Mull were reflective of agricultural modernisation taking place throughout Scotland. One of the most significant improvements being implemented throughout the country was 'enclosure'.[13] The unfenced infields and outfields at the core of the traditional Scottish townships were replaced with fenced, defined holdings. The development meant grass-keepers and moor-herds became redundant.

The Kelp Industry

In selected areas around coastal Scotland, seaweed was the foundation of an important secondary industry that had started on the east coast and in Orkney in the 1720s. Kelp is the name given to large brown seaweeds, and around Scotland many types did and still do abound.

Mull was fortunate in having areas of accessible shoreline where various types of seaweed, also commonly referred to as 'wracks', grew abundantly and rapidly. Wrack is the name for dead seaweed and other marine vegetation left high and dry after being washed ashore. Dead seaweed and seaweed that had reached maturity after about 3 years of growth was prone to be torn away from the seabed by winter storms and washed ashore. From the seashore, the drift weed kelp as it was known (commonly the laminaria species) was collected in creels and horse drawn carts and carried to the machair (a flat grassy seashore area) or a low stone wall where it was laid out to dry.

Seaweed (commonly the Fucus species) was also harvested from the seabed at low tide. Men cut the weed with a sickle and dragged it ashore on the incoming tide using a heather rope. It would regrow in two years, when it would be ready to be cut again.

When burnt, the calcined seaweed was also simply called kelp, and produced a hard, brittle, multi-coloured alkaline powder, rich in soda and potash. It was used to bleach linen and in the manufacture of soap and glass.

Producing kelp was a hard, unpleasant, labour intensive job. It required about 20 tons of raw seaweed to make 1 ton of kelp.[14] One observer of the period described the primitive processing of seaweed after it had dried: "Then a few stones, arranged somewhat in the manner of a prehistoric grave, forming a low and a loose enclosure, was all that was dignified by the name of a kiln. Within this little enclosure a lighted peat or bit of wood was used to set on fire a few fronds of the half-dried weed, and when it burst into a crackling flame, fresh weed had to be added so as to keep it down. In this way the weed was rather melted than burnt into a hot and pasty mass, which finally cooled and consolidated into a glassy and brittle substance not unlike the resin... derived from pine trees."[15]

A different description states the dry kelp was forked into a kiln - a trench about 20 feet (6 m) long by three feet (1 m) wide and two feet (.60 m) deep. The trench had stone walls and a peat bottom. The seaweed was burned over a period of four to eight hours with the assistance of heather or peat, usually watched over by women to ensure the fire kept burning. Once all the seaweed was alight, men with long handled 'kelp irons' would rake and pound the mass together. The kiln would then be covered with turf and stones overnight to keep off the moisture. The following day the kelp could be cut into pieces ready for packing and transport by boat to a major city such as Glasgow or Liverpool. The price of the ash varied greatly, as it was subject to competition from a Spanish product called 'barilla', which was extracted from 'glasswort', a coastal plant.[16]

Kelp production began on the Argyll Estates in the early 1750s, when Archibald Campbell, the 3rd Duke of Argyll, recognised the potential his estates on Mull and

Morvern had for producing the product. Its creation waxed and waned according to the price it fetched. When prices were high, between 130 and 150 tons were made in the parish of Kilfinichen and Kilviceuen, but as was reported in the Old Statistical Account, when prices fell as they did in 1791, output fell to less than 70 tons. Production soared after the start of the Napoleonic Wars (1803-1815), during which time prices skyrocketed.

The kelp industry was an essential part of the economy on Mull as elsewhere. The most important place for the industry on Mull was near the island of Ulva, around Loch na Keal. It required large numbers of men and women from June to August, and as a consequence, it had a great influence on all the inhabitants of the island. The income generated from the kelp industry no doubt encouraged people to stay put and contributed to population increase.

The main beneficiaries of the kelp industry were the landlords. Not only did it help tie their tenants to the land, but it gave them another source of income without the need for any capital outlay. Despite kelp being taken from the seaside and the foreshore, landlords such as the Duke of Argyll saw it as their property and their right to control it.

In 1792 John Campbell, the 5th Duke of Argyll, instructed his agent on Mull, James Maxwell, to ensure that his estate's farming tenants were aware that any kelp on their farms belonged to him.[17] He further noted that his rights to kelp would form part of new leases. Those farmers who did not have leases and did not comply with the Duke's wishes were threatened with eviction.

Four years after receiving his instructions, Maxwell was still having difficulty executing the Duke's policy. Tenants engaged in kelp production on Mull's Argyll Estates were expected to harvest and produce the product, then hand it over to the estate for a price it would determine. The tenants resisted this arrangement, making its implementation difficult. To get over the problem, the 5th Duke of Argyll simply raised their rents to reflect the value of the kelp that could be produced on each farm or by each tenant.[18] A higher rent was often an unfortunate consequence for the tenants who had access to kelp.

Highland Regiments

Less than a decade after the Battle of Culloden, most of the world powers at that time became involved in a war with many theatres. It was a global conflict called the Seven Years War (1754-1763). For Britain, it was not only a fight against her old enemy France in Europe, but the threat to her colonial interests in North America.

In a strange quirk of history, Britain turned for help to the Scottish Highlanders, many of whom had recently been their enemies. An Englishman, William Pitt (1708-1778), as the Secretary of State in the British cabinet in charge of military affairs and colonial policy, was responsible for the decision to raise many new Highland regiments. Following Culloden, there had been strong resistance to the formation of such regiments. Pitt however recognised the many advantages Highlanders offered, not the least being they were cheaper than hiring additional German mercenaries.

Kilted Highland regiments were originally aimed at attracting young men from those clans who had fought against the Crown at Culloden, and raised with the object of sending them overseas to fight for the British Government. Looked on with antipathy by many in the English establishment for their lawless past, the loss of such clansmen on the battlefield was a minor consideration. In their eyes they were expendable.

Highland regiments provided much needed employment and money for those men displaced or unable to find suitable work near home. Some of the money they earned could be remitted back home and was often a significant contributor to their parents' rental obligation to landlords.

The Isle of Mull, like many other places in the Western Isles, saw a significant proportion

24. Kilted Highland soldiers in the 1750s.[19]

of its young men join Highland regiments to fight in the Seven Years War. The attrition rate was horrendous. Dr John Walker's Report in the Hebrides of 1764 and 1771 stated the following about the men from Mull: "There went out of this island to the Army during the late war, 350 men, of which only 50 have returned. A great many were killed in America, and the rest are still in service."[20] Numerous survivors of the war in America elected to stay in the country after demobilisation and start a new life there.

The successful deployment of Highland regiments in the Seven Years War led to their increased use in the American War of Independence (1775-1783). Scotland during that time became a key source of military manpower for Britain. Highland soldiers served with distinction. For over 50 years the regiments provided an important employment opportunity for young Highland men until recruitment was curtailed in the early 1800s.

Two significant changes to English-Gaelic relations can be attributed to the role played by Highland regiments, particularly in relation to the American War of Independence. Firstly, the British no longer saw Gaels and Gaelic culture in quite the same negative light as they did after the Battle of Culloden (the Dress Act was repealed in 1782). Secondly, it facilitated the rehabilitation of the Scottish landowning class and the aristocracy back into the fold of the ruling elite in London. The ability to raise and supply clansmen for Highland regiments in the British army gave them considerable social clout. Their newfound power wasn't perhaps so wonderful for single young men on a Scottish laird's estate, for they were susceptible to being coerced against their will, into joining one of those regiments.

Fishing and the British Fisheries Society

One of the most obvious alternatives for people displaced from farming, or returning home after military service, was fishing. Large numbers of farms were close to the coast. The fact that many Highlanders had an aversion to fishing full-time was apparently not taken into account.

When the Rev. Dr. John Walker toured Mull in 1764, he reported on the complete absence of any commercial fishing around the island. He wrote: "Though the Isle of Mull is almost every year visited by the herring shoals, and though there is plenty of cod and ling upon many parts of the coast, there is not a net or long line in all the Island. None of the inhabitants are acquainted with any kind of fishing, but with the rod, and in this way, they procure the most part of their subsistence in summer, by catching great plenty and variety of fish from the sea rocks."[21]

Fishing for herring was thought to be an untapped resource around the coast and in the lochs. Feeding on plankton and microscopic organisms, herring are a pelagic fish i.e. fish that swim near the surface. They appeared around the Hebrides coast in great spawning shoals between May and September. The Dutch had learnt how to preserve them with salt so they could be consumed in winter and during the following year.

Herring could be caught using hemp drift nets thrown from small, open, undecked sailing boats with only one or two masts, and hauled in by hand. Back on shore, after being salted down and placed in barrels, herring could be sent to distant markets.

To try to organise a fishing industry in Scotland, a number of notables put forward the idea of establishing fishing villages around the country's coast. Principal among them was Scotsman John Knox (1720-1790), a wealthy philanthropist who had made his fortune as a bookseller and publisher in London. Concerned at the poverty he found during many tours of Scotland, he published a proposal in 1784 to establish a commercial fishing industry.[22] His ideas gained public support and government favour.

The Scottish nobility took up the idea and the British Society for Extending the Fisheries and Improving the Sea Coast of this Kingdom (British Fisheries Society) was incorporated in 1786. The first governor of the Society was the cream of the Scottish aristocracy and enthusiastic improver, John Campbell, the 5th Duke of Argyll.

The object of the British Fisheries Society was to establish planned villages to accommodate Highlanders and provide grants to individual landowners. The inhabitants of the villages would primarily support themselves by fishing, and supplement their fishing activities with other jobs. At that time, some among the Scottish nobility wanted to stem the loss of cheap labour from their estates so this improvement was naturally welcomed by them. Some landlords also saw it as a way of supporting demobilised servicemen, especially those from the navy.

The British Fisheries Society commissioned Knox to tour Scotland and report on the feasibility of establishing new fishing enterprises there. The report he submitted after his journey in 1786 was extensive and ambitious. He recommended purchasing land and building fishing towns at regular intervals around the coast. Each of those towns would have a school house, an inn and 16 two storied houses with two rooms.

As the 5th Duke of Argyll was the governor of the British Fisheries Society, it is hardly surprising he applied what the Society was doing to his own estates. He saw the Ross of Mull as an ideal location to establish fishing villages which could be sustained by a commercial fishing industry.

One of the Duke's farms near the coast at Creich was chosen to create a fishing village on the Ross of Mull. Twelve lots and a number of families who had lived in the area as tenant farmers were relocated, so that they could become fishermen. The place at a small inlet, was known by its Gaelic name, Ceann Traigh, meaning head of the beach.[23] The 12 lots that formed the village later became known by the anglicised name of Kintra. Anglicisation of Gaelic place names like this was common because of the differences between the Gaelic and English language and alphabet. The Gaelic alphabet for instance does not have the letter 'k'.[24]

To execute his plan, the 5th Duke instructed his chamberlain on Mull to bring some experienced fishermen to the island so that they could instruct the locals on how best to cure fish correctly and catch not only herring, but fish such as cod and ling using long lines. Fishermen from the Shetland Islands and Uist were settled in Creich, on the Ross of Mull.

Fish caught during the summer of 1787 by fishermen living in Creich were sent to the Liverpool market but had not been sold by the following season. It was reported to the 5th Duke of Argyll that "The fish of 1788 are well cured and intended for the Glasgow market when an opportunity of sending them there offers. When the crofters of Creich are fairly settled in their different crofts and better reconciled to their situation the factor will endeavour to introduce the spinning of yarn and manufacturing of nets amongst them."[25]

If any local tenant did not comply with the direction to engage in fishing, then the Duke's representative on Mull had the power to remove the offending tenant. In Creich, three tenants were removed as examples, to encourage others to comply with the Duke's wishes. In a letter from the 5th Duke to his agent on Mull in 1788, it is clear that his tenants aren't interested in fishing. It is also clear that if their attitude persists he is prepared to evict them: "If the natives continue refractory we must introduce a new colony of strangers from other parts, and at any rate you must persevere in the plan of operations laid down last year. I approve of your having removed three of the tenants by way of example."[26]

One of the 5th Duke of Argyll's large tenants in Creich encouraged the new Kintra tenants to become full time fishermen. He was Lieutenant Colonel John Campbell of the marines, who rented a farm next to Kintra. In his extensive report on fishing in the Old Statistical Account, Rev. Dugald Campbell described how he "fitted out a boat, manned it with natives, and except a little fish for his own table, received no other benefit. But though they were as successful as the other boats, they dropped fishing."[27]

The carrot was used as well as the stick to try and get the fishing venture up and running. To assist people trying the new enterprise, the 5th Duke kept the rent low and supplied some of the equipment needed, such as boats and fishing lines. In 1789, the chamberlain instructed the fishing overseer at Creich to:

> "... let it be known immediately, by an advertisement at the church doors, that all persons residing upon His Grace's estate who are willing to furnish themselves with fishing boats and tackling will be supplied with salt at Creich; and that all well cured, marketable dried ling fish which they shall bring to you in the course of the ensuing season will be taken off their hands at Creich at the rate of £14 per ton..."[28]

Full time fishing commenced in 1789 when five boats, each with a five man crew, commenced fishing in April. They fished in water 25 to 80 fathoms deep, catching haddock, flounder, ling, cod, scates (similar to stingrays), eels and dogfish. Fishing continued the following year but did not continue after that as a full time occupation.[29]

Although well-intentioned, commercial fishing was a dismal failure. To cure fish, the majority of fishermen had to obtain salt from specified government customhouses, and the closest one was at the mainland town of Oban. Fishermen were often stuck in Oban for extended periods because of bad weather. The main problem, however, was the lack of demand caused by an oversupply of the product. There was no market for the cured fish in the local area to compensate for the times when sending the product away was not profitable. Fishing remained a mainly part-time occupation.

It was anticipated that a fishing village would also be established on the 5th Duke's farm at Bunessan, on Loch na Lathaich a few miles from Creich. Being under lease (tack), it couldn't be established until a later date. James Maxwell, the Duke's manager on Mull replied about the instructions he had received in 1788: "The farm of Bunessan, if laid out into such crofts as those of Creich, might accommodate about thirty fishing crofters. It is situated at some distance from the fishing banks and is under tack until the year 1799."[30] Following the experience at Kintra, the Bunessan development did not go ahead as planned.

Rev. Dugald Campbell commented in the Old Statistical Account that "after every exertion, his Grace's benevolent and patriotic intentions are, in a manner frustrated, and the prospect of employing, in this branch of industry, the many idle hands in the country with benefit to themselves, and to the community, is nearly vanished."[31]

The parish minister on Mull, like many others, was to lament that the big problem in the Highlands was the lack of any manufacturing industry in which to employ the growing population. The 5th Duke of Argyll was active in trying to address this problem. Naturally it was in his interest to do so in order to obtain a better return from his holdings. Apart from fishing, he tried linen production and opened granite quarries on Mull. Rather than drive people away, he tried to harness the labour on his estates.

The British Fisheries Society, which started out with such high hopes of establishing a fishing industry, had mixed fortunes. After the 1830s it went into decline, eventually sold off all its assets, and was wound up in the 1890s. It was responsible for establishing the towns of Ullapool on Loch Broom, Tobermory on the Isle of Mull, Lochbay on the Isle of Skye and Pulteneytown in Caithness.

25. Fishing boats in port.[32]   26. Women gutting fish.[33]

Whisky Production

Production of whisky from small farm stills for local consumption and export to other areas had traditionally been an important source of income in some areas. It was not uncommon for the income from the sale of the spirit to pay farm rents. In 1786, restrictions and substantial licence fees were imposed by an Act of Parliament on whisky stills in Scotland. As a result, many small stills common throughout the country were put out of business or rendered illegal.

The illicit production of whisky was one enterprise that grew after the new restrictions were introduced. Small stills, especially in the north and north-east of Scotland, were the source of some supplementary income. Utilising barley grain for making whisky was a seasonal activity that occurred in late autumn when the harvest had finished.

In many aspects, whisky-making was like the kelp industry. It was not a full-time activity, but a crutch that enabled many families to stay put when they otherwise would have been forced to move. Just as with kelp, those making it were not the main financial beneficiaries. The grain growers, smugglers, distributors and complicit landlords usually received most of the rewards.

Landlords who allowed the illegal production of whisky on their estates were able to benefit by raising the rent for their land.[34] That arrangement came to an end in 1823 when another Act of Parliament made the domestic distilling of whisky illegal and landowners jointly responsible for any unauthorised production on their land.

Seasonal Work in the Lowlands

A parish minister on Mull, commented in the Old Statistical Account that the movement of young people to work in the Lowlands during the 1790s was a common practice.[35] People would leave Mull in April or the beginning of May to work in the Lowlands of Scotland. They would normally return home to their families in November before the arrival of winter. It was a bone of contention with outsiders and parish ministers that many of the young men and women did not engage in productive work until they went away again.

The movement of seasonal labour, particularly prior to the 1800s was in part determined by wage rates and economic conditions. Highlanders were commonly attracted to the Lowlands by the higher wage rates offered there. Mull residents, like those from nearby islands, generally sought employment in the central and south-eastern Lowlands as agricultural workers. The movement of labour was made much easier with the introduction of steamboats in the 1820s.

Large numbers of people living in the Highlands moved to the Scottish Lowlands during harvest time. As the improvement era progressed, there was a tide of outgoing and incoming seasonal workers. During this period, harvesting crops was still a labour intensive activity where, until the 1840s, the sickle was used by both men and women to reap grain crops. After the introduction of the more efficient scythe, which required two hands and considerable strength to use, harvesting grain crops was done mainly by men. The Lowlands, being the main cropping area, needed substantial casual labour. Many men also moved away to find casual employment in the fishing industry and many women worked as household servants.

Tenant Farmer Evictions

The 1770s were the years when the old life style in the Highlands began to change from the 'black cattle' economy. Many owners of Highland estates amalgamated small tenant holdings into larger farm units. The new order, based on wool from sheep grazing, had a significantly greater impact on small tenant farmers than it did on the tacksmen. With few resources and no equitable right to their traditional livelihood, small farmers could do little to prevent being thrown off their rented land. After small holdings were consolidated, they were commonly rented out to Lowland wool growers. So commenced another phase of the Highland Clearances, where large numbers of people were removed from their homes.

Agents known as 'factors' were employed by landlords to manage their estates. Factors in turn appointed a 'ground officer' to help them run the landlord's property. Factors assisted in what could be classed as a sort of forced land reform, albeit in some places a cruel one.

The easiest option for the landlords to rid themselves of unwanted tenant farmers was simply to raise their rents. All leaseholders of land were affected. Many tenant farmers earned little income and farmed on what could best be described as a subsistence agriculture basis. Families on small plots of land found it increasingly difficult to live, let alone pay rent. For those who persisted and paid the increased rent, life was hard. Poverty was an obvious consequence. Many farmers could not pay, and the landlords issued eviction orders to force their tenants out.

In the early period of the Clearances, rough justice in the form of widespread evictions generally did not occur on Mull. In this regard, the tenants on the Argyll Estates were more fortunate than many. While ever tenants behaved themselves, they were rarely removed from their holdings. Also, rents were kept at modest levels.

The years during and just after the Napoleonic Wars (1803-1815) saw the removal of Highland families on a larger scale than had occurred previously. High wool prices spurred landowners to cash in on the boom by replacing traditional tenants with larger scale wool growers. This phase of the Clearances was marked by increased hardship in the Highlands and the notoriously brutal removal of thousands of people from estates owned by the Duchess/Countess of Sutherland and her wealthy English husband Lord Stafford in the county of Sutherland.[36]

Evictions saw many families lose their home. In some cases, tenants were physically put out, their simple dwellings were often pulled down and, in some extreme cases such as those that occurred in Sutherland, were set ablaze in front of the former inhabitants. As it was difficult to rebuild elsewhere, burning the homes of the people deprived them of some basic materials for shelter. Often the small farmers' crops, such as potatoes, could not be recovered, further adding to their misery.

The plight of the Highland communities was exacerbated by the failure of their religious leaders to help them. Churches turned their backs on their own flocks and more often than not took up the case of the landlord.[37] Churchmen had a vested interest in supporting the landed gentry because it was they who usually appointed them. Many of those self-serving churchmen threatened the poor souls struggling against eviction with the wrath of God if they didn't do as they were told. It is no wonder that, with a few exceptions, tenants were generally compliant of the orders made against them.

The severity and cruelty with which evictions took place varied from estate to estate. Some areas fared worse than others. Whether cruel or otherwise, it was under these circumstances that if they could afford it, thousands of Scottish Highlanders emigrated in search of a better life in places like Canada, America, Australia and New Zealand. For whatever reason, emigration was to feature throughout the period known as the Highland Clearances that occurred for over 75 years.

Emigration and Ship Passenger Act

On Mull, it was reported in the Old Statistical Account, that only a few families had emigrated to America during the 1790s. The Rev. Dugald Campbell made the point in his report, that no people are more attached to their native country than his parishioners.

Elsewhere, particularly as time went by, large numbers of Scottish Highlanders emigrated to seek a better life. Landlord evictions, together with overpopulation, periodic famines and low commodity prices, had seen emigration blossom and grow. Whether voluntary, forced, assisted by landlords or assisted by government, it was one way of alleviating the abject poverty that many Gaelic people lived with.

Emigration brought with it the usual rogues and unscrupulous operators anxious to make a quick profit from the plight of those involved. The conditions on many vessels used to carry their human cargo were often appalling, due to overcrowding and a lack of fresh food and water. In response to this problem, the British Government in June 1803 passed the Ships' Passenger Act, aimed at improving the conditions on board vessels carrying emigrants, especially those going to North America. The Act regulated a minimum space per passenger and a luggage allowance for each person. It also stipulated sufficient food, water and medical supplies were provided, and a qualified surgeon on vessels carrying more than fifty people. While a laudable piece of legislation, it had the unfortunate consequence of forcing up the cost of the fare, which in turn prevented many families who had saved for such voyages from going.[38]

The Ships' Passenger Act had little effect on the Argyll Estates. This is made clear in an interesting letter dated 7th February 1804 sent to the Duke of Argyll by his Estate Manager for Mull and Morvern, James Maxwell. The letter stated: "The spirit of emigration which was so active last year, though restrained by the regulations of the late Act of Parliament, is by no means extinguished. Some individuals who cannot afford to pay the increased freight have already enlisted in the Canadian Fencibles, on condition of having their wives and children carried free to America; and many single families will probably engage passages on board ships that, by taking out only a few, will not come within the operation of the Act. This spirit does not however extend to your Grace's estate, nor do I understand that, with the exception of one worthless individual, there is a single tenant upon it who has at present any intention of moving."[39]

Not every Scottish estate owner wanted to clear out all the small tenants or see them emigrate. Many of the influential landowners around coastal Scotland were not happy with the high level of emigration because it deprived them of a plentiful supply of cheap labour for the kelp industry. Those landowners were happy to see a fall in the emigration rate to retain their kelp workers and the profits generated from that enterprise.

NOTES

1. Macinnes, A I, 1994, *Land Ownership, Land Use and Elite Enterprise in Scottish Gaeldom: from Clanship to Clearance in Argyllshire 1688-1858,* contained in Scottish Elites, edited by Devine, T M, p. 20.

2. Johnson, S, 1984, *A Journey to the Western Isles of Scotland and the Journal of a Tour to the Hebrides,* p. 73.

3. Richards, E, 1982, *A History of the Highland Clearances,* p. 174.

4. Richards, E, 1982, *A History of the Highland Clearances*, p. 175.
5. Prebble, J, 1963, *The Highland Clearances*, p. 25.
6. Prebble, J, 1963, *The Highland Clearances*, p. 27.
7. Smout, T C, 1969, *A History of the Scottish People 1560-1830,* p. 308-9.
8. Prebble, J, 1963, *The Highland Clearances*, p. 146.
9. Devine, T M, 1994, *Clanship to Crofters' Wars*, p. 39.
10. ROMHC, Bunessan grain mill image.
11. Argyll, Duke of, 1887, *Scotland As It Was and As It Is*, 2nd edn, p. 309.
12. Devine, T M, 2004, *The Great Highland Famine*, p. 15.
13. Lynch, M, 2001, *Oxford Companion to Scottish History*, p. 207.
14. Argyll, Duke of, 1887, *Scotland As It Was and As It Is,* 2nd edn, p. 314.
15. Argyll, Duke of, 1887, *Scotland As It Was and As It Is*, 2nd edn, p. 313.
16. Keay, J & J, 1994, *Encyclopaedia of Scotland*, p. 567.
17. Cregeen, E R, 1998, *Argyll Estate Instructions Mull, Morvern, Tiree 1771-1805*, p. 151.
18. Cregeen, E R, 1998, *Argyll Estate Instructions Mull, Morvern, Tiree 1771-1805*, p. 193.
19. Reid, S, 2000, *Highlander Fearless Celtic Warriors*, p. 101.
20. Walker, J, and McKay, M M, 1980, *The Rev. Dr. John Walker's Report on the Hebrides of 1764 and 1771,* Edinburgh, Donald, J, p. 152.
21. Ibid, p. 162.
22. 'A View of the British Empire, more Especially Scotland, with some Proposals for the Improvement of that Country, for the Extension of its Fisheries, and the Relief of the People'.
23. Maclean, C, 1997, *The Isle of Mull Placenames, Meanings and Stories*, p. 29.
24. Black, G F, 2004, *The Surnames of Scotland*, p. lvii.
25. Cregeen, E R, 1998, *Argyll Estate Instructions Mull, Morvern, Tiree 1771-1805,* p. 151.
26. McGeachy, R A A, 2005, *Argyll 1750-1850*, p. 171.
27. Statistical Account of Scotland, No. xii *Parish of Kilfinichen &Kilviceuen*, p. 178.
28. MacArthur, E M, 2002, *Iona The Living Memory of a Crofting Community*, 2nd edn, p. 30.
29. Statistical Account of Scotland, No. xii, *Parish of Kilfinichen & Kilviceuen*, p. 177 and 179.
30. McGeachy, R A A, 2005, *Argyll 1750-1850*, p. 169.
31. Statistical Account of Scotland, No. xii, *Parish of Kilfinichen & Kilviceuen*, p. 176 and 177.
32. KGPA Ltd, *Alamy stock photo.*
33. www.scotfishmuseum.org/, No sfm - 166, women gutting fish.
34. Devine, T M, 2004, *The Great Highland Famine*, p. 10.
35. Statistical Account of Scotland, Number xii, *Parish of Kilfinichen & Kilviceuen,* p. 196.
36. Richards, E, 1982, *A History of the Highland Clearances*, p. 284.
37. Prebble, J, 1963, *The Highland Clearances*, p. 63.
38. McGeachy, R A A, 2005, *Argyll 1750-1850*, p. 48, 69.
39. Cregeen, E R, 1998, *Argyll Estate Instructions Mull, Morvern, Tiree 1771-1805*, p. 201.

7

Crofting

Small tenant farmers and others among the commonality were provided with an alternative to stay in their native land. They were able to rent farms called crofts. The word croft means small farm or enclosed land, and the tenant farmers on those farms were called crofters.

Croft development varied from estate to estate. Small crofts were often established away from the fertile hills and glens, on poorer ground that had previously been unsuitable for grain crops. Commonly this was coastal land. Near the coast, it was anticipated the displaced families could survive by growing potatoes, fishing and providing their labour for activities such as kelp production.[1] Broadly speaking, crofters were small-scale farmers who maintained themselves and their families by growing high yielding potato crops as their main source of food. For an income, they kept some cattle and could engage in seasonal activities like kelp production or fishing.

Rather than the haphazard old rural holdings or townships that comprised arable land and grazing areas, crofts were laid out in formal blocks, sometimes comprising just a few acres each. Little regard was paid to the suitability of such land to sustain a family.

Stone dykes were erected to enclose what were previously open, unfenced fields. Potatoes formed the main crop with small areas sown to oats and barley. Beyond the arable land, crofting townships had an area of pastureland set aside for grazing cattle on a communal basis. A tenant's rental was commonly based on the head of cattle a tenancy could sustain or was permitted to own. As a rough guide, for each £1 of annual rental, one cow could be grazed.[2] The majority of crofts were too small to support large numbers of livestock or substantial grain growing.

Traditionally, cultivation was done with a Scotch plough pulled by two or three horses in a line abreast, against a beam fastened to them with straps. The plough had two almost perpendicular handles, so the ploughman held them in an erect position as he guided the plough through the ground. A man followed the ploughman with a spade to flatten the furrow not filled in by the two sideboards on the plough. In front of the horses was a man called the driver who held the reins of the horses. In this awkward position the driver navigated the horses as he walked backwards across the field.[3] Such labour intensive cultivation practices on communal farms were not practical on small crofts. The creation of small, fenced, individual farms meant a significant change to past farming practices.

Horses could not always be used on stony or marshy ground developed for crofting, so a foot plough called a 'cas chrom' was sometimes used. The implement was often used when planting and harvesting potatoes. It was a heavy farm tool, consisting of a narrow steel blade with a long wooden handle, and using it was extremely hard work.

On areas where it was impossible to use a horse and cart, a type of carrier referred to in the Argyll Estate papers as a car, was still necessary for farm work. A sled or struts were connected by two shafts, one on either side of a horse, to carry loads. With no wheels, the two ends of the shaft simply dragged along the ground.

Sheep walks and land subdivided into crofts heralded the end of the old runrig system. Tenant farmers on crofts were expected to grow and live primarily on potatoes. As crofts had generally been established on gentle hills with shallow soils and or poor quality marshland, potatoes often had to be grown in raised beds. This was necessary in order to provide adequate soil and facilitate drainage. Raised beds were created by digging drainage ditches and piling the extracted soil onto strips of land. If available, seaweed was spread in a layer on the beds to act as a fertiliser. The raised strips were called 'lazybeds'.[4]

Towards the end of the 1700s and in the early 1800s, many new crofting communities were formed and families established in them.

Crofts were not established evenly throughout Scotland. The main crofting areas were in the Western Isles, Northern Isles and along Scotland's west coast. These three regions encompassed seven shires or counties which were Argyll, Caithness, Inverness, Ross and Cromarty, Sutherland, Orkney and Shetland. Collectively they are sometimes referred to as the Crofting Counties.[5] (fig. 27).

Crofting was a profitable strategy for some landlords. The best land and larger farms could be leased out to wool growers who were able to pay higher rents. Displaced tenants and others could be accommodated on crofts. In addition to paying rent, those people formed a captive labour force that could be used for activities beneficial to the estate owner, such as kelp production or fishing. Some Highland estates were thus divided so as to accommodate a greater number of rent paying tenants. For those not able or desiring to live on a croft, there were new villages being created

The crofting society, however, was fatally flawed. It was based on the availability of part-time work in a few select industries. It also depended on the potato as a reliable source of food for the crofting families. A problem with either could spell disaster.

Subdivision of Communal Farms

Having begun croft development on Tiree in the late 1770s, the 5th Duke of Argyll was in the forefront of changing the land use on Highland estates.

To manage his vast land holdings, the Duke issued written instructions to his chamberlains at an annual meeting in October at Inveraray.[6] The chamberlains brought their reports on the instructions the previous year. The instructions and reports were supplemented with correspondence throughout the year.

In 1787 the Duke appointed James Maxwell as his chamberlain to manage his

27. The shaded portions on the above map indicate the location of the main crofting areas in the seven crofting counties of Scotland.[7] Unlike the old traditional rural townships, crofting communities were established with a planned layout, often based on small farms made up of a rectangular strip of land.

properties on Mull (which included Iona) and Morvern. A capable man, he lived on one of the Duke's farms at Aros, in the northern Mull parish of Kilninian and Kilmore. Chamberlains like Maxwell in turn employed ground officers to help them execute their duties and undertake day to day activities for him.

The 5th Duke of Argyll resolved to start subdividing and improving his farms on Mull and Morvern in the 1790s. Those developments generally commenced when farm leases came up for renewal. In October 1800, he instructed James Maxwell to commence the process of establishing crofts on his estates there:

> "Being satisfied that it will be of great advantage towards the improvement of my estates in Mull and Morvern if the small tenants were to divide their farms, or at least the arable parts of them, and every man to build his house upon his own particular lot, you will turn your attention to this object, and report to me next year what farms you think may admit of this kind of management. I am aware that much cannot be expected from small tenants in this way whilst they posess from year to year, but I will agree to give leases for 9 years and to help such of them as shall undertake to divide their farms and sit down upon the separate lots."[8]

The first crofts were divided up and leased from 1802. During the first few years on new crofts, tenants had to work assiduously to not only build their houses and grow crops, but to erect dividing fences. Enclosing the fields with stone walls was quite a task. The new nine year leases gave those tenants security of tenure for a reasonable term.

The Ross of Mull became one of the principal crofting areas on the island. The gathering and production of kelp was not a major consideration in their establishment. The main objective of the 5th Duke of Argyll was to try and improve the productivity of the agricultural land on his extensive estates. It was also his policy to try and retain all the people who lived on them.

To subdivide existing farms for closer settlement and advise him on improvement generally, the 5th Duke utilised the services of George Langlands, a land surveyor. He worked out the optimum subdivison and drew up plans. To keep abreast of the changes, the Duke instructed James Maxwell to employ a person specifically to monitor the improvements on each farm. Maxwell's choice was confirmed by the Duke in 1801: "I agree to employ Alexander McCallmum at a salary of £25 to superintend the execution of the improvements undertaken by the tenants, and you will cause him to report occassionally to yourself and annually to me, how they advance."[9]

Tenants who had once operated and leased farms in a communal arrangement had to accept a new way of living i.e. a house on their own defined area of land. Advised by James Maxwell that farmers were short of tools to reconstruct their houses or build new ones and other farm buildings, the 5th Duke agreed to help them: "As you say that the tenants will be a loss for tools and cars for quarrying and leading stones for building their houses and dykes, I agree to furnish the tenants of every farm that is to be divided with a sledge-hammer and crow iron amongst them and with as much timber as will make a car to each individual."[10]

One matter the 5th Duke was uncompromising about was the old practice of tenants dividing their farms amongst their children. That was not to be permitted.

The available evidence indicates a report on croft development was submitted every six months, with one being the period between Whitsunday in May until October, and the next report for the remaining six months.

In 1802 one such 'report of improvements executed' from the Argyll Estates on Mull, provides a fascinating example of the details that were recorded on the 5th Duke's vast holdings. Regrettably, the copy of the original document sighted has a considerable amount of detail obscured or missing. The record however demonstrates the meticulous nature of the 5th Duke towards the development of the land under his control.

The 1802 report is provided on pages that appear like those from a type of cash book with 16 columns, and like other records of the era, spelling of names and places is inconsistent with that of today. The headings are all handwritten. Farms including Ardton, Bunessan, Knockvologan, Uskin, Saorphin and Shiaba were recorded in the first column. The name of each tenant in those farms is then listed. Beside each tenant the following information is recorded:[11] The number, length in feet and breadth in feet of dwelling houses, barns and byres that have been built. As well as the buildings, the length in roods and feet of any stone dyke and ditch 'executed' was also noted on the report. In Scotland, walls were known as dykes.

Probably because the crofts were in their early stage of development, there is little information recorded about the barns, byres, stone dykes or ditches from the improvements executed in 1802. However the record provides some interesting measurements for houses that had been built. Built with stone walls (sod or turf not being permitted), they were nearly all between 30 and 33 feet (9-10 m) long, and 18 feet (5.5 m) wide. The cost of house building and fencing was borne by the individual tenants. They were aware that at the end of the lease their landlord might not necessarily renew it.

A report for the period from May 1803 to 12th October 1803[12] required similar, but less comprehensive information to that of the previous year. It provides only for the number of houses, barns and byres built, excluding all the measurements. More information is required under the heading of roods of fencing executed. Measurements are required for double stone dykes, ditches, dyke and ditch and for single stone dykes against hanging ground. Hanging ground refers to the unimproved ground around crofts, usually on the hills away from the arable farmland.

One of 13 tenants shown in the 1803 report, residing on the southern side of the Ross of Mull at Shiaba, is a John McPhee. Was he from one of the three families with that clan name listed on the 1779 census living at Knocknafenaig? Almost certainly, but using such a record to positively identify individuals is virtually impossible. It is fair to conclude however, with such an uncommon surname at that time in the area, he was a member of one of those families. If not an existing tenant at Shiaba, he may have moved there to take up one of the new crofts. Did that particular tenant continue to live on a croft at Shiaba until he died, did he move, or, when the wheel turned full circle, was he among those evicted when crofts were later amalgamated? Like countless others, there is no record to determine what happened to him. Despite decades of occupation throughout the 1800s, few if any detailed records about crofting townships and those who lived in them were ever made or have survived.

At this point it should be noted that in order to emphasize the relevance of some historical occurrences, this book sometimes draws on the life of an individual family in a typical crofting community. It is used as an example because considerable information is known about it. Utilising that material also provides a continuous thread for the story and helps humanise what occurred during the Highland Clearances. Any family on a small croft could be substituted for the one used.

Accommodating the Supernumeraries

Croft development occurred during a time of increasing population on Mull as elsewhere in the Highlands. Communal farms that once could support an extended family were phased out with farm subdivision and enclosure. That meant a large increase in the non-farming population. Those extra people or supernumeraries as they were sometimes referred to, created a problem never before experienced.

Unlike some landlords, the 5th Duke of Argyll took a compassionate approach to the less fortunate residents on his estates. At the meeting with his chamberlains in October 1803, he gave the following instruction to James Maxwell from Mull:

> "... I see a necessity for taking some steps to endeavour to accommodate cottars and the other supernumerary population of the country who cannot be provided in farms. I understand there are many people of this description in the Parish of Ross who formerly found accommodation among the tenants when farms were possessed in common, but who will be more at a loss for settlements now that they are divided and every tenant has his own separate share. My engagements in that part of the country do not at present admit of giving relief to those people to the extent that may be necessary or that I would otherwise incline, but still I wish to do as much for their accommodation as circumstances will allow. I therefore desire that you will consider whether Catechant and perhaps a small part of Salchur, possessed by General John Campbell, lying contiguous to Creich, can without much inconvenience be separated from his farm and cut down into small lots or settlements for such of these people as are the most destitute and maintain the best characters..."[13]

The 5th Duke's compassionate approach to those who lived on his estate is also evident in the instructions he gave to his chamberlain on Tiree at the meeting in October 1803: "... different farms must be broke down into small crofts to accommodate the people who are in want of possessions. Such as were formerly tenants to have from 6 to 10 acres, and those who were only cottars and tradesmen to have four arable acres, and both to have what accommodation can be given in the article of summer grass. As these people will have much to do in the article of building houses and division fences at the beginning, I agree to allow the first year free of rent to such as shall deserve it by building houses and other exertions in that period... It is absolutely necessary that the people be led to manage their crofts in the best possible manner, without which they will soon ruin the land, and become beggars themselves. A scheme of management for such small possessions is annexed to these instructions."[14]

Before croft development was completed on the Argyll Estates, the 5th Duke of Argyll died in 1806. His 38 year old son, George William Campbell (1768-1839), became the 6th Duke of Argyll, and inherited the Argyll Estates. Fortunately for the tenants on Mull and Iona, their new landlord did not pursue a policy of leasing his land to the highest bidder, or a policy of aggressive eviction in order to settle sheep farmers. In consultation with the chamberlain on Mull, the 6th Duke of Argyll set the price for croft leases on how much each should be reasonably able to pay.

The 6th Duke was the antithesis of his father. He not only didn't follow his father's improvement policies, he didn't follow any policy at all. He generally left the management and development of his Estates to others. As a politician and playboy, he preferred to spend his time in London and Edinburgh rather than at Inveraray. Like others of his ilk, he ran up debts and sold off some of the land he inherited to fund his lifestyle, but did retain his land on the Ross of Mull. The Estates on Mull, Iona and Morvern were continued to be managed by his predecessor's chamberlain, James Maxwell.

It seems marriage also played a part in providing crofts to landless labourers. Although it may not have been a stated prerequisite, the records indicate that once a young labourer was married, he was given priority in the allocation of newly created crofts which gave him an opportunity of having a place to build a home, farm and raise a family. Marriage was therefore a blessing in more ways than one.

Regardless of any tangible benefit, Gaelic marriages were a cause for much celebration, observed with formality, feasting and decorum. A few days before the ceremony, verbal wedding invitations were issued to relatives and neighbours by the bride and groom. On Mull, as elsewhere in rural Scotland during the early 1800s, weddings usually took place on a Thursday, commonly during the quiet winter period or a month either side of it.

On the wedding day it was the norm for a bride and groom to have a midday meal of oatmeal bannocks (cakes) and maybe some cheese and whisky, at their respective homes. After lunch, each left home accompanied by family and friends, with a piper possibly leading the way to the church. After the ceremony, everyone headed off to a dance, followed by a lavish evening meal of meat, potatoes, eggs, cheese and butter served up on a long table. Sometimes a barn or local school hall was used for such occasions.

James Maxwell was responsible for croft development on Iona, where many new crofts were established between 1802 and 1804. Around this period, three of John McPhie and Catherine Cameron's children mentioned in an earlier chapter, had for some unknown reason moved from Mull to live or work on Iona. Each was able to lease a croft after their marriage. In 1803, their daughter Flora McPhie married Iona resident Donald MacLean, and the MacLeans were allocated one of the new crofts on the island about the time of their marriage.

Crofts were eventually established at Catchean (spelt previously as Catechant), on the western end of the Ross of Mull as originally proposed by the 5th Duke at the end of 1803. After his marriage to Ann McDonald in 1807, Alexander McPhie was allocated one of the new crofts at Catchean (pronounced Car-chin), a Gaelic word meaning common gathering or common grazing.[15]

In 1816 at the age of 23, Donald McPhie married Mary McInnes on Iona. McInnes was one of the most common names on the island. In the 1700s it was frequently expressed as 'MacGinnis'. When Johnson and Boswell visited Iona, they recorded that "The McGinnises are said to be a branch of the clan of McLean."[16]

The minister at the time of the marriage was the Rev. Donald Campbell, who had replaced his father, the Rev. Dugald Campbell in 1816, as the Church of Scotland minister for the Parish of Kilfinichen and Kilviceuen. Church services were conducted by Rev. Campbell down the length of his large parish at three strategic locations on a rotational basis, alternating between Kilfinichen, Bunessan and Iona.[17] Whatever the preaching schedule, while visiting those places he was also able to marry couples and record baptisms. In remote areas a long way from any church or where the minister routinely preached, weddings were sometimes conducted in the home of the bride.

Rev. Campbell recorded the marriage in the usual way, with a one line entry in the parish register useing the spelling McPhee.[18] Their first child was born the following year with a baptism recorded in November. The registration doesn't ascribe any occupational description to McPhee indicating he worked in some capacity rather than occupy land as a rent paying tenant. A year or two later, the family was able to lease one of the newly created crofts at Braighcreich, in the district of Creich, on the Ross of Mull.

Braighcreich, a Typical Crofting Comunity

Creich (pronounced Kray), is the name of a district that had within it a farm or rural community of the same name. It was one of those old communal townships with a long history going back beyond the 1600s. At the time of the 1779 Argyll Census, Creich was inhabited by only 25 people.

Most Gaelic place names refer to some historical incident or geographical feature. Creich has two possible meanings. It could have come from the Gaelic term Creiche meaning plunder, to signify that some battle or similar event took place there, or the term Criche, meaning boundary.[19] The latter is apparently more likely.

Geologically the district was notable for the fact it was composed of distinctive pink and grey granite. The granite belt around Creich covers an area of about 20 square miles (52 sq km) extending from the Sound of Iona on the coast, and inland to the vicinity of Bunessan.[20] For generations the locals had picked it up off the ground to construct houses, byres, barns, kilns and mills. Although its beauty, strength and durability had long been recognised, it was not until 1839 that commercial quarrying began.

In the crofting era, Creich grew to include a number of subdistricts or what used to be farms. Over the years, various census returns described the district, but probably the 1871 census gives the most informative account for contemporary readers trying to understand the lie of the land. "District of Creich comprising the farms of Ariglass, Creich, Bracreich, Deargphort and the village of Kintra bounded in the north by the Atlantic on the east by the boundary of the parish of Kilfinichen on the south by the district of Fidden and in the west by the district of Catchean. Level arable land a considerable portion of moss land. Length 1 ½ miles Breadth 1 ¼ miles."[21]

The district of Creich described above was the classic crofting locality. It was near the coast and had a considerable amount of 'moss land'. The area known as Braighcreich situated within that locality, was sometimes referred to in old documents as 'Bra Creich' but pronounced Bra Kray. The term most likely translates in Gaelic as something like 'top end of the boundary'.[22]

The crofts at Braighcreich were reached by a small track that passed by the old traditional township of Creich. On the rocky, windswept grassland and moorland of Braighcreich, a string of crofts, rectangular in shape, had been laid out line abreast across a piece of gently sloping country. There were about six small crofts in all, each separated by stone walls .

In all the records researched to write this book, no original documentation has been found which recorded the size of the Braighcreich crofts, when they were developed, who first leased them or a map showing their layout. Being created after the 6th Duke took over the Argyll Estates may be the reason for those deficiencies. It seems certain however, the size of the crofts conformed to the instructions given to the chamberlain of Tiree by the diligent 5th Duke in 1803 i.e. where possible, cottars and tradesmen were to be allocated four arable acres (1.6 ha) of land.

The 1851 government census for Kintra and North Creich adds weight to the assumption that the crofts at Braighcreich were four acres in area. It lists eight individual families, numbered one to eight, living there. Of the eight, six family heads are shown as farmers, five resident on four acres and one on five acres (2 ha). Farming families at North Creich are also shown mostly on four acres of land. It would therefore be fair to assert the Braighcreich crofts were nearly all four acres in area. As some land was better than others, the rentals probably varied for each holding.

All dwellings built on the Braighcreich crofts were located in a rough line across an ill-defined ridge. At the bottom of the slope ran a small stream called 'Allt na Creiche'. Allt na Creiche in essence means the boundary stream.[23] There are many places with similar names across the Highlands and Islands, as a stream was traditionally used to identify boundaries between landowners.

The croft made available for the McPhees' to lease was the last one at the eastern end of Braighcreich. It occupied a site at the base of a hill called Beinn Chladan (pronounced Ben Cladin). As most of the surrounding area was either naturally treeless or had long been denuded of trees, the leafy canopy that shrouded the hill gave rise to a pleasant backdrop to the croft. The trees growing on Beinn Chladan included birch, rowan and oak, and were the remnants of old, native woodlands.

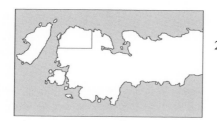

28. The district of Creich on the Ross of Mull is located opposite Iona.

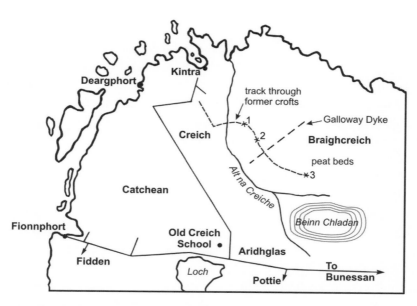

29. The district of Creich. This section of the Ross of Mull had within it Creich and a smaller locality known as Braighcreich where there was a clearly defined crofting community during the 1800s.
1 = MacGillivary; 2 = MacCormick; 3 = MacPhee.

Soggy, open, treeless fields joined the croft at the eastern end of Braighcreich, which, although unsuitable for agriculture, were rich in peat. At various times of the year a carpet of flowering mauve heather, white cotton grass, bogbean and spotted orchid disguised what lay beneath. Over the years, areas the size and shape of football fields were cut into the landscape to extract peat.

Not only locals used the fields at Braighcreich. People from Iona came across and obtained their peat from this location. Rowing boats ferried men, women, horses and carts from Iona to Deargphort on the coast in the Creich district. From Deargphort they made their way over the fields, past the Braighcreich crofts to the peat bogs. Peat was then cut and left nearby for a month or so to dry. It was then carted to the coast where each household stacked their supply in their own spot. When the weather and sea permitted, the dry peat was ferried across to Iona.

The expanse of moist fields near the peat fields attracted a noisy, migratory bird every year called the barnacle goose (Branta bernicla). These birds are small, black and white geese that have a call something like the yapping of a small dog. They breed in Greenland during the summer and spend the winter in parts of the Western Isles of Scotland, including the Ross of Mull. The location of the open field near the peat beds at Braighcreich was known as 'Gortain na Ghibhain' (pronounced Gorchin a Geeblan).[24] It is not certain what the term means, but it may have referred to a field where geese were common or a small calf enclosure.

Croft Houses

New houses, barns and byres were constructed by the first tenants to lease crofts at Braighcreich. Their homes were somewhat like those thatched stone huts described previously, but improved versions. They were still rectangular in shape, but instead of rounded corners, had double dry stone walls that met at right angles. Rather than a place in the middle of the home for an open fire, they had a stone fireplace at one end, sealed with rough mortar, with a chimney for the smoke to escape.

The thatched stone hut built next to the peat field at the eastern end of Braighcreich was typical. It had a similar dimension to the new croft houses recorded in other localities during 1802 and 1803. The inside of the home was 33 feet (10 m) long by 18 feet (5.5 m) wide. The stone walls were over 3 feet (1 m) thick at the base, which tapered up to about 2 feet (61 cm), reaching a height of only about 5 feet (1.5 m) and were in-filled with smaller stones. Croft walls typically inclined inwards about 1 inch (2.5 cm) for roughly every 7 inches (18 cm) of height. The appearance of a section of the rear stone walls of the croft, at the opposite end to the fireplace, seems to have been constructed differently to the rest of the croft. Whether the house was built that way, or like other croft houses in the community altered at some point, is impossible to say.

On Mull, stone houses of the period commonly had a strange looking chimney called a 'loudie brace lum' protruding from their roof (fig. 31). It was a structure made of timber

30. A primitive Mull home in the 1700s with the fireplace in the middle of the building.[25]

31. The type of stone house common on Mull in the 1800s. It has a distinctive chimney called the 'loudie brace lum'. Lum is another name for chimney.[26]

32. An example of a stone house found on the Ross of Mull in the 1800s.[27]

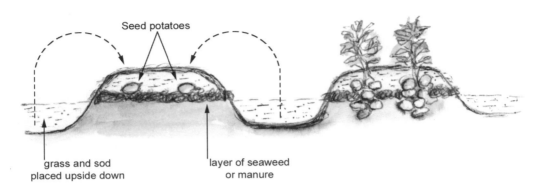

33. Potatoes being grown using the lazybed method of cultivation.

34. Preparation for planting potatoes. The cas chrom or foot plough is being held by each of the men in the photo. One of the women is carrying a creel on her back full of seaweed which will be added to the planting bed. The photo was taken on the Isle of Skye in the 1800s.[28]

sheets nailed together that acted as a chimney, and rather than being perpendicular in the traditional fashion, was built at an angle leading the smoke away from the end of the house. It was a type of chimney commonly found in the border districts of Scotland and probably introduced to Mull by seasonal workers who regularly visited the Lowlands during harvest.

The wooden beams of the house roof supported sods of turf (or peat) that were covered with thatch made of rush, bracken fern or heather, tied down with heather ropes connected to anchor stones, just as had been done by past generations. It covered an interior that had an earth and stone floor. The area inside was not much bigger than the size of a modern single car garage and had an area partitioned off where the parents slept. Despite its limited space and basic nature, the house was weatherproof and cosy.

A few yards away from the house were two other smaller stone buildings constructed with rounded corners. Almost certainly one was a barn to hold grain, animal feed, and possibly some crude farm implements and the other a byre to house the animals. All three buildings seem to conform to those required to be reported in the 1802 and 1803 Report of Improvements on the Mull Estates.

Neighbouring croft houses in the community were roughly 220 yards (200 m) away from each other. Near the croft once leased by the MacCormack family, there used to be a blacksmith's workshop, known as a smiddy, that served the local community. The smith not only shod horses, but repaired farm implements and household goods. As one writer put it,[29] the smiddy was also the local exchange, where crofters would gather on short wet days during winter to discuss crops, market prices and other matters of local interest. It was the social hub in small Highland communities.

North-west of the MacCormack's farm, the MacGillivrays lived on another croft. There were about 18 stone buildings with thatched roofs that eventually made up the crofting community at Braighcreich. Apart from the three crofters mentioned in this chapter, there is no available record to indicate who occupied other individual crofts.

It was in this setting that families in the district farmed their crofts. During the short days of winter, they carried out routine activities necessary to maintain themselves and their farm. Seaweed was collected from the seashore and carried to farms where it was spread on the lazybeds used to plant potatoes in the spring. Potatoes were the main crop, with a limited area also used to grow some oats and barley. Kale and peas may have been grown in a small vegetable patch near the house. On the common grazing nearby, crofters had a few head of sheep and cattle, while nearer to home they kept some fowls, pigs, pet dogs and perhaps a horse.

Spring and summer were seasons of constant activity. The sowing of crops usually commenced in the 3rd week of March and was finished by the middle of May. After the potato crop had been planted, families went to the nearby bog, where for the best part of three weeks they had to cut enough peat for cooking and heating for the coming year. It was an essential task and one that prevented more profitable farming endeavours when the weather was usually fine. Towards the end of summer, cereal crops had to be harvested and the grain dried, threshed and winnowed prior to it being ground into meal. When the potatoes matured, the men dug them up using the cas chrom and the women helped collect the potatoes and carry them home.

In a good season, the crofters grew enough produce on their farm to feed and clothe themselves. The sale of surplus crops and livestock went towards paying the rent for the croft and the purchase of goods produced elsewhere. As some of their children reached adulthood, they contributed to the family's income by working in the Lowlands or perhaps in the local fishing industry.

Living on their croft in the district of Creich, the McPhees had another child. Rev. Donald Campbell recorded the birth with a one line entry in the parish register when the baby was baptised.[30] The entry notes the father's rise in social status, giving his occupation as a crofter.

Like many of their neighbours, the McPhee family living in what was once the crofting township of Braighcreich were to have a large family. With a child born nearly every second year, the parents would raise 10 children on their croft[31] - six boys and four girls (Appendix 2). During the 30 years the family lived there, just as their contemporaries did throughout the Highlands, they would experience one of the most tumultuous and distressing periods in Scottish history.

NOTES

1. Devine, T M, 1994, *Clanship to Crofters' Wars*, p. 35.
2. Devine, T M, 2004, *The Great Highland Famine*, p. 5.
3. Burt, E, 1998, *Burt's Letters from the North of Scotland*, Letter xx, p. 210.
4. NRS, *Jamieson's Scottish Dictionary*, 1880, Paisley, Vol III.
5. Willis, D, 2001, *Crofting*, p. 126.
6. Cregeen, R, 1998, *Argyll Estate Instructions Mull, Morvern, Tiree 1771-1805* p. 104.
7. Willis, D, 2001, *Crofting*, p. x.
8. Cregeen, R, 1998, *Argyll Estate Instructions Mull, Morvern, Tiree 1771-1805*, p. 196.
9. Cregeen, R, 1998, *Argyll Estate Instructions Mull, Morvern, Tiree 1771-1805*, p. 198.
10. Ibid.
11. A&BC file FH344 *Report of Improvements executed upon the following His Grace the Duke of Argyll's Estate in Mull and Morvern betwixt Whitsunday 1802.*
12. A&BC file FH344: *Report of Improvements executed upon His Grace the Duke of Argyll's Estates day of May 1803 and the twelfth day of October.*
13. Cregeen, R, 1998, *Argyll Estate Instructions Mull, Morvern, Tiree 1771-1805*, p. 201-2.
14. Cregeen, R, 1998, *Argyll Estate Instructions Mull, Morvern, Tiree 1771-1805*, p. 73-74.
15. Maclean, C, 1997, *The Isle of Mull Placenames, Meanings and Stories*, p. 22.
16. Johnson, S, and Boswell, J, 1984, *A Journey to the Western Isles of Scotland and The Jounal of a Tour to the Hebrides*, p. 367.

17. Currie, J, 2001, *Mull the Island and its People*, p. 239.

18. Old Parochial Register, Kilfinichen and Kilviceuen. It stated "22nd Aug. 1816 Donald McPhee in Iona & Mary McInnes in Iona were married."

19. Maclean, C, 1997, *The Isle of Mull Placenames, Meanings and Stories*, p. 21.

20. Faithfull, J, 1994, *The Ross of Mull Granite Quarries*, 2nd edn, p. 8 and 9.

21. 1871 Scotland Census, County of Argyll, Reg. district of Creich.

22. ROMHC, *A Guide to the Walks in the District of Creich*, p. 19.

23. Maclean, C, 1997, *The Isle of Mull Placenames, Meanings and Stories*, p. 69.

24. Mull resident and local historian, Attie MacKechnie.

25. Garnett, T, 1811, *Observations on a Tour Through the Higlands and Part of the Western Isles of Scotland*, Vol 1, p.160.

26. Argyll - An Inventory of the Ancient Monuments, Volume 3, Mull, Tiree, Coll and North Argyll: The Royal Commission on the Ancient and Historical Monuments of Scotland; Edinburgh 1980, plate 91.

27. Argyll - An Inventory of the Ancient Monuments, Volume 3, Mull, Tiree, Coll and North Argyll: The Royal Commission on the Ancient and Historical Monuments of Scotland; Edinburgh 1980.

28. Aberdeen University Library: George Washington Wilson Collection.

29. MacCormick, J, 1923, *The Island of Mull Its History, Scenes and Legends*, p. 165.

30. Old Parochial Register, Kilfinichen and Kilviceuen. It stated: "10th October 1819 Donald McPhee crofter in Creich & Mary McInnes 1 S John."

31. Old Parochial Register, Kilfinichen and Kilviceuen and Quoad Sacra Parish of Iona.

8

Increasing Hardship and Emigration

As the population grew during the 1820s and 1830s, change continued to take place in the Highlands and the Islands. Farms and estates had been amalgamated to form sheep walks, and thousands of families had been forced off those areas to live elsewhere or emigrate. The crofts formed to provide an alternative for some tenant farmers and others displaced from fertile areas, were increasingly uneconomic and unable to support large families. Crofters had to pay rents that were often increased beyond the capacity of the farmer, and any untoward event such as a crop failure was disastrous.

Quoad Sacra Parishes and Cholera

Deciphering early records can sometimes be difficult. Some inhabitants on the northern area of the Ross of Mull such as the residents of Braighcreich, were recorded as being born in the Parish of Iona. At first glance, the records would indicate they were born on Iona when in fact they were born on Mull. It is confusing but there is an explanation.

Following victory in the Napoleonic Wars, the British Parliament made funds available for the construction of churches throughout the country. Parliament not only recognised the need for more churches for a greater population, but saw it as an expression of goodwill and thanks to God, after the victorious outcome of the wars. Known as Parliamentary churches, they were built to a design by Thomas Telford.

In 1828 the government built one such church on Iona and a 'quoad sacra' parish was then established. A quoad sacra parish was not a normal parish but one created for ecclesiastical reasons only, i.e. without any civil or state significance. It was a religious parish with its own church and minister to cater for an increased population.

The quoad sacra Parish of Iona also included five farm areas in the district of Ross, on Mull - Fidden, Knockvolagan, Potee, Creich and Catchean. Although included in the Parish of Iona, these areas were located on mainland Mull. Separate registers were kept for the Parish of Iona from 1829.

Dugald Campbell was the minister of Kilfinichen and Kilviceuen Parish between 1780 and 1816. As stated in the previous chapter, keeping things in the family, his son Donald took over from his father as the minister of the parish. Another one of Dugald's sons, Dugald Neil Campbell, became the first minister of the quoad sacra Parish of Iona. The Rev. Donald McVean became the second minister of the Iona Parish in May 1835.

The minister of the Kilfinichen and Kilviceuen Parish was based at Bunessan, where another Church of Scotland had been built in 1804 to replace the dilapidated, ancient

Christian chapel at Kilviceuen. The new church served the united parishes of Kilfinichen and Kilviceuen. The minister used to visit Iona officially only four times a year when it was part of his parish. Following the establishment of the Iona Parish, the minister based on the island visited mainland Creich and Catchean, etc. about twice a year to attend his parishioners. At other times, parishioners living on Mull had to cross the Sound of Iona if they wished to attend their parish church. Apparently a group with boats did this regularly, while others went to the church at Bunessan.

A year after the creation of the new quoad sacra parish, management of the Argyll Estate on Mull and Iona changed with the death in 1829 of James Maxwell, who had been the chamberlain for over 40 years. He was replaced by Alexander MacDonald, who became the Ground Officer.

Populations beset by poverty, hunger, poor housing, overcrowding and ignorance of good hygiene, are prone to contract contagious diseases. Some, if not all, of those conditions were prevalent in many of the crofting communities. The deadly disease cholera arrived in Britain during 1831 and was reported in Scotland during January 1832.[1]

County Boards of Health were given funds to alert the public on precautions required to prevent an outbreak and spread of cholera. Crofters and others who had dungheaps near their doorways as described in Chapter 3 were instructed by inspectors to move them at least 30 yards (33 m) away. Places where pigs rooted about on dungheaps were particularly at risk from the disease. People who rarely changed the straw they slept on were advised to do so, and householders were urged to clean their dwellings. In the villages and towns, manure stances were encouraged to be established at appropriate places. Those dungheaps could then be removed by contractors and sold to farmers.[2]

Fortunately the 1832 cholera outbreak was contained. Unlike some mainland counties, it seems few among the population on Mull, Iona or other Hebridean islands either died or were affected by the outbreak.

During the 1830s, large families on small crofts began to feel the pinch of being forced to depend on poor quality land, meagre assets and low incomes. Some chose emigration while others preferred not to move unless forced. The seven children of John McPhie and Catherine Cameron listed in Chapter 5 were typical of the generation who lived in the crofting era. All married local people. Only two out of the seven children didn't emigrate and continued to live in Scotland. One remained on Mull and the other on Iona.

Of the remaining five, three were fortunate to secure a passage to Canada: Ann to Ontario, Malcolm to Prince Edward Island and Neil, also to Canada. The remaining two stayed on Mull until events that will come to light in the following pages forced them or their families to leave. Alexander at Catchean had 14 children, but several died in infancy.[3] Until his death between 1827 and 1836, he remained a crofter there.[4] His adult son John continued working the croft to support his widowed mother Ann and the family until necessity compelled them to move to Australia. Donald continued as a crofter at Braighcreich, until he was eventually also forced to migrate to an Australian colony.

The 1836-7 Famine

Crofters were more vulnerable to the vagaries of farming than either their forebears who lived in traditional townships, or to those who farmed larger areas of land. Landless cottars and those dependent on employment also faced a tough time during any economic downturn, no matter what the cause.

In 1835 and 1836, cold and wet spring weather throughout Britain delayed crop planting and crop maturity. Wet weather during late harvests exacerbated a difficult situation which caused a substantial drop in potato and grain crop yields. In the Highlands, the potato harvest was down by a quarter to half, while the oat crop was more severely affected, with yields down between half and two thirds.

One poor season was bad enough for crofters, two poor seasons was a disaster. Those unfortunate crop yields led not only to a lack of food, but also the seed required to plant a new crop. In some ways it was reminiscent of the famine during the Ill Years of the 1690s. The food shortage caused great hardship throughout the country, and as one writer put it when referring to the 1690s famine years, "it was a terrible instance of a vulnerable and primitive economy to bad weather..."[5]

In the Highlands the famine coincided with a number of adverse economic conditions. Returns from the sale of black cattle had dropped and were no longer a reliable source of income. In years gone by, Highlanders sold cattle at local fairs or had them sent down drove roads for sale at annual trysts such as that at Falkirk, but now found it difficult to compete against cattle from Aberdeenshire and counties in north-east Scotland.

The price of kelp had also declined after the reduction of duties on an imported substitute called barilla and the availability of other alternatives. The once dependable herring fishery had also become less reliable with a drop in income from that source.

By the 1830s, the income from seasonal employment on public works and on farms in the Lowlands had become crucial for the maintenance of many Highland and Island families. The immigration of large numbers of Irish labourers to Glasgow and rural parts of the Lowlands not only depressed wages, like those for shearers which had halved, but denied many Highlanders the opportunity of any employment. It cost an Irish labourer between sixpence and a shilling to travel from Belfast to Glasgow, whereas from the Highlands or far flung islands, the fare could cost 12 shillings and the journey took days.[6]

The confluence of poor economic circumstances, unrelenting population growth, lack of employment, crop failure and famine led not only to hunger but extensive poverty throughout the Highlands.

Knowledge of the position in the Highlands and Islands was brought to the attention of the government in London by petitions, letters from the Solicitor General of Scotland and a deputation of Scottish members of parliament to the Chancellor of the Exchequer. Although sceptical about the reported extent of the problem, the government commissioned Robert Graham, the Secretary of State for the Home Office, to visit the distressed districts in the north west of Scotland and report on his findings.

The Graham Report

Robert Graham (1784-1859), was a Scotsman from Perthshire who had previously been a lawyer. He was joined on his fact-finding tour by his second cousin, Robert Stewart of Ardvorlich, who acted as his Gaelic interpreter. Both toured the distressed areas of the Highlands and Islands during the months of March and April 1837 in His Majesty's revenue cutter *Swift*.[7] A revenue cutter was a vessel used to deter and apprehend smugglers. With their vast sail area and long bow spit, they were built for speed, strength and fire power. Cutters were heavily armed, as they often encountered violent opposition from smugglers.

Graham did a thorough job of investigating the districts he visited. He documented his findings in a number of letters to the Treasury, the last of which he wrote on 6th May, 1837. The 215 page collection of letters confirmed that more than half the Highland and Island population was in a state of need.[8] While some areas like Sutherland and Wester Ross were relatively unscathed, others in the Outer Hebrides and Skye were severely affected. Skye was in a particularly parlous state, with more than three quarters of the population destitute. Within the distressed areas, it was found the cottars, other landless inhabitants and small crofters suffered most from the famine.

Visiting the Mull district, Graham estimated more than a quarter of the population was in distress, with the Ross of Mull and Iona among the most badly affected places. On the Ross of Mull he found "The failure of potatoes in the District is reckoned fully one third, of grain one half."[9] Like visitors before him, he found travel on the island difficult. For that reason he recommended "making roads which are much wanted in Mull would be the best mode of finding temporary employment for the people."[10]

Letters from Graham described the reality of life in the Western Highlands and Islands. They noted the economic problems that have already been mentioned, described each district's distress, what relief was required, temporary works that could be undertaken and the best way to distribute supplies of meal to the affected areas. On the question of supplying food aid, Graham suggested storage depots in a few key areas to facilitate distribution, and lists of those requiring aid be drawn up by local committees.

Graham made two significant criticisms. Firstly, the proliferation of land subdivision on proprietors' estates that had encouraged an unsustainable increase in the population. Secondly, the failure of the existing voluntary poor relief measures in Scotland (which differed from those in England) to assist the starving and destitute. Graham's letters also made clear that overpopulation was the underlying cause of the poverty and starvation in the areas visited, and government assisted emigration was the way to solve the problem.

Money for famine relief was forthcoming from the government. Funds were also provided by estate proprietors, the church and the public at large. Relief committees set up in Glasgow, Edinburgh and London raised almost £80,000 to buy meal, potatoes and blankets for the starving.[11] On Mull, as elsewhere, a list of those in urgent need was drawn up and they were supplied with meal and seed to replant crops. Mass starvation was avoided.

Emigration and the Bounty Scheme

In the decade leading up to the famine years in the 1830s, there had been a constant stream of emigrants to North America which contrasted sharply to the relatively small number of people who went to Australia.

There is little doubt the residents of Mull were familiar with the colony of New South Wales in Australia. Local man Lachlan Macquarie (1761-1824), born on the nearby island of Ulva, was a distinguished soldier who had been the Governor or New South Wales between 1810 and 1821. After an illustrious career, he returned in 1822 from New South Wales to live on land he owned on Mull. After his death in London on 1st July 1824, his body was transported to Mull where it was buried on his Gruline Estate. Despite knowledge about Australia and the opportunities it provided, few among the poverty stricken tenantry in the Highlands had emigrated there.

Considering the advantages North America offered, that was hardly surprising. The sea journey was comparatively short, the fare was cheap, a significant number of Highlanders were already resident there and settlement conditions were favourable with Canada offering free grants of land. A Highland family could pay the fare to Canada and stock a farm, for the cost of a fare to Australia.[12]

The onset of the famine years precipitated a rise in emigration to Australia that was in part aided by political problems in Canada and less favourable economic conditions in the United States, but fuelled primarily by critical labour shortages in Australia. Scotland's need to alleviate its surplus population through emigration was mirrored by Australia's need of immigration to provide people to help develop the country. Scotland had too many people, Australia did not have enough.

To help finance immigration to Australia, the Colonial Government established a 'Land Fund' from the sale of Crown Land. Money from the fund could then be used to finance emigration to Australia. By 1835 the demand for labour in Australia was so great that Richard Bourke (1777-1837), the Governor of New South Wales,[13] was forced to act. A Bounty Scheme (which had been legislated for in 1831) was introduced as a way of attracting migrants to Australia.

The Bounty Scheme was an arrangement whereby the Colonial Government indirectly paid the fare for immigrants. The government issued a 'Bounty Order' valued at £30 for a married couple, £5 for a child, £15 for a single woman and £10 for a single man.[14] Immigrants were conveyed by private arrangement from the United Kingdom to Australia, with little or no control exercised by the British Government.

Bounty Orders were issued to colonists to bring out migrants of a suitable age and occupation. Those Orders were often signed over to British ship owners and immigration agents, who in turn appointed commission agents to find suitable applicants. Commission agents not surprisingly recruited any likely prospect from city slums willing to accept a free fare to Australia. Such recruiting led to profiteering and other abuses.[15]

One of those who utilised the Bounty Scheme was a prominent Scotsman living in

Australia. Reverend Doctor John Dunmore Lang (1799-1878) was educated at a parish school in Largs, and graduated from Glasgow University. In 1822 he was ordained as a Presbyterian minister, and a year later went to New South Wales to establish Presbyterianism in the new colony.

The Rev. Dr. John Dunmore Lang was elected to the NSW Legislature, where he was often embroiled in controversy over the issue of immigration. He advocated increasing the migrant intake for the colony and was strongly opposed on this issue by the powerful landowners and squatters, who saw this as contrary to their best interests. The squatters, the landed gentry of Australia, were trying to stop people encroaching on their sheep country for exactly the same reason that the Scottish lairds were driving them away.

Leading the squatters was William Wentworth, and it was to these people that Lang directed the following quote: "In short, the squatters, who then ruled the colony under the leadership of Mr. Wentworth, in virtue of an electoral system... characterised by downright chicanery and fraud, had no desire for the settlement of the country with a numerous, industrious, and virtuous population from the United Kingdom. They desired to have it reserved exclusively for their sheep and cattle."[16]

Perhaps Lang's most controversial views were those concerned with the type of migrant that should come to Australia, and the type of assistance, if any, that should be given to them. Lang was strongly opposed to open-ended assisted immigration, and advocated a system whereby immigrants were selected for settlement in Australia according to their suitability. He complained vociferously about unscrupulous immigration agents and the dubious practices they employed.

Still more controversial were Lang's views on the composition of the migrant intake. In his view, immigrants should have been reflective of the population of England, Scotland and Ireland, especially with regard to religion. With this view he contended "The grand desideratum for this colony is a thoroughly British population, coming out as nearly as possible in the proportions of the Three Kingdoms."[17] Not unnaturally for a Presbyterian minister in that era, he was unhappy that the bulk of newcomers to the colony were assisted migrants, dominated by Irish Catholics.

In the famine year of 1836, Lang was making one of his nine voyages to England,[18] a feat in itself in those days, when he saw the plight of his native people as an opportunity not only for them, but also for the colony of New South Wales. He sent out circulars to Presbyterian ministers in places like Mull, which could be read out to parishioners, advising them of the merits of immigration to Australia.

Lang could arrange for impoverished parishioners with little or no money who wanted to emigrate to have their fare paid through the Bounty Scheme, and was able to facilitate that arrangement by chartering ships for the journey to Australia. He had remarkable success in his efforts to attract emigrants from Scotland. Prior to leaving England in 1837, he played a pivotal role that saw the emigration of 4,000 people from Scotland to Australia in 18 ships during the course of the following three years.[19]

Like many others, it was the hardship caused by the 1836-7 famine which prompted the widow Ann McPhie and her family living at Catchean on Mull, to take up Lang's offer. Ann, together with six children, were accepted as emigrants under the protection of Ann's eldest son John. John, as a 29 year old farmer on his widowed mother's croft, paid £15 towards the fare for the family to emigrate to Australia. Documents of the day show how important the church was, with the local parish minister for the Church of Scotland giving a reference for the departing family:

> "The Rev'd D McVean Minister of Iona Certifies from intimate knowledge of his character that he is an exceedingly well conducted man and much respected in his Parish. The Factor to His Grace the Duke of Argyll on whose Estate he was a tenant corroborating the above as also does the Rev. Dugald Neil Campbell late Minister of Iona. These certificates are for the whole family."[20]

On 13th September 1837, the Catchean McPhies from Mull were among between 235 and 280 emigrants and passengers (the number of each being uncertain) on board the *SV Minerva* chartered by Rev. Dr. John Dunmore Lang, that sailed from Greenock for Australia. The passengers included a number of German missionaries from Berlin in what was then called Prussia. They were laymen, agriculturists and artisans, who had volunteered for service in Australia, accompanied by two ministers of the German Reformed or Presbyterian Church. Lang had recruited them in order to establish a mission for aborigines at Moreton Bay in Queensland.[21] He was paid a bounty for every fit person under his charge who landed in New South Wales.

Lang personally organised the charter of three ships to bring English and Scottish emigrants to Australia. The majority of those emigrants were from the Lowlands, many of them skilled tradesmen. In that regard the *Minerva* was an exception as it carried a complement of Highlanders.

Lang's strident criticism of the Bounty Scheme and a recommendation for change from the Legislative Council of New South Wales Committee of Immigration, saw the introduction of a new immigration scheme.

35. The Rev. Dr. John Dunmore Lang.[22]

Government Funded Emigration

Governor Bourke introduced a 'Government System' of immigration to be run in conjunction with the Bounty Scheme. Under this arrangement, all aspects of emigration including migrant selection was placed under the control of the Colonial Office in London. To manage the Government System, Thomas Elliot, a talented career civil servant in the Colonial Office, was appointed to the new position of Agent-General for Emigration.[23]

To bolster government emigration, Governor Bourke appointed naval surgeon Dr. David Boyter in 1836 as the Colonial Emigration Agent in Scotland. His instructions were to "procure and bring out from Scotland a certain number of emigrant mechanics in conformity with the recommendation of the Committee of the Legislative Council of this colony."[24] If there were insufficient mechanics available, married shepherds and agricultural labourers were to be chosen, but whatever the case their employment was guaranteed on arrival in Australia.

Despite the huge number of Highlanders desperate to escape the hardship caused by the famine and a country desperate to receive them, there was political and bureaucratic opposition to opening the emigration gate to relieve starvation and poverty in the Highlands. The British Government refused to allocate funds for emigration to Australia, Canada or anywhere else. It was argued by Thomas Elliot and others that colonial funds available from Australia were not intended for Highland emigration.

Thanks to pressure from the famine relief committees, representations by Rev. Dr. John Dunmore Lang and Robert Graham's tour of the distressed areas, objections to financing an emigration programme were overcome. The Colonial Office recommended to the British Cabinet that money from the Land Fund in Australia be applied to facilitate emigration from the Highlands to Australia.

Dr. David Boyter was instructed to proceed to Scotland and liaise with both the Edinburgh and Glasgow Famine Relief Committees and then "to proceed to the Highlands in order to ascertain whether or not a sufficient number of married persons of good character and of an age not exceeding thirty-five are to be found who are willing to avail themselves of a free passage to New South Wales."[25] Thus began the first significant programme of emigration from the Highlands of Scotland to Australia.

Among the first emigrant ships Boyter was able to charter was the three year old wooden hulled *Brilliant.* When the fully rigged sailing ship arrived in Tobermory on 16th September 1837, it "created a sensation in Mull never before equalled; the Highlanders having only been accustomed to see small vessels fitted for American emigration,..."[26]

An extensive newspaper article about the *Brilliant* was printed soon after it sailed from Tobermory on 27th September 1837: "... on Tuesday afternoon a farewell sermon was preached in Gaelic by the Rev. F. McPherson, of Tobermory,... The people to be conveyed by this vessel... from their knowledge of agriculture, and the management of sheep and cattle, must prove a most valuable acquisition to a Colony like New South Wales... Among the many visitors that came to see the *Brilliant* was a gentleman, a native of the country of their adoption... and presented all he met with letters of introduction, which were joyfully received as passports to sure and profitable employment... The embarkation was superintended by Dr. Boyter, R. N...”[27]

Aboard the *Brilliant* were 318 emigrants: from Ardnamurchan and Strontian, 105; Coll and Tiree, 104; Mull and Iona, 56; Morven, 25; Dunoon, 28 plus 2 teachers and 2 surgeons. It was the third and final ship to take Highlanders to Australia in 1837, the two preceding it being the *William Nicol* and the *Midlothian,* both of which departed from the Isle of Skye.

During early 1838, Dr. Boyter found it hard to deal with a flood of letters from people seeking to emigrate which forced him to insert the following newspaper notice: “Finding it utterly impossible to reply to the numerous applications for information respecting emigration to New South Wales, this is to give notice to all those intending to emigrate, that the terms on which people are sent out are simply, a passage free of all expense, including provisions and bedding. On arriving in the Colony, they are provided by the Government with house and rations for a reasonable time, until employment is offered them; they are at liberty to whom they choose, and no money is either advanced or received by Government on any account whatever. Before entering into any agreement with people, it is necessary for me to see them. In order that it may be known generally when and where I am to be seen, due intimation will be inserted in the *Inverness Courier...*”[28]

The strong demand for emigration to Australia was evident when Dr. Boyter visited Fort William in May 1838. “The news of his arrival... soon spread through every glen of the district, and at an early hour on Monday, thousands of enterprising Gaels might be seen ranked around the Caledonian Hotel, anxious to quit the land of their forefathers and to go and possess the unbounded pastures of Australia... the Highlands will be considerably relieved of its over – plus population.”[29]

During 1838 and 1839, a dozen or so emigrant ships transported Highlanders to Australia. Two of those ships sailed from Tobermory with people from Mull. The *British King* on 18th October 1838 and the *George Fyfe* on 15th September 1839.

Emigration was curtailed after 1839. A drought in Australia, a belief there that the British Government should pay for emigration, criticism of the Government System's high cost compared to the Bounty Scheme, and improving conditions in Scotland, resulted in the cessation of the Government System in 1840. Thomas Elliot's position as Agent-General for Emigration and his office were absorbed into a new government body, the Colonial Land and Emigration Commission.[30]

Crofting Rent Arrears

Famines such as that which occurred in 1836-7 always cause hardship. This was particularly so for small farmers who lived a hand to mouth existence on Mull and Iona. For the hard pressed crofters who remained on their land after the famine, finding the money to pay the yearly rent was one of the many difficulties they faced.

Unless things had changed since the days of the 5th Duke's management of the Argyll Estates, tenants were expected to pay their rent twice a year, "one half at Martinmas and the other half at Whitsunday."[31]

Each year, a list was compiled of tenants on the Argyll Estates who were behind with their rent. At least one such list has survived and is available to provide an insight into not only the management of the Estates, but the lives of some of its inhabitants on the Ross of Mull. The list for 1840 provides the name of each tenant who is behind in rent, how much is owed, the farm district where residing, the amount owed by that district and finally the total amount of rent owed. The following are the tenants shown, and the amounts they owed according to the arrears list for Creich.[32]

Name	£. s. d	Name	£. s. d
Donald MacLean's widow	6. 13. 4	Neil Patterson	4. 9. 10
Peter MacArthur	4. 13. 4	Martin MacGilvra	2. 17. 4
Arch. MacMillan	2. 18. 4	John MacLeod	2. 19. 0
Alexander MacDonald	4. 11. 0	Donald MacPhee	3. 0. 8
William Black	2. 19. 2	Donald MacLachlan	1. 16. 8
Alan MacLean	16. 6	Hugh MacArthur	3. 6. 8
Arch. MacKinnon	2. 14. 4	Hugh MacGilvra	16. 8
Dugald MacCormaig	13. 3. 4	Alexander Campbell	18. 8
John MacGilray's widow	1. 0. 2		

The 1840 arrears list for the district of Creich shows 17 tenants are behind in their rent. The Argyll Estate was owed a total of £59.15.0 from the district. It should be noted that long before famine created hardship, being in arrears was a way of life for some crofters.[33] Such tenants pleaded poor for all sorts of reasons in order to seek a reduction in rent or avoid paying rent when it was due. Famine however, forced many who would usually pay their rent on time into arrears.

NOTES

1. *Inverness Courier*, 4th January 1832.

2. *Inverness Courier*, 11th January 1832.

3. McPhie, H, *A short Journey into the Genealogy and history of Clan Macfie Commander Alexander Carpendale (Sandy) McPhie*, private paper.

4. Old Parochial Register, Kilfinichen and Kilviceuen, Isle of Mull.

5. Smout, T C, 1969, *A History of the Scottish People*, p. 242.

6. Balfour, R A C S, 1973, *Emigration from the Highlands and Western Isles of Scotland to Australia during the Nineteenth Century*, University of Edinburgh Thesis, note 32, p. 62.

7. NRS, HD. 7/9. Graham, R, *Report on the Highland Destitution of the Year 1837*.

8. NRS, HD. 7/9. Graham, R, *Report on the Highland Destitution of the Year 1837*.

9. NRS, HD. 7/9. Graham, R, *Report on the Highland Destitution of the Year 1837*, Combined Parish of Kilfinichen and Kilviceuen, p. 55.

10. NRS, HD. 7/9. Graham, R, *Report on the Highland Destitution of the Year 1837*, Combined Parish of Kilfinichen and Kilviceuen, p. 56.

11. Balfour, R A C S, 1973, *Emigration from the Highlands and Western Isles of Scotland to Australia during the Nineteenth Century*, University of Edinburgh Thesis, p. 63.

12. Balfour, R A C S, 1973, *Emigration from the Highlands and Western Isles of Scotland to Australia during the Nineteenth Century*, University of Edinburgh Thesis, p. 42.

13. Richard Bourke was the Governor of New South Wales between 1831 and 1837.

14. Cannon, M, 1971, *Who's Master? Who's Man?*, p. 121.

15. Cannon, M, 1971, *Who's Master? Who's Man?*, p. 121-122.

16. Lang, Rev. J D, 1978, *The Fatal Mistake*, p. 16.

17. Lang, Rev. J D, 1978, *The Fatal Mistake*, p. 32-33.

18. Gilchrist, A, and Powell, G, 1998, *John Dunmore Lang Australia's Pioneer Republican*, p. 59.

19. Lawson, R, 1966, *Dr. John Dunmore Lang and Immigration*, Australian National University Thesis, p. 79

20. Archives Authority of NSW, *Letter 8/8/1969 to A. C. McPhie*.

21. *The Courier Mail*, 3rd July 1937.

22. Lang, Rev. J D, 1978, *The Fatal Mistake*.

23. Macmillan, D S, 1967, *Scotland and Australia 1788-1850, Emigration, Commerce and Investment*, p. 271.

24. Balfour, R A C S, 1973, *Emigration from the Highlands and Western Isles of Scotland to Australia during the Nineteenth Century*, University of Edinburgh Thesis, p. 61.

25. Balfour, R A C S, 1973, *Emigration from the Highlands and Western Isles of Scotland to Australia during the Nineteenth Century*, University of Edinburgh Thesis, p. 66.

26. *Inverness Courier*, 11th October 1837.

27. Ibid.

28. *Inverness Courier*, 28th March 1838.

29. *Inverness Courier*, 30th May 1838.

30. Macmillan, D S, 1967, *Scotland and Australia 1788-1850, Emigration, Commerce and Investment*, p. 277.

31. Cregeen, E R, 1998, *Argyll Estate Instructions Mull, Morvern, Tiree 1771-1805*, p. 50.

32. A&BC file FH277: *List of Arrears due from His Grace the Duke of Argyll's Estate in Mull, Crop Year 1840*.

33. Currie, J, 2001, *Mull the Island and its People*, p. 235.

9

Population Growth and a
Church Divided

In 1841 the British Government initiated a nationwide census that was undertaken on the 6th and 7th June. It shows how the population of Creich had grown from a small communal village of 25 people in 1779 into a crofting community with a comparatively large population of 282. The first government census has also proved invaluable for later generations with a snapshot of their descendants' families in that year. In remote areas like the Ross of Mull it has provided some definite statistical information not provided beforehand or found elsewhere.

The section of the census for the Parish of Iona shows that the Braighcreich McPhees were still living on their croft at 'Gortan A Chibain' in the district of Creich. The family is listed as: Donald Macfie 50 crofter, Mary (McInnes) 45, Duncan 20, Neil 15, Hector 15, Catherine 13, Mary 11, Alexander 8, Angus 7, Margaret 3, Flory (i.e. Flora) 6 months and Catherine McInnes 20.[1] Catherine McInnes was a member of the extended family, possibly a niece. The family's second oldest son John is not shown on the census. He may have been away working, or had met with some misfortune and died.

The ages shown cannot be taken at face value, as the census taker was required to round down an individual's age to the nearest five or zero. Also, people often were mistaken about their age. Children 15 years or younger were supposed to have their exact age recorded.[2] The information provided by the census was in many ways subject to how the information was related to the census taker.

As the first government initiated census, the 1841 census provided little more than the names and ages of the people. Those conducted in the future recorded more useful, relevant information.

With the birth of Flora just prior to the census, the McPhees had 9 of their 10 children still at home with them. Unless the barn was used for extra living space, conditions in their house must have been cramped. Not long after the above census was taken, it became even more so, when another member of the extended family came to live with them.

Janet McInnes, the wife of Neil Morrison, moved from Iona to live on the croft at Braighcreich after the death of her husband. He was almost certainly a descendant of the only person recorded with that surname on the 1716 Iona Disarming List. It was the accepted practice of those living in the Highlands to offer sanctuary and assistance to extended members of the family whenever the need arose. Crofts in particular were havens where it was common for many less fortunate family members to take up residence on a permanent basis. Janet was one such family member. After a period of ill health, she died at Braighcreich in August 1845.

The New Statistical Account of Scotland

Historians today are fortunate that the early 1840s saw another major report gathered by parish clergy, similar to the Old Statistical Account. The Society for the Benefit of the Sons and Daughters of the Clergy was responsible for what is now generally known as the New Statistical Account of Scotland (NSA). It was published in 1845.

The Rev. Donald Campbell was the minister responsible for providing the information for those who lived in the parish of Kilfinichen and Kilviceuen which covered Iona and the Ross of Mull. Included in his report for the NSA were the following observations:

> "The inhabitants in general are quiet, sober, humane, kindly towards each other, and religiously inclined. They are healthy, and capable of undergoing much fatigue;... They make expert and hardy seamen, being accustomed to the sea from infancy; and they make no less efficient soldiers... the bulk of the population, consisting of crofters possessing small patches of land, agricultural labourers, cottars, and fishermen..."[3]

The majority of the people living on Iona and the Ross of Mull were now crofters. In addition there were agricultural labourers, cottars and fishermen. Rev. Donald Campbell noted that the small crofters would typically have been paying rent of between £4 and £12 per year. They rented their land on an annual basis and did not have the security of a lease, as did the larger tenant farmers.

Whereas earlier generations grew oats as the staple crop, crofters and the population generally now lived on the potato for about nine months of the year, a real indicator of the importance of this crop. Potatoes were sometimes planted in rows after cultivation with a plough, but more often than not, still placed on beds and covered with soil and seaweed manure, using the lazybed method.

Oats were still cultivated and made into meal, and the straw used as cattle feed during winter and spring. Scots barley or 'bere' was grown and sold to distilleries at Tobermory or Oban. Contrary to times past, the parish did not produce enough food now to feed its inhabitants. Prior to the turn of the century, sheep on Mull were mainly Scottish ones but now, like elsewhere, the land was covered with that tough English breed, the Cheviot. As mentioned in an earlier chapter, before the turn of the century, the 5th Duke of Argyll prohibited goats being kept on any of his estates and as a result of this there were still no goats in the parish.

One big change had taken place on Mull that affected the population adversely. The once thriving kelp industry began to decline. The price of kelp had risen dramatically as a result of the Napoleonic Wars in Europe. When they ended, the government protected the local industry by placing an import duty on similar products. In 1825, the government removed the import duties from imported kelp substitutes such as barilla, and the local industry collapsed. The NSA reveals what the Rev. Donald Campbell thought of the government's decision and its consequences:

> "Kelp - This manufacture has entirely disappeared... Before barilla was allowed to enter our market duty free, and thereby exclude the kelp... this manufacture employed... many thousands in the Highlands and Islands, and the price it drew brought money to the country, and this being again circulated through the kingdom at large kept that money at home, which now goes to enrich the foreigner at the poor Highlander's expense; a measure of policy which cannot be too strongly condemned, - for whether it arose from ignorance on the part of Government, or from any other cause, the Highlands have, since the admission, duty free, of barilla and other substances, presented scenes of much distress, bankruptcy, and poverty."[4]

The discovery of mineral potash deposits in Germany that provided a much cheaper product compared to that made from kelp or barilla, was the eventual death knell of the local industry.

Whilst few Gaels could understand English in the early 1800s, most people by about the 1840s could now not only understand it, but also speak it. Although greater interaction with the Lowlands was now possible with the introduction of steamboats, it was primarily a greater awareness of the benefits of education and the easier access to it that had brought about the change. Whereas 50 years previously there were only two schools in the parish, there were now nine, consisting of two parochial schools, one assembly school, two charity schools, two Gaelic schools and two female schools, and all were well attended.

All the Braighcreich crofters sent their children to one of the local schools, possibly one of the parochial schools run by the Church of Scotland. By the early 1840s, government grants were available to landlords such as the Duke of Argyll for the payment of salaries for parish school teachers. This not only encouraged the establishment of new parish schools but meant existing ones were not so dependent on the generosity of the landowner. Nevertheless, all school teachers usually had to negotiate housing needs and the supply of peat for cooking and heating with the landlord.

The charity schools mentioned by the parish minister were those run by the Scottish Society for the Propagation of Christian Knowledge (SSPCK). The Society was granted a royal charter in 1709, and from 1710 it built schools and supplied teachers to areas in the Highlands and Islands it deemed in need of its assistance. Under its charter, the Society was to "eradicate error and sow truth, to teach true religion and loyalty and to strengthen the British Empire by the addition of useful subjects and firm Protestants."[5]

To provide salaries for school teachers, the Society received financial support from the General Assembly of the Church of Scotland, and in return, teachers worked as catechists for a specific number of days a week until that arrangement ended in 1758.

The SSPCK was a staunchly Presbyterian organisation with an anti-Catholic outlook and because Catholicism was still associated with Gaelic speakers, it did not encourage education in the Gaelic language. The SSPCK had inspectors to check on the conduct and performance of their schools, similar to a modern state or private school system today.

Both girls and boys attended school provided it did not interfere with farm work such as that during harvest time, when everyone in the family was expected to help bring in the crop. Schools for girls only run by various individuals and organisations including the SSPCK, taught girls domestic skills such as sewing and spinning. For that reason, although some girls probably attended school, they remained illiterate.

At the turn of the century there were no towns on the Ross of Mull, but by the 1840s the village of Bunessan had become established. The town serviced the local crofting communities. Bunessan had a population of about 250, which included 5 merchants who sold a general array of goods. It was to eventually boast a bakery, tailor, cobbler, smiddy (blacksmith), parish church (Church of Scotland), Baptist Church, school, two piers, a hotel and mill. There was still no post office, the nearest one being at the town of Aros in the Parish of Kilninian and Kilmore. Like the other parishes on Mull, mail was delivered by 'foot post' - carried by foot-runners who delivered it every 3 days.

The Duke of Argyll built the grain mill at Bunessan in the 1700s before it grew into a town. As mentioned in a previous chapter, originally it was a single storey stone structure with an 11 foot (3.4 m) diameter waterwheel. The building was enlarged in the 1830s with the provision of a second storey and a new 14 foot (4.3 m) waterwheel was installed. A drying kiln was also built nearby.[6]

Astonishingly there were still no roads on the island, but fortunately for the residents, the introduction of steamboats improved trade and communications with other islands and the mainland. The propulsion of boats using steam rather than wind was a huge technological advance. In the 1840s the round trip between Mull and Glasgow took less than three days. Regular steamboat services linked the Western Isles with the mainland. Mull was also fortunate that the Skye to Glasgow steamboat also called in at the island.

The Conflict Between Church and State

The Gaelic inhabitants of Mull were God-fearing, church-going people, and for the parish of Kilfinichen and Kilviceuen, all but 40 were members of the established Presbyterian faith. Religion was central to the life of the people, but underlying this seemingly cohesive, peaceful congregation was considerable unrest.

The early 1830s and 1840s saw Church of Scotland ministers dividing into two separate camps. On the one side were those known as 'Evangelicals', who supported fundamental religious doctrines, embraced social issues and placed a high value on the personal conversion experience. Opposing Evangelical ministers were 'Moderates' who had a more broadminded view of the world and took a softer line on matters of faith.

Beyond their religious outlook, a chasm divided Evangelicals and Moderates over the issue of 'patronage'. Patronage came from the word 'patron', who was the person that nominated the minister to the parish. The Patronage Act of 1712 had restored the right of a patron or individual (who was usually the most important landowner in the parish), to appoint whom he so desired to be the minister, rather than the local parishioners.[7] The patron was virtually the minister's employer, and was responsible for supplying him with a manse, and usually a plot of land called a 'glebe', on which to farm.

Evangelicals wished to see an end to patronage and congregations with the authority to make a 'Call' to appoint their own ministers. They repudiated the involvement of the state in church affairs. This was at odds with civil authorities who defined patronage as a property right, and thus expected the Church of Scotland to obey the law of the land and accept the dictates of the Patronage Act. Moderates were prepared to tolerate patronage and the involvement of the state in the church. Those ministers were aligned with the landlords and the Scottish aristocracy.

The two factions were at loggerheads over patronage for 10 years, during which time Evangelical ministers grew in number and influence. Due to their efforts, the General Assembly of the Church of Scotland passed the Veto Act in 1834, which empowered parishes to veto a patron's nominee minister, and restored some rights of congregations to make the 'Call' to engage their own minister.[8] The Assembly also passed the Chapels Act in the same year, which legalised new churches known as 'chapels-of-ease', commonly run by Evangelical ministers which had been built to serve overpopulated parishes like those in the crofting communities.[9] It became another contentious issue as the power of Evangelical ministers grew within church courts, especially the General Assembly.

Conflict soon arose after the introduction of the Veto Act. One of the most notable was a dispute between landowners, the Church of Scotland and the congregation of Marnoch Parish Church in the County of Banff. The Marnoch Congregation accepted a new minister for their church in January 1841 at the same time that an alternative minister was proposed by a patron. Being forced to accept a minister they didn't want, almost the entire congregation "arose from their seats in the body of the church and left the house where they and their fathers had long worshipped..."[10] Their action to leave the Church of Scotland and build their own church nearby was a harbinger of what was to follow.

Evangelicals fought the state in various court cases over the legality of the Veto Act. In January 1843, the Court of Session, Scotland's highest civil court, found the Veto Act to be illegal - church courts were subservient to the law of the land and therefore, a patron's choice of minister had to be accepted. An appeal against the ruling to the House of Lords was unsuccessful.[11] For the Evangelicals, their spiritual independence was thus compromised and their influence diminished.

The dispute between Evangelicals and Moderates did not end there.

'The Disruption'

A momentous turning point in Scottish history occurred on 18th May 1843 at the General Assembly of the Church of Scotland, which was held at St. Andrew's in Edinburgh. On that day the leader of the Evangelical ministers, Dr. Chalmers, led 190 dissenting ministers attending the Assembly out onto nearby George Street, where thousands of people waited in anticipation.[12] After walking to a rallying point not far from the church, Dr. Chalmers, joined by over 400 ministers, signed a 'Deed of Demission', separating them from the established Church of Scotland and forming a new church called the 'Free Church of Scotland'. It was called Free because by relinquishing all state support, it was not beholden to government. This event became known as 'The Disruption'.

The Disruption was the climax of a 10 year conflict that saw 474 ministers out of a total clergy of 1,203 leave the established church.[13] In the Highlands, few clergymen joined the new church. Less than a quarter of the Church of Scotland ministers in the huge Synod of Argyll, which included places like Mull, joined. The vast bulk of the clergy that formed the Free Church of Scotland came from the Lowlands.

The reaction of the clergy throughout the Highlands stood in stark contrast to the ordinary worshipper. In the Western Isles, about 90% of congregations, mostly rural in nature, joined the Free Church. In the Lowlands parishioners in urban centres like Glasgow and Edinburgh supported it.[14] About 40% of all parishioners joined the new church.

The Rev. Donald Campbell was still the parish minister responsible for the Ross of Mull district at this time. Like many others, he had no manse but received an allowance of £42 annually in lieu, had a glebe of 70 to 80 Scotch acres, and a healthy stipend on which to support himself. He remained as the Church of Scotland minister for the parish of Kilfinichen and Kilviceuen until 1856.

36. Rev. Donald McVean, the Church of Scotland minister for the Parish of Iona 1835 - 1843 and Free Church of Scotland minister 1843 - 1878.[15]

There was a great deal of excitement among the local parishioners when The Disruption occurred, to see who would join the new church. One of the first to declare himself as a Free Church minister on Mull was the minister of Iona, Reverend Donald McVean.[16]

No matter what the denomination, in places like Mull, clergymen had to put up with primitive conditions. Parishes were large, and travelling in muddy conditions was difficult. Manses were often not provided and church buildings and facilities were usually poorly maintained by landlords. Ministers were reliant on their patron (landlord) for an income, a place to live and a place to preach.

It was no bed of roses being a minister in the new church. Free Church ministers were denied the most basic of conveniences and suffered considerably for the stand they took. Men strongly committed to their cause risked the loss of their homes and livelihoods. The Free Church clergy did not have churches in which to conduct their services or to train in, so local houses became places of worship and study, and in extreme cases, services were held in the open. They did not receive a salary, manse or glebe from a wealthy patron, so they all made a significant financial sacrifice.

The Rev. Donald McVean, his wife and young children, were forced to vacate the manse on Iona and find accommodation in private homes as best they could. With the 7th Duke of Argyll opposed to the new church, worship had to be conducted on the island in a gravel pit below the high water mark. Eventually the 7th Duke of Argyll permitted another church and manse to be built on Iona at Martyr's Bay in 1845. Years later the Free Church congregation funded construction of a new manse for Donald McVean at Achaban overlooking Loch Potee on the Ross of Mull, but still within the quoad sacra parish of Iona.[17] The new manse was next to an ancient standing stone.

To fill Donald McVean's position, the established Church of Scotland appointed the Rev. Alexander MacGregor to the quoad sacra parish of Iona, so that the parish then had two ministers.

On Mull, the Free Church of Scotland appointed the Rev. Duncan Fergusson as its minister in the parish of Kilfinichen and Kilviceuen. He lived in the northern part of the Ross at Tiraghoil. Free Church parishioners worshipped on the Ross of Mull in a building at Monachuich, about 3 miles (4.8 km) west of Bunessan.[18]

One member among the Campbell nobility who did embrace the Free Church of Scotland was John Campbell, the 2nd Marquess of Breadalbane. He donated money so the new church could build a ship to transport its ministers to remote areas throughout the islands and Highlands of Scotland. The church had a 30 ton schooner rigged vessel built (which is one characterised by having fore and aft masts of the same height), made of oak. To recognise the Marquess' generosity, it was called *The Breadalbane*. The ship had a captain's cabin, an aft cabin where meals were served, two cabins to accommodate ministers and a main cabin with two benches for additional passengers and where acts of worship could take place. It was not a large sailing vessel, but it was a sturdy, safe one, manned by a religiously devout captain and a crew of four, which could carry six church ministers to spread the word of God primarily to the underprivileged and neglected souls around the Hebrides.

Generally speaking, the skilled people in the community such as the school teachers, joiners, millers and other reasonably educated people so often taken for granted by the ruling elite, joined the Free Church. The split in the Presbyterian Church affected many individual families. Members and branches of the same family took different sides and that caused considerable unhappiness in some communities. Like many other Gaelic people in the Western Isles, it was during those turbulent times that the majority (and probably all) of those living in the Braighcreich crofting community became members of the new branch of Presbyterianism called the Free Church of Scotland.

The Disruption precipitated the demise of the parish state. History went on to vindicate the change sought by the Evangelicals, as parliament repealed the Patronage Act in 1874.[19]

NOTES

1.   1841 Census, Quoad Sacra Parish of Iona, District of Creich.

2.   Jonas, L and Milner, P, 2002, *A Genealogist's Guide to Discovering Your Scottish Ancestors*, p. 111.

3.   New Statistical Account, *Parish of Kilfinichen and Kilviceuen*, p. 307 and 308.

4.   New Statistical Account, *Parish of Kilfinichen and Kilviceuen*, p. 309.

5.   Walker, J, and McKay, M M, 1980, *The Rev. Dr. John Walker's Report on the Hebrides of 1764 and 1771*, Edinburgh, Donald, J, p. 20.

6.   Anon, ROMHC, *Discover the Ross*, p. 35.

7.   Hume Brown, P, 1995, *Scotland A Concise History*, p. 320.

8.   Lynch, M, 2001, *Oxford Companion to Scottish History*, p. 172.

9.   MacLeod, J L, 2000, *The Second Disruption, The Free Church in Victorian Scotland and the Origins of the Free Presbyterian Church*, p. 2.

10. *The Banner*, 23rd January 1841, Aberdeen Newspaper.

11. Lynch, M, 2001, *Oxford Companion to Scottish History*, p. 172.

12. Lynch, M, 2001, *Oxford Companion to Scottish History*, p. 91.

13. Keay, J & J, 1994, *Encyclopaedia of Scotland*, p. 230.

14. MacLeod, J L, 2000, *The Second Disruption, The Free Church in Victorian Scotland and the Origins of the Free Presbyterian Church*, p. 3.

15. MacArthur, E M, 2002, *Iona the Living Memory of a Crofting Community.*

16. MacArthur, E M, 2002, *Iona the Living Memory of a Crofting Community*, p. 242-3.

17. Cameron, J S, 2013, *A History of the Ross of Mull*, p. 315.

18. Anon, *The Story of St. Ernan's Church Creich, Isle of Mull Centenary 1899-1999*, p. 6.

19. Hume Brown, P, 1995, *Scotland A Concise History*, p. 321.

10

The Potato Famine

Famines occurred periodically in Scotland, as they did elsewhere. Such events not only caused hunger but also poverty. The middle years of the 19th Century, especially during the famine years of the 1830s and 1840s, marked the final phase of the Highland Clearances.

While famines were periodic, there were always those who for some reason or other became poor and unable to look after themselves. In Scotland it was the church that by tradition had provided assistance to such individuals. Parish churches distributed money raised from the voluntary donations among their congregations.[1] At the time of the Reformation, when the Church of Scotland (the kirk) came into existence, it repudiated any involvement of government in providing relief to the needy. No matter how poor, fit, able-bodied people in Scotland were expected to maintain themselves by working.

Rev. Donald Campbell documented how the disadvantaged in his parish on Mull were looked after. The congregations at his two churches in the parish of Kilfinichen and Kilviceuen made a combined annual contribution of about £11 for those in need. Added to the collections for the poor were "occasional fines for immoralities imposed by the kirk-session".[2] The church was the only source of funds available for the indigent. No matter how impoverished, Highlanders were renowned for their sense of pride, so to be dependent on fellow parishioners who were friends and neighbours was something of which to be ashamed. Such a predicament was to be avoided if at all possible.

Following the turmoil of The Disruption in the Presbyterian Church and an economic depression in 1843, a Royal Commission, The Poor Law Inquiry Commission (PLIC), was set up to investigate the plight of the poor. From this followed the Act of Parliament for the Amendment and Better Administration of the Laws relating to the Relief of the Poor in Scotland (the Poor Law Amendment Act (Scotland) of 1845).[3]

The new law had the potential to adversely affect all those who owned or leased Highland estates. In addition to the church, the community and the family, the poor also became the responsibility of the landholder on whose property they resided. Landowners could be issued with annual assessments for the cost of caring for destitute residents based on the value of their property. If the land was leased, the landowners paid half and the tenant the other half. Rich and poor landholders alike had to pay the new impost.

The 1845 Act established a Board of Supervision in Scotland. Individual parishes retained responsibility for their poor via 'parochial boards' (destitution boards) that were appointed each year.[4] The boards could raise money from voluntary donations as had been done in the past, but could also send out notices of 'Assessment for Poor's Money' to landlords in order to fund their operation. The parochial boards compiled rolls that placed people in one of three categories depending on their level of poverty. Assistance was only given to the most desperate of people and only after a means test. By any measure it was a harsh regime. The new law centralised control of poor relief with the British Government.

Potato Blight 1846

In 1846, blight (Phytophthora Infestans) affected the potato crop in the Highlands of Scotland, just as it had done all over Europe and Ireland a year earlier. Virtually the entire crop was wiped out. In this aspect it differed from previous crop failures which had not been so widespread. The crofting communities, dependent on potatoes, felt the full impact of the crisis. It heralded years of hunger, poverty and dislocation.

At the end of July 1846, the Argyll Estate's Ground Officer on the Ross of Mull, Alexander MacDonald, wrote from his office at Bunessan to the Duke's Chamberlain at Inveraray to advise him about the potato crop on the Mull Estate: "I consider it my duty as Ground Officer to say that since you have left the place, the disease in the potato crop has made an alarming progress both in the Ross of Mull and Iona. The fields that then appeared beautiful and in full bloom and promised an abundant harvest to the consumer are this day as if overun by fire. I tremble at what may be the consequence from the complete failure of this staple article of consumption on this district and unless some means may be advised (and that without loss of time) of providing for the starving population, the issue will be most appalling."[5]

By this time, Lord John Douglas Campbell (1777-1847) the 7th Duke of Argyll, who had replaced his brother George William Campbell after his death in 1839, was quite old. Due to his age, many of his responsibilities and duties were handed to his son, George Douglas Campbell.[6]

George Douglas Campbell appointed John Campbell of Ardmore, from Islay, as his business manager or factor, to manage the Argyll Estates on Mull and Iona. He commenced his duties there in September 1846 and took over the lease of Ardfenaig Farm that had previously been leased to a prominent family of MacLeans.[7] It was a substantial farm, a mile (2 km) or so to the east of the Braighcreich crofting community. Unlike his predecessors, the new manager would live among the tenants under his charge.

John Campbell was an extremely large man and as such attracted the name 'Factor Mor', which translated to 'the big factor'.[8] As was the case in many places throughout the Highlands, factors wielded considerable power and in many respects were a law unto themselves. John Campbell became a renowned cattle breeder and leading farmer on Mull. He relished his role of improving the agricultural output of the Argyll Estates and carrying out development projects to the benefit of his boss, the 7th Duke of Argyll.

One significant improvement to the Duke of Argyll's Estate prompted by the outbreak of the potato blight not only provided work for the local people, but made life a little easier for them as well. In return for food aid, men from the Ross of Mull helped build a deepwater pier near Bunessan, which assisted the transfer of famine relief from ship to shore. It was made of locally quarried granite and built on the southern side of Loch na Lathaich in 1846.[9] It allowed steam boats to tie up alongside to unload supplies. Prior to the Bunessan pier being built, goods and people were ferried by small boats to and from larger vessels anchored out in the loch. Once unloaded at the pier, famine relief was transported to a store at Bunessan where it was held until it was distributed to the needy.

The Provision of Famine Relief

Recognising the gravity of the situation soon after the potato crop failed, the Free Church of Scotland was the first organisation to provide significant aid during the famine. In November 1846 it established its own famine relief or Destitution Committee which raised thousands of pounds from church congregations to purchase food for starving people. Having not long beforehand taken delivery of its own sailing vessel *The Breadalbane*, it was able to distribute supplies quickly and efficiently using its own ship.[10] As many of its congregations lived in the worst affected areas, it was in a good position to help those most in need. The most impoverished were the destitute cottars rather than rent paying crofters. It established unofficial local relief committees to distribute food to them, and did so regardless of their religious persuasion.

After the Free Church's decisive action to supply famine relief, two other relief committees were established like they were during the 1836-7 famine, one in Edinburgh in December 1846, and another in Glasgow in January 1847. By February the three separate relief committees had amalgamated to form the Central Board of Management for Highland Relief (the Central Board). It had two sections, one in Edinburgh and one in Glasgow, each responsible for specific geographical areas. The Glasgow Section was responsible for Argyll, Western Inverness, the Outer Hebrides and with the exception of Skye, the Inner Hebrides.[11]

Like the three original relief committees, the Central Board was a non-government charitable organisation. Its fundraising was facilitated by widespread publicity in newspapers which alerted the public to the hardship caused by the potato famine. A sympathetic Christian society donated generously to provide relief. The Central Board was a God-send for landowners. The activities of the Board prevented tenants being listed on parish poor rolls where they would have become subject to Poor Law relief.

Once money had been raised and relief supplies purchased, there remained the problem of distribution. It was fortuitous that by the time of the potato famine, communication with the Highlands and Islands of Scotland had been revolutionised by the introduction of steamboats.

Action by the English Government prevented a disaster. Government Commissioners toured the distressed areas in 1846 and at the start of 1847 to assess the situation. Government relief efforts fell under the direction of Commissary General, Edward Pine Coffin who ensured Royal Navy steamboats played a pivotal role in delivering relief supplies quickly to coastal communities. Two meal depots were established in the Highlands, one at Tobermory on Mull and the other at Portree on Skye. In 1847, the Board of Supervision, established to administer the Poor Law in Scotland, employed David Boyter, the former Colonial Emigration Agent for New South Wales. A man with ideal experience, his job was to organise the distribution of food aid to the starving and deploy relief workers where most needed.

Relief rations were hardly luxurious, and indeed, were just sufficient to prevent starvation. Daily food allowances consisted of wheatmeal, oatmeal and peasemeal. Men received 1 ½ lb. (700 g), women ¾ lb. (400 g) and children less than ½ lb. (200 g) each.[12] To distribute rations, local relief committees were established in distressed areas from names supplied by parish ministers. Handouts to able-bodied people during that era was generally frowned upon, so every effort was made to avoid that happening.

The winter of 1846-47, after the potato blight struck, was a particularly desperate one for all who were relying on the potato. Naturally the degree of hardship varied as people did everything they could to stave off hunger. Those living around the coast for example, stripped every rock of any sort of shellfish that could be consumed. Malnutrition was an early consequence of the potato crop failure, which not only caused outbreaks of disease and sickness in most families, but increased the loss of life, especially among the young and the old, who were the most vulnerable.

A letter from Donald Maclean, a merchant in Bunessan, to the Destitution Committee of the Free Church of Scotland on 13th January 1847, gave a first-hand account of how bad the situation was on the Duke of Argyll's Estate: "There are several families in this district actually in a dying state from starvation and sickness. The sickness is so great, with other calamities, that the number of deaths some days are between Ross and Iona from two to five. I am sorry to add that sickness is still on the increase, particularly British cholera and dysentry."[13]

Crofters Petition for Meal

Crofters living all over Mull required help to overcome the reduction in their food supplies. On 22nd January 1847, some 30 crofters from the southern Ross of Mull townships of Uisken and Ardchiavaig signed a petition addressed to The Honourable Her Majesty's Commission for examining into the Destitution of the Highlands requesting advances of meal.

The petitioning crofters had run out of meal and run out of money to buy it. Their petition advised the commissioners that "... unless immediate relief is afforded us we can have no prospect but of starvation as all our means that in the mean time we can make use of are exhausted and although there is meal in the place it is of no use to us as we will not get a grain of it without ready money." In order to obtain meal, the crofters went on to request they be supplied with meal on credit "until May next when we could get our little remaining stock sold to pay for what we receive as your Petitioners shall ever pray".[14]

Accompanying the petition was a letter signed by parish minister Donald Campbell and the Inspector of Poor in the parish, John McDonald, penned at Bunessan on the same day as the petition. It was written for Factor Mor, noted on the bottom of the letter as "John Campbell Esq, Chamberlain of Ross and Tyree."[15]

The letter is interesting on several counts. It shows the petition is to be presented to Commissioners onboard their ship at Bunessan. It shows the importance of Factor Mor on the Estate. It shows the influence of the local minister and his desire not to offend the Duke of Argyll. The letter states: "The foregoing petition has been presented to us this day with a request that we should attest the truth thereof and present the same to Her Majesty's Commissioner Capt. Bynlow lying at anchor here, we cannot deny but the Petition is correct, but at the same time we considered that by attending to the Petitioner's request it might be offensive to His Grace the Duke of Argyle, we therefore advised the Petitioners to forward the same to you for your consideration. The state of this district is very alarming..."[16]

While the response to the crofters petition is not known, it is probably fair to assume that if credit was not forthcoming, they received charitable relief supplies to stop them starving to death.

The catastrophic humanitarian disaster that had happened in Ireland was fortunately averted in Scotland. To save people from mass starvation, food was purchased, shipped and distributed to those areas of greatest need. The public rose to the occasion and after the experience of the potato famine in Ireland, the English Government had the experience and where-with-all to ensure there was no widespread loss of life in Scotland.

Petition for Emigration to Canada

On the 29th January 1847, many Church of Scotland parishioners in the Creich district attended a meeting convened by their local minister, Rev. Alexander MacGregor. At that meeting he read out a letter from the 7th Duke of Argyll, which apparently indicated emigration was one of the main ways of relieving the people of their plight. He also read out a circular from the Reverend Dr. John Dunmore Lang about emigration to Australia. The church minister pointed out to his congregation the positive aspects of emigration, compared to the hardship of remaining where they were.

It was about this time that the Destitution Committee of the Free Church of Scotland made a visit to the famine affected areas. Their observations were reported in the *Glasgow Times*, part of which described the magnitude of the situation leading up to the potato harvest that year in Argyll: "... and it is surely a grave question how the fifty thousand, now suffering destitution on the shores and islands of Argyllshire, are to be fed during the next six months that yet remain till harvest. It covers a space equal in extent to about a third of Scotland – it affects at this date about two hundred thousand of our countrymen, and this number is daily augmenting."[17]

The Free Church of Scotland minister for the quoad sacra Parish of Iona, Reverend McVean, was acutely aware of the issues that confronted his parishioners. In a letter to the Duke of Argyll on 16th March 1847 he wrote, "It seems quite clear that a considerable number of them must move and I have no doubt will, for I believe it is universally felt that it would be for the benefit of all. A good many of the Ross people I understand have thoroughly made up their minds for America and I make no doubt a considerable portion of the poor crofters of Iona will do so also..."[18] Ordinary folk may well have come to accept the idea of emigration, but few could actually afford a fare.

People were undoubtedly desperate to escape the hunger and poverty caused by the potato famine. Following on from the January meeting, a petition dated 23rd March 1847, was sent to the 7th Duke of Argyll, with the names of families that wished to leave their homes and go to Canada. The members of those families represented about half the population of the Ross of Mull. The petition was titled 'List of Names Wishing to Emigrate to Upper Canada North America.'[19] The term Upper Canada generally referred to the area around Toronto in Ontario whereas Lower Canada could be taken to mean Nova Scotia and coastal areas such as Prince Edward Island, where many Scots had emigrated in previous years.

The petition showed the head of the household or name of the individual, his occupation, the number of adults, the number of children over seven, the number of children under seven, and 'supposed means' that is, if they could pay the passage.

The 1847 document is a graphic indicator of just how desperate and impoverished people had become. The fathers, husbands or heads of 149 household residences, including 24 from Iona, representing a staggering 963 people, sought to emigrate. The petitioners included 88 cottars, 39 crofters and 22 others, including fishermen, shoemen, ploughmen and workmen. The ability of the 963 people to pay their passage according to the 'supposed means' of the petitioner is summarised as follows:

'supposed means'	
can pay their own passage:	4 %
uncertain if they can pay their passage:	9 %
can pay part of their passage:	32 %
destitute:	55 %
	100 %

Among the petitioners were struggling small crofters living in the district of Creich. It is unlikely however, that any of the Braighcreich crofters were successful in their bid to leave the Ross of Mull for Canada.[20] That may have been because they couldn't contribute enough towards the fare, which at that time was about £4 per adult. Those in that position wishing to leave were denied any assistance from the Argyll Estates to emigrate. If the 7th Duke of Argyll accepted advice from Factor Mor, then only tenants who could pay at least half the fare were given financial help to leave his Estates on Mull, Iona and Tiree.

Documentation to establish how many tenants were successful in their bid to emigrate, and who they were, is not available and may not exist. The Argyll Estate provided financial assistance for over 250 people to depart from Mull, Iona and Tiree in at least two ships, the *Eglington* and *Jamaica,* during 1847. The Duke's banker at Greenock made the arrangements for those tenants. He co-ordinated their travel to Greenock, their accommodation there and the supply of suitable clothing. From the port of Greenock the emigrants sailed to Canada.

The Drainage Act

What was expected to be a one-off year of famine lasted a number of years. Many able-bodied men became incapable of feeding themselves or their families and food had to be provided for them. This went against the accepted economic principles of those administering relief in London. It was the commonly held belief that giving charity led to dependency and laziness. To obtain help in the form of food, fit men, women and children had to work for it.

It has been seen that although the government provided assistance for the distressed areas in the Highlands, it relied on charities to purchase food for famine relief. The government also expected landowners to shoulder a large part of the burden of looking after starving tenants on their estates. Some landlords accepted responsibility for their tenants but others did not.

To assist landlords bear the cost of supporting their tenants, the government offered them finance under the Drainage Act 1846. Landlords were able to access low interest loans at 6 ½ % per annum, repayable over 22 years.[21] Initially there was a poor response because loans could not be used for any of the associated work that accompanied drainage. Once the rules were relaxed, government funding to Highland landowners increased.

It was a good deal for landowners. They could utilise cheap money to employ people to improve their estates and at the same time prevent people starving. Crofters who were behind in their rent could also be employed to pay off their rent arrears.

Soon after his appointment as the business manager on the Ross of Mull, Factor Mor encouraged the Duke of Argyll to utilise the benefits offered by the Drainage Act. In a letter sent to the Duke's office, he stated money from such a loan would "... keep the Tiree, Mull and Iona poor from starving and enable the crofters to pay the rent. As they might make the drains on their own possessions and receive the benefit, a double benefit would accrue... Drainage is the only salvation for the property."[22]

Through his estate manager Factor Mor, the Duke of Argyll was one of those who used the Drainage Act to good effect. As was a common practice, Factor Mor gave the tenants under his supervision meal rations for the work they performed. The work demanded for the minimal rations he provided was a bone of contention for all those forced to rely on it. Two supervisors were employed to oversee labourers working for their famine relief. One lived at Creich on the Ross of Mull and the other on Iona.[23]

Cutting through the Braighcreich crofting community, an imposing stone wall called the Galloway Dyke, stood out (and still stands out) in the fields. It was called the Galloway Dyke because it was built in the 'Galloway' style. Looking at it today, it is not clear what the original purpose for the structure was, assuming there was one, but it is known local people from the crofting community received food as payment for building it, so that they might avoid starvation.[24]

Seasonal Work

Although food shortages had been severe during 1846 and 1847 and many cottars, crofters and others had petitioned to leave, there was not a mass exodus of people from Mull or the nearby islands during those years. Food relief had been provided and widespread starvation averted. Landlords had also played a part in assisting some of their tenants.

Families themselves did everything they could to survive the potato famine. As seen in an earlier chapter, for many years there had been a temporary outflow of people from the Highlands during the summer months to seek employment elsewhere. The failure of the potato crop and a sharp drop in cattle prices saw this movement increase during the early famine years. Not only did more people leave to seek work, they left much earlier in the season, sometimes as early as February and stayed away from home longer.

Single men and women of working age were usually the members of a family that sought work elsewhere. During the famine years, a significant percentage of the heads of some crofting families on the Ross of Mull and Iona also left their families in order to earn some income. This particularly applied to the small crofters with a croft rental of less than £5 per annum.

When the potato famine took hold, it was the Duke of Argyll's policy to encourage healthy young adults to leave his estate and take up work elsewhere to minimise his obligation of providing famine relief. Withholding aid was a strong inducement.[25]

Single women from Mull and Iona found work as domestic servants and farm help in the Lowlands. They were also employed in the fishing industry, gutting and cleaning fish. Men typically worked on Lowland farms and as fishermen. During 1846 and 1847, thousands of Highland men were able to work as navvies on booming railway construction projects. Seasonal work was probably the salvation for many tenants during the first two years of the potato famine.

NOTES

1.   Cullen, K J, 2010, *Famine in Scotland: The 'Ill Years' of the 1690s*, p.94.

2.   New Statistical Account, *Parish Kilfinichen and Kilviceuen*, p. 311.

3. Devine, T M, 2004, *The Great Highland Famine*, p. 84.
4. Devine, T M, 2004, *The Great Highland Famine*, p. 84.
5. ROMHC: Letters to the Chamberlain of Argyll.
6. Currie, J, 2001, *Mull the Island and its People*, p. 349.
7. Ibid.
8. Ibid.
9. ROMHC, *Discover the Ross*, p. 37.
10. Rothney, S J, 2011, *The Presbyterian Response to the Famine Years 1845-1855 within Ireland and in the Highlands of Scotland*, University of Glasgow Thesis, p. 149.
11. Devine, T M, 2004, *The Great Highland Famine*, p. 39.
12. Devine, T M, 1994, *Clanship to Crofters' War*, p. 167.
13. ROMHC: Letter from Donald Maclean, merchant, Bunessan to the Destitution Committee of the Free Church, 13th January 1847.
14. A&BC file FH357, *Petitions of Crofters in the Ross of Mull for Meal 1847*.
15. Ibid.
16. Ibid.
17. *Glasgow Times*, Saturday 20th February 1847.
18. MacArthur, E M, 1991, Talk to the Gaelic Society of Inverness, titled *The Potatoe Famine of 1846 and its Aftermath in Iona and the Ross of Mull*, courtesy ROMHC.
19. A&BC file FH 274, *List of Tenants and cottars warned (to remove) on His Grace's estates of Tiree and Ross of Mull, 1850: Mull Parish of Kilfinichen and Kilvickeon.*
20. The Braighcreich McPhees were listed as 'uncertain' if they could pay the fare to Canada. Among the family of 14 which unsuccessfully sought to emigrate, were nine adults (including extended family), three children over seven and two under seven years of age.
21. Devine, T M, 2004, *The Great Highland Famine*, p. 100.
22. MacArthur, E M, 1991, Talk to the Gaelic Society of Inverness, titled *The Potatoe Famine of 1846 and its Aftermath in Iona and the Ross of Mull*, courtesy ROMHC.
23. MacArthur, E M, 2002, *Iona the Living Memory of a Crofting Community*, p. 103.
24. ROMHC, *Discover the Ross*, p. 25.
25. Devine, T M, 2004, *The Great Highland Famine*, p. 158.

11

Repression and Crofter Evictions

It was during those famine years that George Douglas Campbell (1823-1900), the Marquess of Lorne, inherited the Argyll Estates and became the 8th Duke of Argyll in April 1847 after the death of his predecessor that month. His elevation heralded a continuing but more decisive approach to emigration and famine relief. The policy towards recovering outstanding rents changed significantly. The Duke instructed his factor to take assertive action against those in arrears, by seizing and selling their cattle in lieu of a cash payment.[1] There was further misery for a tenant if cattle prices were low. For those with no cattle to sell or money for rent, eviction became a certain fate.

Eviction notices were familiar to crofters throughout the Highlands by this time. When issued, they did not just result in the eviction of one man or one family, but usually included aged parents, extended family members and others, so that possibly 10 to 20 people may have been displaced. Eviction notices used the following language and terminology: "flitt and remove themselves their wives bairns families servants subtenants cottars dependents, goods and gear forth from their occupation and possessions of the subjects..."[2] Proprietors and their managers had the right to evict tenants even if their rent was not in arrears. In the crofting era, Factor Mor had his own "Special Rules and Regulations as to the Removing of Crofters" from their farms on the Argyll Estates:[3]

"1. Indolent crofters who cultivate their lands in a careless, slovenly manner and do not adhere to the given rules of cultivation.
2. Widows and families of deceased crofters ... exceptions when there is a young family with grown up unmarried sons of industrious habits.
3. Crofters who are quarrelsome and troublesome to their neighbours and of reputed bad character.
4. Crofters taking married sons and daughters into possession when the rent is under £20.
5. Crofters who keep idle grown up families about them and of no benefit to the property.
6. Crofters keeping dogs or infringing any of the regulations laid down for the management of the estates.
7. All crofters who do not pay up their rents at the stated periods of collection and not having sufficient stock on their land."

Where a tenant failed to obey a landlord's eviction notice, the law was used to forcibly eject those concerned. Landlords had the full force of the law behind them in expelling unwanted tenants from their land. Sheriff court officers issued a removing summons whenever they were requested to do so by landlords.

Although the position of the crofters was bad, that of the landless cottars was worse. Landowners definitely wanted to be rid of such people, as they became an increasing financial burden on their estates. On the Ross of Mull, Factor Mor wrote to his employer in 1847 about the cottars on his estate. When advising his employer to get rid of them as soon as possible, he was scathing in his criticism:

> "The cottar tribe, who are the locusts of the land... must remain a dead weight upon His Grace's estate... With few exceptions, they comprise the indolent, uncivilised and pauperism of the Estate and in my humble opinion, His Grace never speculated money to such advantage as to get rid of them by all possible speed."[4]

In the crofting era, the term cottar had come to have a different meaning to that in the old days. Cottars were still labourers, but in this period they commonly occupied a house on a croft rented by one of their relatives. In this regard, they had some right to live where they did. Being casual workers whose survival depended on working as labourers on fishing boats or on farms, they were usually poor. They occupied a position at the bottom of the socio-economic scale, detested by estate owners and their factors, who regarded them as little more than squatters. In the old days the working population was characterised by numerous occupations. In the late 1840s, landless cottars dominated the workforce.

Despite the relief and the avoidance of a catastrophe, the crofters and cottars in the crofting communities still faced an unpredictable future. On the Ross of Mull, Factor Mor added to the misery of the crofters by setting about trying to dislodge the small tenant farmers on the Argyll Estates where it suited him. As a prominent farmer, he supported the Duke of Argyll's policy of removing such farmers in favour of larger scale tenants. His friends from the nearby island of Islay benefited from his influence, and those larger tenant farmers were able to increase the size of their holdings.

Factor Mor made plain his intentions towards the crofting community in a letter to his employer on 14th March 1847: "I have been doing all in my power to urge the crofters to sow as largely as possible this spring and using every means to stimulate them to greater exertions by telling them that I would watch them and all who were not industrious would most assuredly be deprived of their possessions. Nothing but harshness and dread, I find will do. I have put a stop to their grinding of any of their grain and give them meal in exchange. I am making lists of emigrants. It is of utmost importance to have as many off this year as possible."[5] It was little wonder the local crofters resented the man with a passion.

37. John Campbell, known as 'Factor Mor', managed the Argyll Estates on Mull and Iona. He was feared for his harsh treatment of the crofters and others under his charge.[6]

38. George Douglas Campbell, 8th Duke of Argyll. He owned large estates not only on Mull and Iona but the island of Tiree.[7]

39. Inveraray Castle, a mansion home built in the style of a castle, is home to the incumbent Duke of Argyll. A foundation stone was laid in October 1746 not long after the Battle of Culloden, but it was many years before the Duke of Argyll's home was completed.[8]

Clearance of Tenants at Shiaba

Shiaba was an early casualty of Estate consolidation on the Ross of Mull. The land around Shiaba had been held by a single tenant prior to the 5th Duke of Argyll establishing the crofting township there around 1802. On fertile land and with good communal grazing pasture, the isolated Shiaba community had grown from a population of 41 at the time of the 1779 Argyll Census, to almost 150 when the 1841 census was taken.

Although its residents suffered like others, the cultivation of extra oats and the retention of livestock contributed to ameliorating the effects of the potato crop failure. Regardless of their situation, the 8th Duke of Argyll, together with Factor Mor, wanted to be rid of the Shiaba residents.

The tenants at Shiaba had been notified of their intended removal by Factor Mor's predecessor a year before the failure of the potato crop, but no further action was taken. In 1847 all the tenants were again advised of the intention to remove them from their properties. The motive to remove them was two-fold. Firstly, to consolidate the land into a single rental. After that consolidation, it could then be used as a sheep run and leased to a man from Islay for a greater return. Secondly, there was less expense incurred in removing the tenants than keeping them alive with famine relief.

To stave off eviction, seven Shiaba tenants petitioned the 8th Duke of Argyll on 1st July 1847. The petition stated: "That the petitioners and their forefathers had been tenants in Shiaba about sixty years and on other parts of the Estate of Ross from time immemorial. That the petitioners were lately warned to flit and remove from their respective possessions although they were not in arrears of rent but, on the contrary, have paid the same regularly, though they had large families to support - numbering, including cottars, upwards of one hundred persons neither of whom received any aid or were a burden on the parish. The whole farm has been let in one lot to one individual who is not native of the Ross and neither he nor any of his ancestors ever possessed any lands under your Grace's noble ancestors..."[9]

If eviction could not be avoided, the Shiaba petitioners requested to be accommodated on other farms on the Estate.

The petition was sent to the Duke with a letter from Neil McDonald, the oldest resident of Shiaba which stated: "... I am now verging on one hundred years of age and... I beg leave to send prefixed a petition by myself and the other tenants in Shiaba. Trusting that your grace will give us a favourable reply... as it would be a great hardship and quite unprecedented to remove a man of my age who, as natural to suppose, is drawing to the house appointed for all living. Trusting that your grace will order an answer soon."[10]

Pleas by the tenants to stay fell on deaf ears. The exact details of the eviction are unknown, but all the residents of the township were forced from their homes. After their departure, Shiaba's stone dwellings were largely demolished to prevent any resident returning. Some of the former residents relocated to poorer areas on the Ross, others went to Glasgow and some emigrated to Canada.

The Destitution Test

While the worst of the potato famine may have passed, blight continued to depress yields. For those in the crofting communities, hardship continued. The price of black cattle had slumped and the demand for seasonal labour in the Lowlands had not picked up following the economic recession in the early 1840s. To make matters worse, 1848 saw another slump in the economy. There was no reprieve from hardship in the Highlands.

The activities of the Central Board for Famine Relief in the Highlands continued in 1848. It had always been influenced by the Government and this increased as the famine years wore on. The two key government officials involved were the Commissary General, Sir Edward Pine Coffin and Assistant to the Treasury, Charles Trevelyan. Their influence manifested itself in a Board that became a more sophisticated tougher organisation.

In 1848, paid Central Board staff replaced the somewhat inefficient volunteer relief workers on local committees. Paid inspectors implemented a tough Destitution Test to ensure those seeking help had nothing on which to live. Starving men had to be prepared to work for eight hours to receive a reduced ration of 1 lb (.45 kg) of meal. This was intended to deter any but the most desperate seeking help and be just sufficient food for a man to survive. Any able-bodied crofter with any means of support was denied assistance.

The Central Board also began to work hand-in-glove with proprietors to provide employment and famine relief. This Cooperative System as it was called was based on funds being provided by both parties for agreed projects. Its critics attacked it for allowing Central Board funds to be used to improve landlord estates.

To cope with the loss of their crops during the famine years, crofters sold off anything they could in order to buy meal. This applied particularly after 1848 when the Destitution Test could be implemented. Cattle and any other livestock would have been the first to go. With no income and the need to purchase food, it was common for rents to go unpaid. How could a crofter afford to pay rent when the family was starving and there was no work?

As in any farming community during bad times, some fared worse than others. Tenant farmers on small areas of land found it the hardest. When potatoes continued to fail, those with larger areas sowed more grain crops such as oats and barley. Possibly they were able to retain some of their livestock, especially their black cattle. Crofters were reluctant to dispose of all their cattle, as they were a prized asset and one of the few ways of obtaining cash. Any croft large enough to run a few extra sheep could also share in the improved prices for wool.

The small crofters with just a few acres (1-2 ha) were hardest hit during those calamitous years. They were forced to sell off cattle and slaughter other livestock such as pigs and sheep, just to survive. If they had some spare land, extra cabbages or some other crops may have been planted. The Braighcreich crofters were in this category. In the Creich district where they were located, nearly half of all the small farmers had sold all their livestock by 1851. In such circumstances, restocking and catching up on unpaid rent was impossible for crofters.

Debts Caused by the Road Tax

Rent wasn't the only expense tenants on Mull and Iona had to meet. Crofters and other residents on the islands were also obliged to pay a road tax. They had to do so even if they had no road to use.

The Argyllshire Road Act of 1843 was passed by parliament "for the making and maintaining highways, roads, bridges and quays, and for regulating ferries in the Shire of Argyll..." The 47 page Act was an update of similar legislation dating back to 1775. Individuals who had lands, houses or other assets with a value or rental of £200 or more, could be appointed as trustees to a Roads Board set up to administer the Act. The Board's Annual General Meeting was legislated to be held at Inveraray, home to the Duke of Argyll, who not surprisingly was one of its trustees. District meetings were held elsewhere when and where deemed appropriate.

To raise money, the Board was empowered to "assess all lands, houses and other heritages... in a sum not exceeding eightpence nor less than fourpence sterling on every pound sterling (i.e. from 4d to 8d in the £1) of the real annual value of such lands houses and heritages; one half... payable by the landlord, and the other half by the tenant or occupier."[11] However, if houses had been built by a tenant on leased land, the tenant was deemed a proprietor and that was the position of nearly every crofter on Mull.

Proprietors like the Duke of Argyll were able to provide the Roads Board with every tenant's annual rent, which saved it the necessity of employing valuers to provide a tax assessment. Each year on or before the 1st February, proprietors had to furnish a list of their tenants with the amount of rent payable by each as well as details of his own land.

Collectors were employed in each district not only to receive proprietors' rent rolls, but to issue the assessments and collect the tax. District collectors gave written notices "to all persons assessed of the sums payable by them respectively, and of the day and place when and where the assessments are proposed to be collected",[12] which had to be done as soon as possible after the first Tuesday in March each year.

Between 1846 and 1850, large numbers of tenants on the Ross of Mull were in arrears paying their road tax. In most cases the amount owed by each was 2/-. In the district of Creich, the number of tenants that had fallen into arrears paying their road tax had quadrupled by 1848, compared to the two previous years. The tenants from Creich, who were all crofters, are all listed owing 2/- each during the following years:[13]

1846/47	1847/48	1848/49	1849/50
Niel Paterson	William Beaton	William Beaton	William Beaton
Donald MacPhee	Donald MacPhee	Donald MacPhee	Donald MacPhee
		Dugald MacCallum	Dugald MacCallum
		Hugh MacArthur's heirs	Hugh MacArthur's heirs
		Hugh McGillivray	Hugh McGillivray
		Martin McGillivray	

Central Board of Management Report

In October 1849, a deputation of the Glasgow section of the Central Board of Management for Highland Relief reported on the state of affairs on a number of islands including Mull and Iona. Generally it painted a dismal picture of the crofting communities in 1849. The extensive report on the various districts included details about the landlords, the number of tenants they had according to the yearly rental, work carried out and prospects for the coming year.[14]

The Ross of Mull or the 'Bunessan District' on Mull is described as wholly the property of the Duke of Argyll. His estate at that time had "11 tenants or tacksmen paying rents of £20 or upwards; 23 crofters from £10 to £20; 40 from £5 to £10; 101 from £2 to £5; and 58 under £2; besides 130 cottars."[15] All the crofters at Braighcreich were tenants in the £2 to £5 category.

The report gave the total population of the Ross of Mull as 2,350. Out of that population, up to 1,401, or a staggering 60%, received supplies of food to prevent starvation. The report also noted that "Taking into consideration the large number of recipients, and the amount of supplies given, we are sorry to say that comparatively little work has been done in this district." The little work they referred to was for some road works.

Under a byline subheading titled 'Employment by the proprietor' the Highland Relief Board Deputation described what had been done during the year, and the prospect for the year ahead: "During this year, the Duke of Argyll, through his factor, Mr. Campbell, Ardfinaig, employed a considerable number of men at trenching, draining, &c. a good many women and young persons in planting, weeding, and other light work; but we were sorry to learn that there was little prospect of employment next year, and therefore many of the small crofters, and nearly all the cottars, will be very ill off. We urged on Mr. Campbell the necessity of providing as much work as possible; but fear… the Committee must resume operations in this district."

Continual crop failure, increased rents and little local employment made for increasing hardship for all those living on the Duke of Argyll's Estate on Mull. A burgeoning population exacerbated the situation. Eviction from the land was a constant fear among the tenant population. Mention of the Duke of Argyll was enough to bring fear to any local tenant. Despite the potato famine and hard times, some farm rents in the area had been raised substantially. On Iona, they were increased by 50% in 1847 from the previous year. To the small crofters on the Ross of Mull, paying rent arrears was difficult enough without paying a higher rent.

The Process of Evicting Tenants

Perhaps the worst year since the start of the famine for all the small crofters and cottars in the Highlands was 1849. Mull was no exception. In his book *The Great Highland Famine*, T. M. Devine records that during 1849, the Central Board was supplying meal for 7,893 people or 47% of the island's population.[16] In addition to that, parochial boards operating under the Scottish Poor Law were providing assistance to a further 385 people.

Another telling record was that for Summonses of Removal and Sequestration from the Tobermory Sheriff Court. Devine notes that summonses to evict tenants from Mull leapt from seven in 1848 to 122 in 1849, a 17 fold increase. In 1850, they increased to 166 and in 1851 increased again to 181 before declining to 88 in 1852.[17]

The procedure to evict a crofter reluctant to move from his leasehold farm probably varied to some degree from estate to estate, but whatever the circumstances, eviction was subject to a well established legal process. Of course that didn't stop some unscrupulous landlords evicting tenants unlawfully. A landlord did not have to give a reason for issuing an eviction notice. A crofter may initially be issued with a notice to vacate his farm by a proprietor or his agent such as Factor Mor. If that crofter (or any tenant) failed to obey the direction, court proceedings would commence.

In England, judges and magistrates presided over courts of law and an officer of the court was called a bailiff. In Scotland, a judge was known as a sheriff (or sheriff substitute) and an officer of the court was a sheriff officer.

Legal action to evict a tenant fell under an 1555 Act of Parliament entitled 'Act anent the Warning of Tenants'. The Act required landlords to give a tenant at least 40 days notice before the lease term date, (usually Whitsunday), to vacate their property. It states: "It is statute and ordained that in all time coming the warning of all tenants and others to flit and remove from lands, mills, fishing and possessions whatsoever shall be used in the following manner: that is to say, lawful warning being made at anytime within the year forty days before the feast of Whitsunday (May/June), either personally or at their dwelling places and at the ground of the lands, and one copy delivered to the wife or servants, and failing thereof to be fixed upon the gates or doors of the dwelling places of the said lands, if there are any, and thereafter the same precept of warning to be read in the parish kirk where the lands lie upon a Sunday before noon at the time of the high mass, and one copy left affixed upon the most patent door of the kirk forty days before the term and no further..."[18]

If the tenant did not 'flit and remove' as instructed, landlords, at the time of their own choosing, could apply to the Sheriff's Court for legal action to be taken. The court would then proceed to issue the defendant a removing summons requesting the person appear before the court to explain why they failed to obey the eviction notice. The tenant was required to attend court within seven days, or the first available court sitting day. In that era, the Sheriff Court did not work on a daily basis.

A court officer responsible for the district where the tenant resided would then visit the tenant and hand the notice to the person, or leave it with a member of his family. A Sheriff Court Officer would sometimes have a number of summonses to deliver in a designated area to the tenants in question. Cost aside, for a crofter on the Ross of Mull to travel to the Tobermory Sheriff's Court in 1849 was no easy task. Few would contemplate such an appearance.

40. A view of Beinn Chladan, the hill which overlooks the former crofting community of Braighcreich. The ruin at the eastern end (McPhees' Ruin) is in the foreground.

41. The massive Galloway Dyke that cuts through the old Braighcreich crofts.

42. An internal view of the house ruin at the eastern end of Braighcreich looking west towards Kintra. A stone enclosure on the left was added to the ruin when it became a place to yard sheep.

Upon receiving a summons, some tenants would move out as directed. Others, sometimes with a large family that included aged parents, would stay in their homes until the law was brought to bear.

Failure to appear before the court or obey a lawful direction, would see the Sheriff's Court issue a decreet or final judgement, and an order directing the offending tenant to move out. Any tenant who successfully challenged their eviction could expect redress "15 days immediately following the feast of Trinity Sunday for the doing of justice"[19], Trinity Sunday being the week after Whitsunday.

A review of the summonses issued from the Tobermory Sheriff Court in 1849 for Mull shows that 44 removing summonses were taken out at the request of the 8th Duke of Argyll, the majority of them dated 4th April. Thirty-five out of the 44 were issued for tenants on the Ross of Mull and Iona. Included in the 35 removing summonses were four crofters in the Creich District and two in the nearby Catchean District.

A summons for the Creich and Catchean crofters to appear before the court was issued on 19th March. A statement to the Tobermory Sheriff's Court by officer Alex MacDonald, verified by his junior witness Alexander MacDonald (possibly his son), stated the crofters in both districts had been "lawfully summoned warned and charged"[20] on 22nd and 24th March to appear in court. Despite the summons, none of the crofters responded. Subsequently an eviction notice was issued to the tenants on 4th April which stated the defenders "ought and should be discerned and ordained by Decreet of Court to flitt and remove themselves... at the said term of Whitsunday next..."[21] Whitsunday in 1849 was on 27th May.

The four crofters at Creich and two crofters at Catchean, were all listed on an eight page removing summons recorded on 4th April. With the exception of Euphemia McInnes, a number in brackets is shown after each crofter's name, but it is not apparent what the number refers to. Possibly it is a court item number or a croft number. Point four of the summons states the six crofters had been warned often and at various times to vacate their farms by Whitsunday. As the approaching deadline loomed, none of them had moved. In addition to being asked to leave their farms, the crofters had been warned not to plant another crop following the previous harvest. The following is a brief summary of the removing summons issued to the crofters at Creich and Catchean.[22]

Date	Place	Name and Number	Sheriff Officer	Amount	Location
4/4/1849	Ross	Arthur MacArthur (3)	Lachlan McLean	not specified	Catchean
4/4/1849	Ross	Euphemia McInnes	Lachlan McLean	not specified	Catchean
4/4/1849	Ross	Archd McKinnon (9)	Lachlan McLean	not specified	Creich
4/4/1849	Ross	William Beaton (14)	Lachlan McLean	not specified	Creich
4/4/1849	Ross	Donald McPhee (6)	Lachlan McLean	not specified	Creich
4/4/1849	Ross	Alex. Campbell (23)	Lachlan McLean	not specified	Creich

Although money owed to the Duke of Argyll is not specified as the reason for issuing the removing summons to the four tenants at Creich and the two tenants at Catchean, it is hard not to assume they were being evicted for failing to pay rent.

Tenants who were served with a removing summons and ignored it, would see the sheriff's officers arrive at the house with his bullyboys in tow. Often dogs accompanied them. Where a croft home was no longer required, or a truculent crofter was involved, a stonemason was sometimes brought along. He was employed to prise the corners of the croft house apart so as to dislodge the roof timbers. Dust and mayhem would accompany such action. Eventually the occupants would literally be driven out of their homes.

Whatever the circumstances, the four crofters at Creich (which included Braighcreigh), along with their two counterparts at Catchean, were evicted from their properties on, or about, 27th May 1849. In the abscence of any available record to the contrary, all six crofts were apparently re-leased after being vacated, rather than amalgamated, and there is no record to indicate any removal was anything other than orderly.

NOTES

1. Riddell, C, 1996, *The History of 'Tireragan' Township, Ross of Mull. A Study in Local History*, p. 13.
2. NRS, SC 59/2/6/1, Sheriff Court Records, Tobermory.
3. Riddell, C, 1996, *The History of 'Tireragan' Township, Ross of Mull. A Study in Local History*, p. 10.
4. Riddell, C, 1996, *The History of 'Tireragan' Township, Ross of Mull. A Study in Local History*, p. 11.
5. ROMHC: Letter from Factor Mor.
6. Currie, J, 2001, *Mull the Island and its People*, Monochrome Plate Section.
7. Classic Image, *Alamy Stock Photo*.
8. Wikipedia commons, StarBlazcova, 13/3/2007, Inveraray Castle.
9. A&BC file FH 358, *Petition of Tenants from Shiaba*.
10. Ibid.
11. A&BC, *Argyllshire Road Act 1843*, p. 8.
12. A&BC, *Argyllshire Road Act 1843*, p. 11.
13. NRS, SC59/3/2 West Register House.
14. NLS, *Report on The Islands of Mull, Ulva, Iona, Tiree and Coll, and on Part of the Parish of Morvern, by A Deputation of the Glasgow Section of The Highland Relief Board, October, 1849*, p. 1.
15. NLS, *Report on The Islands of Mull, Ulva, Iona, Tiree and Coll, and on Part of the Parish of Morvern, by A Deputation of the Glasgow Section of The Highland Relief Board, October, 1849*, p. 18.
16. Devine, T M, 2004, *The Great Highland Famine*, p. 104.
17. Devine, T M, 2004, *The Great Highland Famine*, p. 179, table 7.3.

18. NRS, PA7/1/14 ff2v-4r, *Acts and Conventions of the Realm of Scotland made in Parliament 1555*. Mary I. As catalogued by NRS as Edinburgh Parliament Legislation, A1555/6/13.

19. Ibid.

20. NRS, PA7/1/14 ff2v-4r, *Acts and Conventions of the Realm of Scotland made in Parliament 1555*. Mary I. As catalogued by NRS as Edinburgh Parliament Legislation, A1555/6/13.

21. NRS, SC59/2/6/1, Sheriff Court Records, Tobermory, Summons of Removal.

22. Ibid.

12

Cottars and Poor Law Relief

Some of the six families evicted from their crofts in May 1849 ended up in the nearby fishing village of Kintra. Included among them were the Braighcreich McPhees. In the single row of 12 houses that fronted the little bay at Kintra, they were able to live in one of the 8th Duke of Argyll's houses, 3rd from the northern end.

At that time, Kintra was one of the places where the Central Board of Management for Highland Relief had been conducting a fishing initiative to try and improve the lot of the local people. A number of the inspectors employed by the Board to facilitate such operations were naval officers with the rank of captain. Mr. McLean at Bunessan was engaged by one of the Board's inspectors to administer the provision of funding for fishing at several places on the Ross of Mull.

According to the report submitted by the Deputation of the Glasgow Section of the Central Board in October 1849, the fishing operation at Kintra was doing well. After payment for fish sent to Glasgow, fish on hand, funds from fishermen and materials paid for by the Board, it had a small surplus of funds.

The report went on to state: "Mr. McLean had men employed in fishing at four different stations, Bunessan, Kintra, Port Uisken and Carsaig, and assured us that, were proper boats and sufficient materials provided, and a little more encouragement given, or a higher price paid for fish caught, he had no doubt that a large number of the people might be profitably employed in this lucrative occupation."[1]

In addition to fishing, the Central Board sought to provide work for women and the elderly in the community, by introducing net-making, spinning and knitting to areas like the Ross of Mull and Iona. Unfortunately those schemes met with little success. In the case of knitting, the price received for the sale of socks and cloth did not cover the cost of the raw materials used to make them.

Fishing and other activities organised by the Central Board were complemented with the relief work of trenching, draining and so on provided by the Argyll Estates. In June 1850, the Argyll Estates also commenced a knitting scheme similar to that of the Board when a hosier was contracted to supply yarn and buy the finished product. Out of a total of 194 women employed by the Argyll Estates on Mull, Iona and Tiree, 108 were employed from the Ross of Mull. That list has now apparently been lost or misplaced, so who was on it is unknown. Despite minimal wages, the scheme was a dismal failure, incurring a considerable loss. It was thus discontinued after about 18 months of operation.

The cottar families living at Kintra supported by the Central Board were also probably assisted by younger family members capable of working. Cottars with sons who could work as fishermen helped in this regard. For those tenants who had been evicted from their crofts and become cottars, having children capable of being employed meant they could avoid being listed on a poor roll, and becoming dependent on food aid.

The Central Board's fishing initiative at Kintra offered the destitute cottars and other residents in the village some hope for survival. Although life was undoubtedly tough, it appears for as long as fishing was viable, the families that lived there had a means to support themselves.

Warning to Remove Tenants and Cottars

In addition to the daily toil of trying to maintain themselves, the cottars and small crofters on the Ross of Mull always lived with the possibility of being evicted from their premises, or being forced to leave the Duke of Argyll's Estate.

Among the Argyll Estates papers, is a copy of one titled "List of Tenants and Cottars Warned (to remove) in his Grace The Duke of Argyll's Estates of Tyree and Ross of Mull 1850".[2] This fascinating document lists the Argyll Estate on the island of Tiree and island of Mull separately, and each Estate lists both tenants and cottars. The document reveals that as to be expected, none of the people listed as cottars are paying rent. Those listed as tenants, have the annual rent they were being charged and the 'amount due at martinmas'.

Eight tenants at Creich (presumably all crofters), were warned mostly for failing to pay their rent. Under the heading Cottars on the Mull Estates, Kintra is shown to have five cottars who were warned together with the reason for the warning. Categorised as cottars, they are the people described by Factor Mor as "locusts of the land... the indolent, uncivilised and pauperism of the Estate". They, and a sample of some of the others warned of being removed from the Ross of Mull, are shown as follows:

Kintra

Archibald Campbell	Retailing spirits
John MacArthur	Keeping a cow and paying no rent
Angus Macfarlane	Keeping a cow and paying no rent
William Suthers	Keeping a cow and paying no rent
Donald Macphee	Fighting and disorderly conduct

Elsewhere on the Ross of Mull

William MacEachern	Poaching salmon
Archibald McDonald	Being destitute
Alexander Macfarlane	Not being a native of Ross
Dugald MacInnes	Arrears & misbehaviour
Widow & Hugh McCormick	Retailing whisky
Widow MacArthur	Stealing turnips from Ardfenaig

43. The fishing village of Kintra on the Isle of Mull circa 1900 - a single row of homes close to the water's edge when the tide is high.[3]

44. A photo of the fishing village of Kintra on the Isle of Mull, early to mid 1900s.[4]

Eighteen-fifty was another tough year for all those in the crofting communities. As blight continued to depress potato yields, more relief was required. Towards the end of 1850, both the Edinburgh and Glasgow boards of the Central Board of Management for Highland Relief had almost exhausted their relief funds. By September it was clear operations had to be curtailed, and eventually would have to cease.

Cessation of large scale voluntary relief forced the government to review its position on famine relief in the Highlands. Despite requests from numerous quarters for action, the government rejected making specific allocations of money for famine relief, or extra assistance for people to emigrate.

Up to that point, the provision of aid under the Scottish Poor Law had not been provided to the majority of the desperate people in the Highlands and Islands. That was because under the Act, able-bodied people who could work were ineligible for any sort of relief. In that era, it was the widely held view that welfare of any kind to support such people led to indolence and the abrogation of personal responsibility. The Scottish Poor Law was designed specifically to make provision only for the sick, the injured, the elderly and generally those incapable of work to maintain themselves.

However, if loss of life from starvation was to be avoided, something had to be done. As a solution, the government found a way to utilise the Scottish Poor Law. It used a clause in the legislation which gave the Board of Supervision the power to provide aid through local destitution committees for the 'occasional poor' as a way around the strict provisions of the Act.[5] If ever a term was a misnomer, it would be hard to find a better one than occasional poor, to describe the cottars and small crofters in the Highlands of Scotland in the 1840s and 1850s.

Using this interpretation, the starving, able-bodied, unemployed, were able to receive famine relief under the Scottish Poor Law. That policy exposed landlords to a legal obligation of making a greater contribution to famine relief. The new policy brought with it more pressure for change in the following year.

The 8th Duke of Argyll was among the large estate owners who sought to rid his land of unwanted people. The main targets for removal were the cottars and poorer crofters. As he was to write in 1851, "I think I must proceed with emigration and wish to send a man to Ardfenaig to tell him (i.e. Factor Mor) to make out a list of the poorest and who are able bodied who will be prepared at any moment. I wish to send out those whom we would be obliged to feed if they stayed at home; to get rid of that class is the object".[6]

Landlords had many ways of forcing unwanted tenants from their property. There was little any tenant could do about the situation. Raising the rent was a tried and trusted method, but there were other options. Tenant farmers owing rent could have their livestock confiscated; those suffering hardship could simply be refused famine relief, the right to cut peat used for cooking and heating could be withdrawn. The crofters and cottars on the Argyll Estates, like estates elsewhere, were like goldfish in a bowl with little control over their station in life.

The 1851 Census in Scotland

At the end of March in 1851, there was another government census. The census was more comprehensive than the first one in 1841, as it included the name of each person in the house, their relationship to the head of the family, their marital status, age, sex, occupation and birthplace (such as the parish).[7]

In Scotland, chief magistrates and sheriffs were given authority by the Registrar General in London, to appoint schoolmasters in each parish as enumerators (census takers) for specific areas, who would distribute a schedule to every household before census night on 30th March.[8] In the Highlands and other Gaelic areas it is doubtful that census schedules were actually distributed, as many of the people could not write. It is more commonly thought that the census enumerator 'interviewed' whoever was in the house when he arrived. Often that was a child, which led to many errors in the census.

The completed schedules were collected the following day and the information copied into an enumerator's book, which was later forwarded to London.[9] The original householder's schedules no longer exist as they have been destroyed. After civil registration of births, deaths and marriages was adopted in 1855, the Registrar General for Scotland became responsible for the census.

The government census for Kintra and North Creich showed the former Braighcreich McPhees still living in Kintra. During that year Kintra was bursting at the seams with 112 residents from 20 families, the largest number of people it was to ever have. Many of the older local men had no employment other than perhaps working as casual day labourers. All the families that lived there at that time were extremely poor.

The 1851 census listed the family as follows: 66 year old Donald McPhie as head of the family, his 56 year old wife Mary (McInnes), 38 year old Neil as a fisherman, 26 year old Hector, also a fisherman, 18 year old Alexander as an agricultural labourer, 15 year old Angus as a scholar, 13 year old Margaret as a scholar and 10 year old Flory as a scholar. Their eldest son Duncan is not shown. By that time he had his own family and resided elsewhere. Their son John is again not accounted for. Their two daughters, Catherine and Mary, are also not recorded as they were working as servants in the Lowlands. Was Mary really 46 years old when she had her youngest child as shown in the census? It seems hard to believe, but women with large families in that era, often had their last child in their mid-forties.

The 1851 McNeill Report on Highland Destitution

In 1845, former naval surgeon and diplomat Sir John McNeill (1795-1883) was appointed chairman of the Board of Supervision, which had been set up to administer and oversee the Scottish Poor Law Act.

By 1851, the situation in a number of Highland areas was reaching crisis point, with continuing hunger and poverty bedevilling the people. Funds available from the Central Board of Management for Highland Relief were no longer available, which added a sense of urgency to the problem. To try and determine the extent of the problem and find some solution, the Board of Supervision instructed Sir John to visit the affected areas and make a report on his findings.

On his travels which commenced on 3rd February 1851 to the affected parishes of the Highlands and Islands, Sir John McNeill made his way from Oban to Bunessan on the Ross of Mull. There, as would be done in every locality visited, he met initially with the Parochial Board. The seven members of the Kilfinichen and Kilviceuen Parish Board present included Factor Mor as a proxy for the 8th Duke of Argyll. The Board advised McNeill that destitution was widespread and more aid would be needed for the coming year. Four Board members present on 10th February made written submissions to McNeill that day. They were Rev. Donald Campbell, Church of Scotland minister of the parish; Rev. Donald McVean, Rev. Alexander MacGregor and Dugald McLachlane.

In the days that followed, reports were provided by Bunessan merchant Charles MacQuarie, the Duke of Argyll's estate manager Factor Mor and his ground officer Alexander MacDonald, the inspector of the poor and collector of assessments, three crofters from Creich, and many others from across the length and breadth of Mull.

All those who made submissions described the terrible plight of the local people and their dependence on relief supplies. It was pointed out by Charles MacQuarie that without growing potatoes, "not less than 12 acres (5 ha) of arable land under crop"[10] would be necessary to sustain an average family of about six to eight people. Donald MacLachlan, who paid £4 rent for his croft at Creich and over a 26 year period had lived on four different crofts, stated that no one could survive on his croft without supplementary work.

Factor Mor made a similar observation to the two mentioned above, that the average sized croft could only support an average family for about half the year. His submission went on to advise that emigration was required to avoid the necessity of famine relief, which he said, without doubt led to people becoming lazy and indolent. It further stated that "the population on the Duke's property in this parish cannot be made self-sustaining, unless it is reduced by at least one-half."[11]

The lack of secure tenure over land was submitted as a significant impediment for small tenant farmers, but two issues that had contributed so much to the local crofters parlous state were not. One, crofters being forced to live on small unviable holdings, and the other, the raising of rents beyond their capacity to pay.

After visiting 27 parishes, Sir John McNeill returned on 17th April and submitted his report in July 1851. Despite being over 200 pages with an enormous amount of detail, it recommended little other than emigration as a way of solving the problem of starvation and poverty in the Highlands, a view that reflected the landowner's wishes.

Taking his report into account, the Board of Supervision strongly recommended government assisted emigration as the only solution to the problems of overcrowding, hunger and poverty in Highland areas. Landlords naturally didn't like being responsible for an ever increasing number of poverty stricken people on their estates, so they also lobbied hard for the government to solve the problem by promoting and funding emigration.

In response to this and the recommendations of the Board of Supervision, the government passed the Emigration Advances Act in 1851. The owners of Highland estates could use public funds to take up low interest loans to assist them to remove unwanted cottars, crofters and others from their lands.

That was a necessary move by the government, because by 1851 some estate proprietors were in the same position which ended the operation of the Central Board of Management for Highland Relief. They had run out of money. Others had nearly exhausted the funds available for their dependents.

The cost of providing famine relief had resulted in some proprietors being placed in the hands of creditors and others bankrupted. Norman MacLeod, the 22nd chief of Clan MacLeod was one of those unfortunate landlords.[12] He looked upon his tenants as would a clan chief in years gone by. As the population on his estate increased, employment was provided for them by initiating brickmaking, and shipping enterprises. He also had the family's ancestral home, Dunvegan Castle on Skye, repaired. Those measures incurred large debts for Norman MacLeod.

When the famine struck in 1846, Norman MacLeod sent out a printed circular to his tenants reassuring them he would look after them, which he did. Over the following three years he spent £13,000 predominantly on meal for famine relief. His benevolence ruined him, forcing him to take a job as a clerk in London at £3 a week. Little wonder he felt aggrieved that the Edinburgh and Glasgow sections of the Central Board had mostly provided relief for people on estates where the proprietors had failed to help their tenants.

Distribution of Meal

During the cold, wet winter of early 1852, life got a little tougher for all those in the crofting and fishing communities on the Ross of Mull. Food continued to be in short supply and little money could be earned from fishing or labouring. Many were forced to seek emergency relief to avoid starvation.

Meal was distributed on the Ross of Mull and to Iona using horse-drawn carts and boats by people such as Bunessan merchant Charles MacQuarie. Poor Law relief supplies were not given out willy-nilly or to other than the most needy. Accurate records that detailed meal distribution on a quarterly basis were kept at various distribution points. Those meticulous records listed the name of each person who received assistance, together with the type and quantity of food given out. Today those records are held at the National Records of Scotland in Edinburgh.

The increasing need for famine relief in places like Kintra and the reduction in number of crofters and others at places like Creich can be seen in a comparison of the meal distribution lists for 1849 and for 1852. Not only do they show more people required relief in total, but fewer people in some crofting communities like Creich required meal, probably because so many had emigrated or been evicted.

In the crofting community of Creich there were 12 people receiving Poor Law relief in 1849. Of those, six were widows who presumably were unable to look after themselves or their family by working. For the same period, there were only five people receiving meal in the fishing village of Kintra and only one of those was a widow. By 1852, the situation had changed. At Creich, the number of people receiving meal had dropped by half to six. Of those, half were widows. At Kintra, the number of residents receiving meal had grown from six to 15 with only four of those being widows. Many more people were receiving meal to avoid starvation. Some of those were receiving Poor Law relief for the first time. The following lists show those who received meal at Creich and Kintra in 1849 and 1852:[13]

1849 Creich	1852 Creich	1849 Kintra	1852 Kintra
Dun. McGilvra	Dun. McGilvra	Lachlan McKinnon	Angus McLeod
Malcolm McCallum	Wid. Cracken	Hugh McGilvra	Beaton Orphans
Widow Beaton	Malcolm McCallum	Marion McGilvra	John McLean's children
Marion McAulay	Flora McCallum	Orphans W. Morrison	Lach McKinnon
Widow Cracken	Widow Cameron	Wid. Allan McArthur	W. Morrison Orphans
Widow Patterson	Widow Beaton		Wid. A. McArthur
Angus McLeod			Marion McGilvra
Widow Cameron			Wid. D. Eachern
William Beaton			Wid. Setton
Widow McCormack			Willm. Setton
Widow Stuart			Janet McLean
John McLean & children			Donald Mcphie
			Wid. McLean
			Arch. McEachern
			Mrs. Arch McKinnon

Quantities of oatmeal and Indian meal (maize) were dispensed to the people listed above. The weight of each was recorded in terms of bolls 140 lbs (63.5kg), stones 14 lbs (6.4kg) and pounds 16 ounces (448g).[14]

The difference in the meal distribution records for 1849 and 1852, which showed a reduction in the number of people in Creich requiring meal (assuming there are fewer of them), and the increasing number of residents in the little village of Kintra receiving it, was symptomatic of life on the Argyll Estates.[15] Small crofters were being displaced, the number of cottars or day labourers was increasing, blight was still depressing potato yields and food relief was still required.

It is difficult to imagine how grim it must have been for all the small crofters and the cottars on the Ross of Mull in 1852. During the last month of winter that year, a soup kitchen had even been established by Factor Mor at his Ardfenaig home. He provided the

8th Duke of Argyll with a list of his daily expenses incurred from February. It included 24 lbs of mutton, 10 lbs of Indian corn, 6 lbs of oatmeal, turnips, fuel and cook's wages costing 5 shillings and 8 pence. Factor Mor went on to say that 'the soup made from the above ingredients is considered a good wholesome meal of which from 40 to 50 individuals partake once a day at an average cost of about 1 ½ d each.[16]

It is hardly surprising that by 1852 the 8th Duke of Argyll's policy of trying to rid his Estate of small unprofitable tenant farmers was continuing apace. Even if they could pay their rent, the small tenants weren't wanted. Crofting areas like those at Creich were gradually being depopulated so that farms could be amalgamated into larger holdings. Those larger farms could then be let for sheep grazing and a more profitable, secure rent.

The problem of ridding the Estate of the cottars and others who made up a large pool of unwanted, unemployed, poverty-stricken people would be addressed increasingly through emigration.

NOTES

1. NLS, *Report on The Islands of Mull, Ulva, Iona, Tiree and Coll, and on Part of the Parish of Morvern, by A Deputation of the Glasgow Section of The Highland Relief Board, October, 1849*, p. 19-20.

2. A&BC file FH 274, *List of Tenants and cottars warned (to remove) on His Grace's estates of Tiree and Ross of Mull, 1850, Mull Parish of Kilfinichen and Kilvickeon*.

3. ROMHC, Fishing village of Kintra.

4. ROMHC, Fishing village of Kintra.

5. Devine, T M, 2004, *The Great Highland Famine*, p. 84.

6. MacArthur, E M, 2002, *Iona the Living Memory of a Crofting Community*, p. 104.

7. Jonas, L, and Milner, P, 2002, *A Genealogist's Guide to Discovering Your Scottish Ancestors*, p. 111.

8. Ibid, p. 109.

9. Ibid.

10. McNeill, J, *Report to the Board of Supervision on the Western Highlands*, Appendix A.

11. McNeill, J, *Report to the Board of Supervision on the Western Highlands*, Appx. A, p. 5.

12. Devine, T M, 2004, *The Great Highland Famine*, p. 86.

13. NRS, 02024 SC59/15/5, Meal Distribution 1848-53, Sheriffs Court Records, Tobermory.

14. Ibid.

15. Ibid.

16. A&BC file FH 213, *Daily Expenses of Soup Kitchen Supplied for People at Ardfenaig Commencing 5th February 1852*.

13

The Highland and Island
Emigration Society

From as far back as about 1848, there had been a change of sentiment among tenants, landlords and government officials towards the desirability of emigration as a way of dealing with the potato famine. Crofters, cottars and other poor tenants began to seek escape from the land to which they had always been so strongly attached. Landlords grew more determined to remove the poor from their estates. The government began to view assisted emigration, rather than famine relief, as a solution to destitution in the Highlands.

Famine relief and various work schemes had failed to solve destitution, poverty and overpopulation in the Highlands. Following on from the passing of the Emigration Advances Act and the McNeill Report, the government sought to use emigration as the ultimate way to solve the problems caused by the potato famine.

To handle government emigration, the British Government had established the Colonial Land and Emigration Commission in January 1840. Three public servants called Her Majesty's Colonial Land and Emigration Commissioners were appointed to the body by the government. Thomas Elliot, the former Agent-General for Emigration was one of the early commissioners who went on to become chairman. During the potato famine years, Sir Thomas Murdoch was the chairman. The Commission operated from an office at 9 Park Street, Westminster.[1]

The task of the Commissioners was to receive applications from people desirous of emigrating with government assistance.[2] They examined the character of the applicants and decided upon the amount each should contribute. This usually varied between £1 and £5, depending on things like age and occupation.[3]

The Commissioners also organised the shipping. They advertised for tenders, and officers were employed to examine and survey the ships, and upon their report, vessels were either accepted or rejected. Contracts or charters were then signed and the ship would proceed to be outfitted, take on stores and other necessities as provided in the charter. The dietary scale, listing daily rations to be provided to emigrants, was an important part of the ship's charter.[4]

Migration to Australia was not the unsupervised free-for-all it once was on the shorter trans-Atlantic voyage to Canada and the United States. On that route, overcrowding and other unhealthy conditions in the early years of migration had resulted in a high death rate on sailing vessels. As the distance was so great, passengers to Australia were fortunate the authorities took a responsible approach to their welfare. In large measure that was due to the efforts of Thomas Elliot and his experience with the emigrant ship *Asia*, when he was Agent-General for Emigration.

Transporting Scottish emigrants to Australia at the end of 1838, the *Asia* was forced into the port at Plymouth for repairs, with many sick passengers on board. Not only was the ship unseaworthy, the passengers were dirty and in unhygienic living conditions. After conducting an enquiry and personally inspecting the *Asia*, Elliot instituted a set of regulations to improve orderliness and cleanliness for those sailing on emigrant ships that contributed to improved passenger protection and a safer journey (see Appendix 9). He was also instrumental in contributing to a more effective Ship Passenger Act passed in 1842 that replaced the Ship Passenger Act of 1835.[5]

The Emigration Commission enforced stricter government regulations which improved the conditions on emigrant ships. Ship owners had to comply with stipulated dietary scales, medical provisions and had to provide details of their stores. Emigrant ships became larger, and passenger ratios improved. Passengers also had to agree to various conditons set by the Emigration Commission to qualify as assisted emigrants.

The cost of a fare to Australia was about £14.[6] To qualify for that benefit, Government assisted migrants had to conform to the Colonial Land and Emigration Commission's rules. A deposit of £1 to £2 for adults and 10 shillings for children had to be paid. For persons exceeding a specified age, a larger deposit was required. There were strict rules regarding the acceptance of children and the elderly as prospective migrants.

The emigrants had to take adequate clothing, which was inspected at the port by an officer of the Emigration Commission. Minimum quantities were stipulated. For males, not less than six pairs of stockings, two pairs of shoes and two complete suits of exterior clothing. For females, not less than six shifts, two flannel petticoats, six pairs of stockings, two pairs of shoes, two gowns with sheets, towels and soap. To cater for extremes of hot and cold weather, it was recommended men take two or three serge shirts and women and children take flannel clothing.

There was also a maximum quantity, weight and volume for luggage. The whole quantity of baggage for each adult could not measure more than 20 cubic or solid feet, nor exceed half a ton in weight. It had to be closely packed in one or more boxes, but no box was permitted to exceed 10 cubic feet in size.

The Skye Emigration Society

Skye, by the end of 1851, was one of the most distressed areas in Scotland. To alleviate the peoples' plight, the Sheriff-Substitute (magistrate or judge) of Skye, Mr. Thomas Fraser and some influential islanders encouraged local residents to emigrate to Australia, as government assisted migrants.

Australia was singled out, as the gold rush there in the 1850s had caused a serious shortage of pastoral labour, so shepherds and other agricultural workers were desperately needed. It was for that reason Australia was chosen as the most suitable destination rather than Canada. Most Highlanders would have preferred Canada, where many of their countrymen had settled since the 1780s. The constant flow of emigrants from that period to Canada had resulted in Canadian provinces such as Prince Edward Island, Nova Scotia and New Brunswick having a distinctly Scottish character.

Destitution however, stopped those wanting to leave from going. The cost of a fare to an emigration port, the cost of meals while travelling to such a port, paying the deposit required by the Emigration Commission and the high cost for new clothing were insurmountable objects to applying for assistance from the government.

To overcome those stumbling blocks, the Skye Emigration Society was formed in September 1851 under the chairmanship of Mr. Thomas Fraser. Its object was to raise funds by public subscription, to pay the expenses for families wishing to emigrate as government assisted migrants to Australia. The response to this initiative was overwhelming. "Upwards of 400 families, over two thousand souls... applied to the Committee for aid to go abroad."[7] After a public meeting in Edinburgh on 23rd February 1852 to further the cause, Sir John McNeill was appointed the chairman. About £600 was subscribed to the Society by the residents of Edinburgh.

It was no coincidence that by early 1852, the Colonial Land and Emigration Commissioners decided to relax the conditions for those emigrating with government assistance. In January it advertised the new conditions in the *Glasgow Herald* under the heading 'Free Emigration to Australia'.[8] The advertisement stated: "In consequence of the recent events, Her Majesty's Colonial Land and Emigration Commissioners have decided to relax in certain particulars their regulations on the selection of Emigrants for Sydney, Port Phillip and Adelaide. The object of this relaxation is not only to increase the present stream of Emigration, but also to facilitate, to a greater extent than hitherto, the Emigration of Families with Young Children, and to admit those having four children under 12, at 10s per head. The following Contributions are required from persons producing undoubted certificates of respectability and ability in the occupations they profess:

1. Married Agricultural Labourers, Ploughmen, Shepherds Iron Stone Miners and their Wives; also Female Domestic Servants, under 45, £1 a head; 45, and under 50, £5 a head; 50, and under 60, £11 a head.
2. Single Men, between 14 and 36, £2 a head.
3. Country Mechanics, such as Blacksmiths, Bricklayers, Carpenters, Masons, Sawyers, Wheelwrights, and Gardeners and their wives, when they can be taken, £5 a head.
4. All Children under 14, 10s a head.
5. As the regulations do not admit of a greater number of Single Men than Single Women on board each Ship, it is of importance that,... each Single Man should be balanced by that of a Single Woman..."

Formation of the Highland Emigration Society

The formation of the Skye Emigration Society and the success of the Edinburgh meeting sparked attention from the London establishment. That was probably helped by the involvement and communication between Sir John McNeill and the Assistant Secretary to the Treasury, Sir Charles Trevelyan, in London, where it was decided a larger, permanent, more effective organisation was required to tackle the problem. Trevelyan was a powerful bureaucrat who was in reality the permanent head of the Treasury.[9]

From a meeting in London presided over by the Earl of Shaftsbury in the Freemasons' Hall, a committee was formed to facilitate emigration from the Highlands and Islands to Australia, with Sir Charles Trevelyan as the chairman and the Hon. Arthur Kinnaird as the treasurer.[10] The committee then formed the Highland and Island Emigration Society (HIES), which ratified a constitution that incorporated all the rules previously incorporated in the Skye Emigration Society.

The Highland and Island Emigration Society was established in April 1852. When details of its formation became known to those leading the Skye Emigration Society in Edinburgh, they decided to cease fundraising and act only to co-operate and assist the new Society in London.

A month or so after it was established, the Society published a brief report listing those on its management committee, its objectives, a list of donors who had contributed to the Society and the amount of money it had raised.[11]

Thirty distinguished individuals made up the Society's Management Committee. They included the Lord Mayor of London, Governor of the Bank of England, eight members of the British Parliament which included the Society's Treasurer Arthur Kinnaird, members of the English and Scottish aristocracy including the Duke of Buccleuch, the Earl of Shaftesbury, Baron L. de Rothschild, MacLeod of MacLeod and Cluny MacPherson of Cluny; the Rev. H. Mackenzie, Vicar of St. Martin-in-the-Fields; Thomas Fraser of Skye and treasury bureaucrat Sir Charles Trevelyan.

The Society was given a significant boost when His Royal Highness Prince Albert approved of the organisation's objectives and became its patron. When a subscription list opened with a donation of £300 from Queen Victoria and £105 from Prince Albert, leading members of the aristocracy were quick to follow suit and make a contribution. Funds from others followed. The British public was sympathetic to the cause and numerous individuals subscribed to the Society. The Australian Colonies, desperate for new immigrants, were also keen to support the Society and see it succeed. Colonial governments such as that in South Australia provided money.

Donations were received at the office of the Society's Committee located at 4 St. Martin's Place, Trafalgar Square in London. Five bankers in London's West End and three in the city were also nominated to accept donations on behalf of the Society. A subscription list published soon after the Society was formed showed it had raised £5,129.5.7. Part of the preamble in the Society's Report stated the following:

"The attention of the benevolent British Public has long been awakened by the lamentable destitution prevailing in the Island of Skye and other overpopulated Highland and Island districts. For five years past a great part of the people of these districts has been supported out of that portion of the magnificant subscription raised in the winter of 1846-7, for the relief of the Famine in Ireland and Scotland, which has been administered by the Edinburgh and Glasgow Relief Committees.

This fund is now exhausted, and the condition of the people remains unimproved. They cannot support themselves in the land of their fathers; and the hardy and loyal Highlander is in danger of being converted into a professional mendicant.

There is need of a complete and final remedy.

Happily there are in other parts of Queen Victoria's dominions, favoured climes, where the labour which at home has no field for its employment will become highly productive and remunerative. They who are a burden to the British community, will become a support to it when they have been transferred to the colonies. Instead of living on our alms, they will give valuable equivalents for our manufactures; and, above all, they will exchange a life of demoralising dependence for one which will abound with the rewards of industry and enterprise."[12]

Sir Thomas Murdoch, as chairman of Her Majesty's Colonial Land and Emigration Commissioners, was very forthcoming in his willingness to help Sir Charles Trevelyan overcome some of the difficulties faced by the Society. An immediate problem was the selection of suitable emigrants. Trevelyan requested that an Emigration Commission official be sent to the Highlands to undertake this task. The Commission appointed experienced emigration officer James Chant as the Benevolent and Intelligent Officer, to liaise with Highland proprietors and assist the Society in arranging the selection and shipment of emigrants.[13] He began work in Glasgow soon after being appointed. The Commissioners also placed shipping at the disposal of the Society.

The Society was faced with enormous costs. There were huge numbers of people involved, many of them destitute, who had to be fed and supplied with a complete outfit of clothing. An enormous cost the Society faced was the transport of emigrants from their home districts to a port of embarkation. Ships under the conrol of the Colonial Land and Emigration Commission were only permitted to sail from a port where an emigration depot was located. The main embarkation port was at Liverpool on the River Mersey. A request from Trevelyan to Sir Thomas Murdoch to establish an emigration depot at Portree on Skye, and another one at Tobermory on Mull, was turned down. Murdoch wrote to Trevelyan advising him that such a proposal "would be expensive and a most inconvenient cost."[14]

HIES Assistance and Funding

The Highland and Island Emigration Society had strict guidelines for people it was prepared to help. Family groups were preferred, but elderly relatives would not be encouraged. Under no circumstances would the HIES countenance the separation of husbands and wives or parents from children under 18 in order to emigrate. Single women, widows or widowers with young children were not accepted under the scheme.

The Society's emigrants were given similar assistance to other government emigrants. As passages were provided by the Colonial Land and Emigration Commission, the HIES emigrants had to conform to the Commission's rules.

The Commissioners agreed to waive some of the usual strict conditions for assistance by allowing children and older family members to be eligible. Many Highlanders simply refused to emigrate unless they did so as a family unit. A big hurdle for the Society and the Highlanders was thus overcome.

The Society's success was contingent on the co-operation of all the key participants. Among them were the British Government, the Australian colonies, the landlords who wanted to be rid of their destitute tenants and the desperate Highlanders themselves. The other essential component was the raising of funds to make the scheme possible.

Highlanders relying on assistance to emigrate had to comply with rules set not only by the Highland and Island Emigration Society but by the government.

The rules adopted by the Highland and Island Emigration Society were practical and effective. Just as John Dunmore Lang years earlier had advocated, emigrants were to be chosen according to their occupations and their suitability for the Australian colonies.

With the fares paid by the government, the role of the Society was to raise funds for all the other costs. Money had to be found for each emigrant's deposit and the clothing mentioned previously. It was a huge logistical exercise transporting thousands of people over such a long distance. As the people were mostly destitute, everything had to be provided. There was considerable expense in just transporting people to emigration ports, not to mention supplying them with adequate food, clothing, eating utensils and bedding. Assistance was given to emigrants based on five key conditions set by the Society:[15]

1. The emigration will be conducted, as much as possible, by entire families, and in accordance with the rules of the Colonial Land and Emigration Commissioners.

2. Passages to Australia are provided by the Commissioners, from Colonial funds, for able-bodied men and women of good character, and not exceeding a specified age, with a certain proportion of children, on production of a stated quantity and description of clothing, and on payment of a deposit of from £1 to £2 for adults, and 10s for children. For persons exceeding a specified age, a larger amount of deposit is required. The emigrants asking for aid will be required to apply all their

available means to defraying the expenses of their outfit and deposits.

3. The Society will advance the sum necessary to make good whatever may be deficient for these purposes.

4. The owners or trustees of the properties from which the emigrants depart, will be expected to pay one-third of the sum disbursed on account of the emigrants by the Society.

5. The emigrants will be required to repay the Society the whole of the sums advanced to them, which will again be applied in the same manner as the original fund.

The deposit and outfit for each emigrant mentioned in point two of the Society's conditions were the two most substantial expenses incurred. Moneyless emigrants were not required to make any financial contribution to their passage in order to depart their home-land, and few had the ability to do so. In fact, many of the emigrants were so poor they were provided with stamps or money for stamps so they could correspond with family and friends left behind in Scotland.

The condition that would contribute to the scheme's success was the role of the landlords and the way the scheme was funded. Co-operation and financial assistance was sought from any Highland landlord who would benefit from the removal of penniless tenants. As already mentioned, to that end, two-thirds of the emigrant's costs were paid by the Society, but the other third was paid by the landlord who owned the estate on which the emigrant lived. This was an ingenious move because it was in the landlord's own interest to be rid of those indigent people for whom they were responsible. Some landlords were more willing to pay than others.

The Society not only paid the government's deposit, but purchased the clothing and other necessities required by government assisted emigrants. Clothing was either distributed at a port like Glasgow, or delivered to the place where the emigrants were departing. A list of expenses was drawn up and the total amount owing by each landlord's estate calculated. Once that had been done, one-third of the relevant estate's total expenses was charged back to it.

Promissory Notes and Emigrant Debt Recovery

Assistance given to the destitute and poor by the Highland and Island Emigration Society was not done by way of gift or donation. The price was a debt that had to be repaid. Emigrants had to repay the Society's expenses advanced to them after they were settled in Australia. The head of each family emigrating had to sign a promissory note.[16]

The promissory note stated "... having advanced to me... in money, and clothing, to the value of... in order to enable me and my family to emigrate to Australia, upon the condition that the whole amount so advanced being in all... should be repaid by me and my family, in order to be again used by the said Society in assisting other poor persons to emigrate, I hereby bind and oblige myself on the expiration of twelve months from the date of my landing in Australia, to pay... such Chairman to receive... the said sum of... and on the part of my wife and children I engage that in the event of my not paying the said sum at the time above mentioned, the sum shall be repaid by my wife and children."[17]

Collection of outstanding debts from the emigrants in Australia posed a problem for the authorities. To tackle the situation, Charles Trevelyan, back in London, was notified that "A Society composed principally of Highland gentlemen, and of which Mr. Lachlan McKinnon, Member of the Legislative Council, is chairman, has been formed at Melbourne, under the patronage of the Government, for the recovery of the sums advanced to the emigrants, who are dispersed over the Colony."[18] Known as the 'Highland Emigration Society', it fulfilled its duties with the help of a full time secretary and had the Victorian governor as its patron.

The Society's secretary was paid a handsome gross income of £500 per annum. His job was to ride over the colony in order to collect the promissory note instalments. Despite his best efforts, he found it difficult to collect enough money to offset his own wages and expenses because many Highlanders repudiated their obligations.[19]

Emigrants had 5 years to pay the amount stipulated on their promissory notes. It is impossible to know how many families repaid their loans, but a significant number, especially in Victoria where a majority of the Highlanders ended up, were unwilling to honour their obligation. Some didn't want to pay for the the poor quality of clothing issued to them, described as "a most miserable rubbish of cloth",[20] while others were agrieved that little provision had been made for Free Presbyterian ministers to accompany them to the colony. These resentments were compounded by a widespread anti-authority mood among the colonial population after trouble on the gold fields.[21]

Complaints about the lack of money returned to the Society in London led to advice from the Melbourne committee, that their agent could not get the Highlanders to make their repayments. This predicament also came to the attention of the Melbourne press and Free Presbyterian ministers in the colony. After a scathing article in a newspaper with the largest circulation in Australia, a meeting was convened so that members of the Melbourne Committee could appeal directly to Society emigrants to repay their loans.

A meeting in the Gaelic Church at Geelong was also attended by Free Presbyterian minister Dr. MacIntosh Mackay, a fervent supporter of the Highland and Island Emigration Society. Addressing his countrymen in Gaelic, he encouraged them to repay their loans and "thus deliver themselves from disgrace and the Gaelic world from dishonour."[22] The emigrants however, remained largely unresponsive to his appeal.

NOTES

1. Ray, M, 2001, *Administering emigration: Thomas Elliot and government-assisted emigration from Britain to Australia 1831-1855*, Durham University Thesis, p. 26 and 172.
2. *London Illustrated News*, 10th July 1852.

3. *London Illustrated News*, 10th July 1852.

4. Ibid.

5. Ray, M, 2001, *Administering emigration: Thomas Elliot and government-assisted emigration from Britain to Australia 1831-1855*, Durham University Thesis 2001, p. 160.

6. *The Glasgow Herald*, 30th July 1852.

7. *Inverness Courier*, 19th February 1852.

8. *The Glasgow Herald*, 16th January 1852.

9. Balfour, R A C S, 1973, *Emigration from the Highlands and Western Isles of Scotland to Australia during the Nineteenth Century*, University of Edinburgh Thesis, p. 107.

10. Report of the Highland Emigration Society, from its Formation in April 1852 - 1853, p. 8.

11. NLS, George IV Bridge Shelf Mark APS.2.85.70, HIES Leaflet, p. 1.

12. Ibid.

13. Devine, T M, 2004, *The Great Highland Famine*, p. 252.

14. Balfour, R A C S, 1973, *Emigration from the Highlands and Western Isles of Scotland to Australia during the Nineteenth Century*, University of Edinburgh Thesis, p. 115.

15. NLS, George IV Bridge Shelf Mark APS.2.85.70, HIES Leaflet, p. 2.

16. NRS, HIES file HD4_6, Promissory Note Book: Recorded the date, drawer's name, drawer's residence, the estate emigrating from, emigrant ship and its sailing date, the destination and the amount owed.

17. www.scan.org.uk/researchrtools/emigration.htm, Scottish Archives Network.

18. Report of the Highland Emigration Society, from its Formation in April 1852 - 1853.

19. Sutherland, R, 1877, *The History of the Presbyterian Church of Victoria*, p. 130.

20. Ibid.

21. Balfour, R A C S, 1973, *Emigration from the Highlands and Western Isles of Scotland to Australia during the Nineteenth Century*, University of Edinburgh Thesis, p. 128.

22. Sutherland, R, 1877, *The History of the Presbyterian Church of Victoria*, p. 132.

14

The 1850s Exodus

Sir Charles Trevelyan had worked assiduously through early 1852, to gain the co-operation of those required, to ensure the exodus of people from Highlands and Islands on a mass scale became a reality.

By the time the Highland and Island Emigration Society came into official existence in April 1852, Trevelyan had selected Skye as the starting point for the Society's operation. Not only was Skye one of the most distressed areas of Scotland, with thousands of desperate people, many of those people were loyal to Norman MacLeod, the chief of Clan MacLeod, who now resided in London. His forthcoming co-operation was a valuable asset to Trevelyan because he was the most highly regarded clan leader from the island.

At that early stage, 200 people had applied to leave Skye. The Colonial Land and Emigration Commissioners had provided places for them in four of their ships, to travel with other non-Society passengers, with another two ships that could be chartered solely to carry the Society's beneficiaries. Those people had to be transported to the main emigration port of Liverpool, nearly 400 miles south of Skye.[1]

All prospective emigrants residing in far flung areas of Scotland made their way to emigration ports by boat. Although Royal Navy boats were used for some pick-ups, one of the regular steamboats that traversed the Western Isles out of Glasgow transported many of the Society's passengers.

The first batches of emigrants from Skye sailed on the open deck of small steamers directly to the port of Liverpool. Those who travelled on the steamer *Princess Royal* complained about a lack of food and when they transferred to the *Marco Polo*, complained about the heat, confusion and discomfort on the ship. The complaints were not received kindly by Trevelyan in London. As he was to write: "I suspect that the people of Skye have been accustomed of late years to consider themselves as peculiar objects of general care and sympathy, that they have in great measure lost the manly tone which belongs to our population and are disposed to complain of every slight inconvenience... I should have been ashamed of any Somersetshire man who would have written such a letter."[2]

Fortunately, by the end of May, Trevelyan had persuaded the Colonial Land and Emigration Commissioners to establish one of their depots at Glasgow, on the River Clyde. Emigrants could be taken there initially by a paddle steamer, and from there to Liverpool by one of the Glasgow to Liverpool steamers.

During the first six months of 1852, four ships sailing from Liverpool took a modest number of migrants before the *Georgiana* sailed from Greenock on 13th July, carrying a full complement of 372 Society passengers. By then a list of 3,000 Skye residents wishing to emigrate had been drawn up.

Emigration from the Argyll Estates

Between 1841 and 1851, economic hardship and the famine, saw the Ross of Mull lose 33% of its population. There was an explosion in emigration in the early 1850s. Between 1851 and 1861, the Ross would loose another 25% of its inhabitants.

Towards the latter part of 1852, with the days growing shorter and another winter looming, the cottars and small crofters on the Argyll Estates had little to look forward to other than cold weather, unemployment and hunger.

Under those circumstances, being able to emigrate was a godsend. In August 1852, probably after being nominated by the Duke of Argyll's factor, the Highland and Island Emigration Society accepted 10 families from the Argyll Estates as suitable emigrants. Documentation shows they were residents of Mull and Iona, who were booked to sail on the *Marmion*.[3] There were 68 people in all.

Five families were from Iona: eight members of crofter Colin Campbell's family who left a four acre (1.6 ha) farm, six members listed under cottar Mary McFarlan, a widow who had worked previously as a hoseknitter; three members listed under Hugh McPhail, the other two being his wife Janet and brother Colin; 12 members of crofter John McInnes family who left an eight acre (3.2 ha) farm and two members listed under cottar John McDonald, he and his younger sister, 21 year old Marion.

Three families from Kintra were all described as cottars i.e. destitute: 10 members listed under Donald McFee; five members under Colin Campbell including his wife Ann, a former hoseknitter and 13 members under Peter McArthur who had once been a crofter living on four acres (1.6 ha) in Creich. The two remaining families included seven members listed under Alexander McLean, a labourer from Ardfenaig, and two members listed under Angus McDonald, a cottar from Bunessan.

Clothing was a major concern to all involved with the Society's emigration programme. Before it got into full stride, Trevelyan wrote to Sir Edward Pine Coffin suggesting depots be established for clothing at Portree on Skye and Tobermory on Mull.[4]

It appears Trevelyan's suggestion did not get off the ground, at least at Tobermory. After the *Marmion* had been booked and passenger numbers finalised, Trevelyan wrote to Benevolent and Intelligence Officer James Chant at the end of July 1852, advising him that clothing for 250 emigrants would be sent from London to Glasgow by rail, and from there, forwarded by 'the Irish steamer' to an address he had nominated at Aros on Mull.[5] It could then be distributed to emigrants. The steamer referred to by Trevelyan was one of those that normally plied the waters between Glasgow and Ireland. Who organised the delivery? Surprisingly, the Treasury Office in London played a key role in arranging such deliveries. Treasury staff were used not only to organise and transport emigrants, but to convey clothing, literature and stores for the Society.

By August, James Chant was able to advise Trevelyan, that a list of promissory notes dated 18th August had been made, and that a note had been signed by the head of each family emigrating from Iona and the Ross of Mull. The signatures had all been witnessed, often by a fellow emigrant who had previously been a neighbour.[6] With their documentation complete and clothing in hand, the emigrants could begin their journey.

Steamers to Glasgow

By 1852 David Hutcheson & Co was the dominant operator of steamboats sailing between Glasgow and the Highlands. The firm advertised their steamers together with their routes and sailing times regularly in *The Glasgow Herald* and *Grenock Advertiser*.

The emigrants from the Argyll Estates however were not transported to Glasgow by a steamer that called in regularly at either Iona or Mull. They were picked up by the *Dunoon Castle*, a 107 feet (33 m) long wooden hulled passenger paddle steamer built in 1826. It was owned by the Glasgow & Lochfine Steam Packet Company based in Glasgow.

Despite much searching, no mention of the vessel's sailing route was found in any Glasgow newspaper advertisement during 1851 or 1852. It was however found in a commercial directory. The listing states "To and from Glasgow and Inveraray (calling at Tarbert and intermediate places) *Dunoon Castle* and *Inverness Castle* on alternate days."[7]

As one of the vessels that serviced Inveraray, the *Dunoon Castle* was a regular attendant during 1852 at a pier near the Duke of Argyll's doorstep at Inveraray Castle on the shore of Loch Fyne. No details have been found about utilising the steamer to pick up the emigrants from Mull and Iona, but it is fair to assume if it wasn't hired by the HIES, then the Argyll Estate may have been responsible for engaging the vessel.

The *Dunoon Castle* took the 68 emigrants to Glasgow on 19th August 1852. No record has been found to verify either where James Chant vetted them prior to their departure, or the place (or places) they were picked up from. Most probably they were collected from Bunessan, and then taken directly to Glasgow. It is also unknown if other emigrants from Morvern or Ardnamurchan, booked to sail on the *Marmion*, were on the *Dunoon Castle* when it collected those leaving from Mull and Iona

Travelling between Mull and Glasgow by steamer meant a journey either around the coast or via the Crinan Canal. Opened in 1801, the nine mile (14 km) Crinan Canal with 15 locks provided a short cut between Glasgow and West Highlands communities in the Inner Hebrides, like that of Mull. After a trip along the canal by Queen Victoria in 1847, shipping companies such as David Hutchison & Co advertised sailing routes using the canal under the heading 'Royal Route'.

The *Dunoon Castle* took the Royal Route which many emigrants were thankful was the case rather than an unpredictable journey in the open ocean. Eventually, the former residents from Mull and Iona ended up on a Glasgow dock after a long day's travel. James Chant almost certainly accompanied them to ensure their safe arrival.

45. Above is the steamer *Dunara Castle,* loading sheep at Bunessan Pier.[8]

46. The paddle steamer *Mountaineer.* Similar types of paddle steamers transported goods and people around the coast of Scotland and England in the 1850s.[9]

From either Glasgow or the growing port of Greenock, 27 miles (43 km) away at the mouth of the River Clyde, a steamer took them on to Liverpool. A steam train service connected both ports with some vessels picking up passengers and cargo from both places. The following advertisement that appeared in *The Glasgow Herald* in 1851 is typical for such a situation: "The Royal Mail Steam Packet *Pioneer* sails every morning (Sunday excepted) from Glasgow Bridge, at 6 o'clock, and from Greenock about 8, on the arrival of the 7 a.m. Train from Glasgow..."[10]

Whether it was from Glasgow or Greenock, the emigrants were possibly transported on one of the ships that departed for Liverpool regularly on Tuesdays, Thursdays and Sundays for a journey of about 220 miles (354 km), that took the best part of a full day and night. If not a regular steamer or the *Dunoon Castle,* some other vessel chartered by the HIES could have been used to carry them on to Liverpool.

Questions such as: how long did the emigrants spend in Glasgow? If they stayed there, where did they stay? Which steamer took them to Liverpool? How long did they stay at Liverpool? How were the financial arrangements organised? All remain unanswered. Although a great deal of documentation surrounding the Society's passengers has been preserved, the answers to many such questions still remain a mystery.

One piece of valuable information retained in the Duke of Argyll's private archives is a 12 column table which provides a costing for each of the 10 Argyll Estate families transported on the *Dunoon Castle* to Glasgow who were booked to sail on the *Marmion.* Bearing no date, it may have formed part of a more comprehensive report. The expenses list was signed by John Campbell, Factor Mor. The costs for the five families emigrating from the Ross of Mull are as follows:[11]

	Donald McFee	Colin Campbell	Peter McArthur	Alexander McLean	Angus McDonald
residence	Kintra	Kintra	Kintra	Ardfenaig	Bunessan
souls emigrating	10	5	13	7	2
cost	£. s. d	£. s. d	£. s. d	£. s. d	£. s. d
passage money	22. 0. 0	15. 0. 0	22. 0. 0	4. 10. 0	2. 0. 0
amount for clothing	15. 4. 6	7. 12. 6	18. 0. 3	0	0
fare to Glasgow	1. 10. 0	0. 15. 0	1. 10. 0	0. 13. 6	0. 6. 1
food to Glasgow	3. 5. 0	1. 12. 6	3. 5. 0	1. 9. 3	0. 3. 0
arrears of rent	0	0	0	0	0
stamps	0. 4. 0	0. 2. 6	0. 4. 0	0	0
total expenses	42. 3. 6	25. 2. 6	45. 10. 3	6. 12. 9	0
payment by emigrant	0	0	0	6. 12. 9	0. 19. 0
promissory note[12]	42. 3. 6	25. 2. 6	45. 10. 3	0	[13]2. 0. 0

The Emigration Port of Liverpool

The *Marmion,* like the *Georgiana,* had been chartered exclusively for the Society's passengers. The ship's home port was the English city of Liverpool, and it was from the dock at Birkenhead near Liverpool that the *Marmion* would leave for Australia. One hundred miles (160 km) south of the Scottish border, Liverpool was the closest port where the government had an emigration depot and it was the busiest in England. People not only from Britain, but Europe and other places, made their way there in order to board a ship to one of the colonies.

What a scene it was for the emigrants to reach the Birkenhead dock and see the *Marmion.* They must have all had mixed emotions at that stage because, although they were leaving a life of great hardship behind, they were also leaving their homeland for good and about to take a long and hazardous voyage.

If the emigrants had not been accompanied from Glasgow by the Benevolent and Intelligent Officer James Chant, then he may have made contact with them again while finalising the passenger list onboard the *Marmion* after their stay at the Birkenhead Emigration Depot. The depot was to be their temporary accommodation until the ship was ready to sail. Usually this was only a matter of days, depending on the fit-out required for the ship's human cargo. There was separate accommodation for the three types of passengers - unaccompanied women, men and families.

The Birkenhead Emigration Depot was a substantial building. The Emigration Commissioners previously despatched ships to Australia predominantly from Plymouth and Deptford, but the quality of the facilities at Birkenhead had encouraged them to use the port of Liverpool. About three or four emigrant ships a month sailed from the Birkenhead dock.[14]

Apprehension may have been the first reaction many husbands and wives had at the first sight of their temporary accommodation. Several hundred emigrants were all to sleep in one great dormitory. Down the length of both sides of the long room, 4 feet (120 cm) off the ground, a 6 foot (1.8 m) wide wooden bench catered for bedding. The two long benches were partitioned every 4 feet with planks a mere 18 inches (45 cm) high which formed open bunks for bedding. Similar partitioning existed below the bunks at floor level. With passengers sleeping in sight of each other, privacy was at a minimum. Everyone had to put up with loud snoring, unruly children and the like.[15]

The dining room at the Birkenhead Emigration Depot was also a huge, open expanse that could comfortably accommodate 600 people. It had trestle tables and bench seats with a wide access stairway that led to the dormitory above.[16] For many impoverished Highlanders familiar with hunger and starvation rations, the quantity and quality of food provided was probably better than they were used to. Irish, Scottish and English emigrants dined at separate tables that were labelled accordingly. Despite being surrounded by the noise and commotion created by the large number of people that used the dining hall, it was not unusual for the Highlanders to sit down and conduct family prayer at the tables

47. The Birkenhead Emigration Depot at the port of Liverpool. Alongside the wharf is the *Bourneff,* one of the sailing ships used by the Highland and Island Emigration Society to take emigrants to Australia.[17]

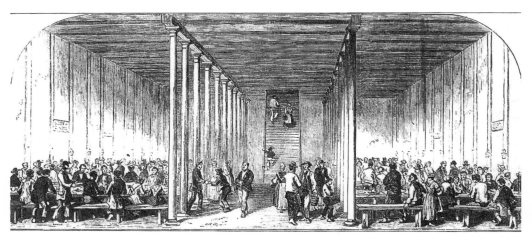

48. The Birkenhead Emigration Depot dining hall. It was capable of seating 600 emigrants.[18]

assigned to them.

The crowded dormitory was a foretaste of things to come. The unhealthy conditions at emigration depots sometimes led to disease outbreaks on board ships. People could easily pick up an infection from bedding that had been previously occupied by a person with a contagious disease. In this regard, children were particularly vulnerable.

Although the stay at the Birkenhead Emigration Depot was a trial for many, in some ways the emigrants were fortunate. Families no longer had to wonder where their next meal was coming from and were probably better fed than they had been back home. Many had friends and acquaintances around them. They had not been thrust into a difficult situation among a body of total strangers. For the people and the time, this advantage should not be underestimated.

NOTES

1. RAHS, Vol 49, Nov. 1963, p. 175.
2. NRS, HIES file HD4/1, Trevelyan to Sir Edward Pine Coffin, 5/7/1852, p. 262.
3. A&BC file FH 213A, *List and Expenses of Passage money, Outfit for Emigrants to Australia from Ross and Iona the property of His Grace the Duke of Argyll shipped per Dunoon Castle Steamer for Clyde 19th August 1852.*
4. NRS, HIES file HD4/1, Trevelyan to Sir Edward Pine Coffin, 5/7/1852, p. 262.
5. NRS, HIES file HD4/2, Trevelyan to James Chant, 31/7/1852, p. 88.
6. NRS, HIES file HD4/2, James Chant to Trevelyan, 18/8/1852, p. 165-6.
    As an example, 'Donald McPhie,' had his signature witnessed by former Kintra neighbour Colin Campbell, and Campbell's signature was witnessed by McPhie.
7. NLS, 1852, *Slater's Commercial Directory*, p. 247.
8. http://meekwrite.blogspot.com/2014/01/transport-to-and-from-tiree.html, Passages from Tiree, Dunara Castle at Bunessan
9. www.clydeships.co.uk/view.php?ref=22190, paddle steamer *Mountaineer*.
10. *The Glasgow Herald*, 4th August 1851.
11. A&BC file FH 213A, *List and Expenses of Passage money, Outfit for Emigrants to Australia from Ross and Iona the property of His Grace the Duke of Argyll shipped per Dunoon Castle Steamer for Clyde 19th August 1852.*
12. NRS, HIES file HD4_6, Promissory Note Book verifies the amounts shown, p. 30.
13. The amount of the promissory note for Angus McDonald is recorded in the Promissory Note Book as £2. 1. 0 not £2. 0. 0.
14. *Illustrated London News*, 10th July 1852.
15. Charlwood, D, 1981, *The Long Farewell, Settlers Under Sail*, p. 84-85.
16. *Illustrated London News*, 10th July 1852.
17. Ibid.
18. Ibid.

15

Life on Board an Emigrant Sailing Ship

Some of the more literate emigrants may have recognised the name of the ship they were about to board as the name of a poem written by Sir Walter Scott in 1808. *Marmion* was the name given to one of Scott's most famous historical romances set in 1513, where Lord Marmion attempted to marry the wealthy Lady Clare. The name may have had a romantic connection to Scotland, but the vessel was in fact an American owned ship of 903 tons.

Shipping records show that the *Marmion* was originally destined for Moreton Bay in Queensland. For ease of administration, the Highland and Island Emigration Society originally decided to send emigrants from Mull and Ardnamurchan to Moreton Bay. Highlanders not from those two areas were to go to various other Australian colonies. The demand for labour in Victoria however was at crisis point. The Victorian goldfields had lured pastoral workers away from the land, creating a serious shortage for employers. For this reason the vessel was re-chartered to Portland Bay in Victoria.

The 10 members of the McPhee family who sailed on the *Marmion* were a typical emigrant family. They were on the ship's passenger list as follows:[1] 50 year old Donald, an agricultural labourer; his 48 year old wife Mary; 30 year old Neil, a fisherman in Aran; 28 year old Hector, also a fisherman in Aran; 26 year old Catherine who worked in service near Glasgow; 24 year old Mary; 22 year old Alexander, an agricultural labourer in the Lowlands; 19 year old Angus, an agricultural labourer; 14 year old Margaret, a domestic servant and 11 year old Flora.

The *Marmion's* passenger list shows the McPhees' surname as McFee, but beneath it, in brackets, is given the alternative spelling McPhee. It is another example of how inconsistent the spelling of surnames was in early records. That wasn't the only inconsistency. There is a discrepancy in the appearance of the former Braigchreich crofter who became a destitute cottar and his recorded age of 50.

The remarks column of the passenger list states: 'man looks old but is healthy, is employed as a day labourer'. Considering the former cottar's age was recorded as 66 in the previous year, was he really only 50 years old? Did he put his age down to gain acceptance as a suitable assisted emigrant? Did he put his age down to minimise the cost of his fare? Did he just look old after a hard life? It is fair to say that the ages of people shown in many old Scottish records are consistently inconsistent. Those old records also have a habit of raising more questions than they sometimes answer.

Primitive Accommodation

For an everyday passenger on a 19th century sailing ship, life was not exactly comfortable. Those on board were segregated according to age, sex, marital status and social position. Only a few privileged fare paying passengers were able to secure the use of the limited number of individual cabins. They were located beneath the raised poop deck at the rear of the vessel. In the same vicinity were quarters for the captain, ship's officers, matron and surgeon-superintendent. Those travellers had access to a generous dining room where they were served meals by members of the crew. They also had the exclusive use of the spacious poop deck where the ship's wheel was located.

One of the three cabin passengers that every Gael was happy to have on board the *Marmion* was Reverend McVean. He was a Free Church of Scotland minister with a name familiar to all those from the Parish of Iona. He was also leaving his homeland bound for a ministry in Melbourne.

Prior to 1839, passengers on sailing ships had the services of a doctor who was known as a surgeon. Despite their position, such men often had few skills and even fewer morals. Long voyages gave rise to carelessness, drunkenness and immoral behaviour. The temptation by those in authority to take extra care of single women was a constant problem. To stamp out malpractice and encourage medical practitioners of better calibre, doctors on sailing ships to the Australian colonies were given permanent positions called surgeon-superintendents. Their role was to provide medical services and look after all aspects of the passengers' welfare. Their new role was a powerful one. They were responsible for ensuring passengers were given their rightful food and water rations, changed their linen once a week, received divine services on Sunday and so on. Generally speaking, they were advocates and umpires for the passengers.[2]

The vast bulk of the people travelled as steerage class passengers. The single males occupied a section enclosed by a bulkhead at the front of the ship. Single females were kept well away in another section at the rear of the vessel below the poop deck. Married couples with young children were accommodated in one large space between the two.

Steerage accommodation was the same as that at the emigration depot - dormitory style but much worse. The area below deck was cluttered, claustrophobic, poorly ventilated and with little light. Lamps were usually forbidden below decks because they posed a serious fire risk. The only available light came through open hatches or perhaps a small porthole. At night and during periods of bad weather during the day, passengers had to endure total darkness.

Bunks were like those at the emigration depot but smaller. Timber benches with plank partitions formed bunks down both sides of the ship that were only 3 feet (1 m) wide. As the head room was only a bit over 6 feet (1.8 m) and the bunks were doubled one above the other, conditions were cramped.[3] Infestations of lice, fleas, and other verminous creatures further added to the discomfort of passengers.

Privacy was non-existent. Two people sleeping in a space only 3 feet wide for several

	Sun	Mon	Tues	Wed	Thur	Fri	Sat	Total
biscuit oz	8	8	8	8	8	8	8	3.5 lb
beef oz							6	6.0 oz
pork oz		6		6		6		1.1 lb
pres. meat oz	6		6		6			1.1 lb
flour oz	6	6	6	6	6	6	6	2.6 lb
oatmeal oz	3	3	3	3	3	3	3	1.3 lb
raisins oz	2		2		2		2	.5 lb
suet oz	1.5		1.5		1.5		1.5	.4 lb
peas pint		0.25		0.25		0.25		.75 pint
rice oz			4				4	.5 lb
pres. potatoes oz	4				4			.5 lb
tea oz	0.25		0.25		0.25		0.25	1.0 oz
coffee roasted oz		0.5		0.5		0.5		1.5 oz
sugar oz		4		4		4		.75 lb
treacle oz	2		2		2		2	.5 lb
butter oz		2				2		.25 lb
water qts	3	3	3	3	3	3	3	5.25 gal

49. In 1852 the *Illustrated London News* published the dietary scale above for government assisted emigrants. The scale is for one adult. Women received the same as men, children between 1 and 14 received half the adult ration and infants under 1 year were allowed one quarter of the daily water allocation, but no rations. In addition to the food items above, passengers were issued a weekly allowance of mixed pickles, ½ oz. mustard, 2 oz. salt and ½ oz. pepper. The minimum acceptable quality biscuit was stated as well as the source of beef and pork - prime new Irish or American East India beef, and prime Irish India pork. It was also noted that from September to March inclusive, parties had the option of taking a supply of fresh potatoes rather than preserved (pres.) potatoes for the first month or 6 weeks, substituting one pound for the quarter of a pound of preserved potatoes. The same issues continue on the same days of the week as above.[4]

months would be a trial in itself let alone on a sailing ship. The partitions between bunks were so low that the occupants of the bunks either side were in easy reach. Everyone was in sight of one another although the dim light gave comfort to the more modest among the emigrant passengers. If a couple in the top bunk did not have their children sleeping below them, another couple occupied the bunk.

Dining and Shipboard Life

During the era of sail, all migrants had to supply their own bedding, cooking and eating utensils. Government sponsored emigrants received assistance in this regard. The Highland and Island Emigration Society provided the Highlanders on board the *Marmion* with the necessities stipulated by the Emigration Commissioners:

> "The commissioners supply provisions, medical attendants, and cooking utensils at their Depot and on board ship. Also, new mattresses, bolsters, blankets, and counterpanes, canvas bags to contain linen etc., their knives and forks, spoons, metal plates and drinking mugs, which articles will be given after arrival in the Colony to the Emigrants who have behaved well on the voyage..."[5]

Between the two rows of double bunks ran a long, wide table. On either side of the table were fixed bench seats. Beneath the table were places for plates, mugs etc. As can be imagined, using the dining table and the availability of acceptable food was an important consideration for all passengers.[6]

Steerage passengers had to fend for themselves when it came to meals. Rations were issued for cooking - meat twice a week and other rations on a weekly basis. It was up to individuals, families or groups to prepare their own meals and take them to the galley for cooking. Cooked meals had to be then taken back to the steerage quarters. The ship rolling in rough weather was the cause of many spoilt and lost meals.

It had long been the custom on sailing ships for people to eat in a small group called a mess. Such groups of half a dozen or so elected a mess captain whose job it was to help organise meal time. The captain drew the mess' rations and basically he was responsible for the conduct of the group. Nearly all men in steerage on emigrant ships took their turn as a mess captain. Married women took it in turns usually on a weekly basis to prepare meals for the group. After each mess had eaten, the task of cleaning the communal table and the floor was rotated among both men and women. This was a situation where families and those with friends they could trust had an advantage.

Food for the emigrant passengers on the *Marmion* was basic, with little variation. A generous supply of biscuits kept hunger pangs at bay, and was the single largest food item stipulated in the victualing scales for government chartered ships. Thick and about four inches (10 cm) square in size, they were often baked until they were as hard as a rock which no doubt helped their storage life but did little for their appeal.[7] Flour and oatmeal were supplemented with meager quantities of preserved meat, such as salted beef and salted pork. Potatoes, rice, peas, suet (beef or mutton fat), coffee, tea, sugar, treacle and butter were also mainstays of the rations. Lime juice was issued regularly to stop scurvy. On all HIES ships, oatmeal was provided as a staple ration, so the Highlanders were fortunate to have a reasonable supply of food they were accustomed to.

The food for the ship's officers and cabin passengers was completely different to that for the steerage passengers and crew. Luxuries such as alcohol, cheese and sweets broke the monotony. Livestock kept on board provided them with fresh eggs, milk and meat. Any pigs or goats also helped dispose of unwanted kitchen scraps. Such animals were usually kept on the perimeter of the poop deck, well away from any desperate poacher from the lower decks.

On many voyages, water was more of a problem than food. Drinking water was supposed to be filtered before being put into barrels for storage, but this did not always happen. Contaminated and poor quality water taken on board ship at port was often putrid by the time it was issued. Additions such as tea, coffee or raspberry vinegar had little effect in disguising its repugnance.[8]

Fresh water was a precious commodity on sailing ships and was replaced with sea water where possible. Steerage passengers washed their own clothes and their dining utensils in salt water. Whenever there was a downpour of rain, they scrambled onto the deck with their tubs, dirty clothes and any dirty dishes on hand, to take advantage of the water that flowed from the ship's sails. Any such water saved for drinking may have had a canvas flavour, but was usually more palatable than the ship's stored water.[9] People also washed and bathed on deck with sea water. That necessity was not such a problem for men but was difficult for women. Their modesty and the norms of decency during the era of sail inhibited many women from washing regularly.

All emigrants experienced uncertainty, anxiety and fear during their voyage. Gales and bad storms at sea tossed sailing ships about like corks in the surf. When bad weather blew up, water often entered the lower decks. In wild weather hatches were fastened down by the ship's carpenters, which confined all the steerage passengers below decks. They were sometimes thrown about in those dark, wet, stifling conditions for long periods until it was safe for the hatches to be removed.[10] Such times were indeed terrifying.

Rough weather and confinement below decks made attending to the call of nature difficult and uncomfortable for both sexes, but particularly so for men. Water closets that had a direct chute to the sea with a protective flap to keep the elements at bay, were provided in steerage for women but not for men. They had to use facilities on the edge of the main deck of the ship.[11] To navigate their way to them on a dark night in a rolling sea was onerous, but not as bad as being confined below decks where there were no facilities for relief.

The Highland and Island Emigration Society was aware of the trauma experienced by

50. Emigrants gathered on the poop deck of a sailing ship. Below the poop deck are the cabins reserved for fare paying passengers and the ship's officers.[12]

51. An emigrant ship being towed out from the Birkenhead Dock into the Mersey River at the port of Liverpool. Once out in the stream, the ship would await a favourable wind to commence its journey. The sketch above appeared in the *Illustrated London News*.[13]

52. Steerage passengers below deck, showing the cramped eating and sleeping facilities.[14]

53. This sketch shows the quarters for unaccompanied women on an emigrant ship. Their bunks are on either side of the long table which had fixed seating.[15]

those unfortunate people. For entertainment, bagpipes, fiddles and various other items were supplied to keep the children and adult passengers occupied and amused. Trevelyan had ensured a library of non-religious books was also included on all Society vessels.

To ease the difficulties of the long sea voyage, a minister of the same denomination as the majority of the passengers sailed on each of the Society's ships. To cater for their religious outlook, passengers were also provided with Gaelic Bibles, New Testaments, books containing religious instruction and prayers (psalters), religious pamphlets (tracts), books of Christian doctrine (catechisms), plus an array of other material.

Poor they may have been, but at least the Highlanders on the *Marmion* were afforded the benefits of rules which had taken their special needs into consideration. The conditions specified by the HIES translated into more bearable travel for the emigrants. In contrast, many Bounty Scheme migrants and private fare paying passengers were exploited by greedy private entrepreneurs. Some ship owners and their agents charged high rates for appalling conditions of travel, and cheated passengers by failing to give them rations to which they were entitled.

Despite considerable government supervision, the death rates on some vessels sailing to Australia during the gold rush period were very high. Ship captains, trying to break sailing records and reduce turnaround times for their owners, took many risks that caused enormous suffering to passengers. To achieve their aims they drove their ships hard during storms and sailed a long way south into the Southern Ocean, where icebergs were a serious hazard.

Departure and Voyage into the Unknown

The original route taken by ships sailing to Australia had been set down by the British Admiralty. It was a slow trip, taking about four months, with at least one stop, usually at Cape Town. In the late 1840s a faster route was devised by Englishman John Towson but was not acted on by the Admiralty.[16]

The 1851 Australian gold rush spurred English ship owners and captains into action. There was a big increase in demand for passages to Australia by emigrants trying to reach the colonies as fast as possible, and towards the end of 1852, the cost of a fare to Australia rose from £14 to £23. Not surprisingly these pressures led to the adoption of Towson's route called the Great Circle Route or Composite Great Circle Route, because ships using it, utilised the curved surface of the earth and favourable winds etc, rather than just a straight line between two points. It was the route taken by the *Marmion*.

The faster route cut the average sailing time between Liverpool and Australia from 120 days to 80 days but did have its disadvantages. Although the voyage took less time, there were no stops along the way to pick up fresh provisions. Food and water taken on board before departure had to be sufficient for the whole journey. Ships had to sail close to Antarctica, where bitterly cold weather caused hardship to many poorly clad passengers.

Departures were very passionate affairs. It was the usual practice for those devoutly religious passengers to gather on deck and receive stirring addresses and sermons from Gaelic speaking ministers that were followed by the singing of well known hymns. Psalm 23 *The Lord is My Shepherd*, was a popular choice on such occasions. Those emotion-charged gatherings were sometimes accompanied by sadness and tears. Drained of their feelings, the trusting souls believed they went forth in the hands of God.

When the *Marmion* was ready to sail, a steam tug towed the ship from its berth to open water so that it could await a favourable wind to take it to sea. So it was that on 28th August 1852, Captain J. E. Headley sailed his ship out of Liverpool Harbour with 400 Scottish emigrants on board, bound for Australia.

Beyond Liverpool Harbour, the *Marmion* turned south and headed into the great space of the Atlantic Ocean. After sailing for a week or so in that wilderness, those on board began to experience noticeably warmer weather and sighted the first land since commencing their voyage. About 350 miles (563 km) off the coast of North Africa, west of Morocco, they sighted Madeira Island and some of the smaller islands near it.

Progressing into tropical waters on their way to the equator, commonly known by all on board as 'the line', passengers were amazed to see fish that could fly. Sailing for over a month, they saw many such fish which could stay airborne for about 30 seconds and cover a distance of several hundred yards (metres) at a time. To their further amazement, some of those fish, about the size of a large herring, glided onto the deck of their ship. Many of the letters sent home by Scottish immigrants in Australia remarked on the feats of this strange creature and their astonishment at seeing it.[17]

Heading south, other sailing ships on their way to Australia were sighted, but convoys never formed, each ship determining its own destiny and making its own way. It was every captain's hope that as his ship sailed near the equator, it did not fall victim to the 'Doldrums', the name given to that area where there is commonly little or no wind for days at a time.

Successfully past the Doldrums, the *Marmion* sailed on towards the South American coast where it probably came within 100 miles (160 km) of land. From there it continued south into the Southern Ocean where it could pick up the Roaring Forties to take it east past Antarctica and on towards Australia.

No matter what was provided on board, such long, non-stop sea voyages were usually difficult, with disease and misadventure never far away. Outbreaks of measles, typhus fever, (known as ship's fever), smallpox, scarlet fever, whooping cough, diarrhoea and pneumonia were not uncommon on emigrant ships. There was little to stop disease outbreaks spreading quickly, with devastating consequences for the young and the infirm. On the *Marmion's* voyage to Australia, there were 27 deaths - 24 infants and 3 adults.[18]

Although there was no land in sight, the emigrants on the *Marmion* sensed they were nearing the Australian coast. They could actually detect a difference in the sea air - an offshore breeze had carried the aroma of the Australian bush across the waves which tantalised people who had spent nearly three months at sea without a break. More obvious

54. Emigrants on the deck of a sailing ship. In the foreground, children are being taught to read. At the rear of the ship, women can be seen drawing water rations.[19]

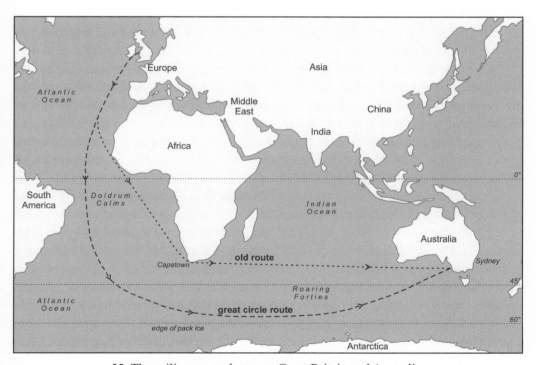

55. The sailing routes between Great Britain and Australia.

to the passengers was the businesslike manner of the sailors who were tidying up the vessel. A new set of sails had even been hoisted so that the ship would look its best on arrival at port. So that the emigrants could also look their best and change their clothes, they were given final access to their trunks in the hold.

On Saturday 4th December 1852, a cry of 'land ahead' startled the *Marmion's* passengers. While there had been great sadness at leaving Scotland, there was now tremendous excitement as men, women and children jostled one another, trying to reach the deck to take their first look at Australia. The curiosity of all the passengers was eventually satisfied and calm returned as the ship sailed closer to land, heading east along the Victorian coast.

The Destination

Having sailed close to the coast for several hours, a number of islands heralded journey's end. Beyond the horizon about 20 miles (30 km) off the coast was Lady Julia Percy Island, a rugged mass of rock over 2 miles (4 km) in length and rising to a height of about 300 feet (100 m). Clearly visible to the *Marmion's* passengers however, were the Lawrence Rocks, situated about 1 mile (2 km) from the shore and looming towards them. Their precipitous nature and location near the entrance to a sheltered bay gave that area of the coast a picturesque appearance.[20]

After rounding the rocks, the *Marmion* turned landward towards a large bay - Portland Bay, which caused another bout of excitement and mad scramble as passengers tried to see another new sight, that being a settlement in their new country. The captain tried to restore calm by ordering all the passengers below deck, but his order was a futile one.

Fortunately for this group of emigrants, the *Marmion* was a fine ship for the period, and although the voyage was marred by unusually strong head winds, she still made the trip in a respectable 96 days. Had the ship sailed with favourable winds, the voyage of about 12,000 miles (26,000 km) could have been made in less than 80 days.[21]

Portland Bay is about half way between Melbourne and Adelaide. With a bay protected from stormy seas caused by boisterous weather from the southeast, it provides one of the best and safest harbours on the southern coast.

Whales were common in the vicinity of Portland Bay, and from the earliest days of white settlement, whale hunters from Launceston in Van Diemen's Land found the shores of Portland Bay a convenient place to stay. Seeing an opportunity, Launceston merchant Thomas Henty established a supply store to service the whalers' needs. From this basic commerce had grown the thriving township of Portland.

As the *Marmion* entered the bay, a pilot boat with a Customs House officer and a government official came out to meet the ship.[22] After boarding, the pilot guided the immigrant vessel to anchor not far from a number of other vessels, including the *Mary Queen, Helen* and *Himalaya,* all from London, and a number of smaller barques.[23] Once anchored, the passengers were able to view from a distance the town of Portland, and to the Highlanders who had spent three months at sea without a break, what a picturesque and inviting sight it was.

When the immigrants arrived at Portland in December 1852, they saw a thriving, prosperous town with a population of about 2,500. Portland rose from the bay on a gentle slope. The town had been laid out in 1840 with streets in a grid pattern running east west and north south. Many of the streets leading towards the coast opened out near the seashore.

On arrival in the colony, all Highland and Island Emigration Society emigrants were at perfect liberty to work for anyone willing to employ them, and to make their own bargain for wages. However, if they quit the colony within four years after landing, they had to repay to the Colonial Government, a proportionate part of their passage money, at the rate of £3 per adult, for each year wanting to complete four years' residence.

The great majority of the new arrivals, were employed on a one year contract to work on pastoral properties in the Hamilton district, not far north of Portland. Nearly all the emigrants were employed as shepherds, labourers and servants. In addition to wages, their employment included the provision of generous rations, which meant they had all the food they could eat.

Relatives back in Scotland nearly always received letters from Society emigrants who made their way to Australia. Donald MacCaskill, who sailed on the *Araminta* from Skye was one. Soon after arriving at the end of 1852, he wrote to his sister back in Skye telling her of his safe arrival and early impressions. A light-hearted postscript added to his letter stated: "Tha mi, slan, lan tolichte, ann fasach Australia" i.e. "I am alive, well, quite happy, in the wilderness of Australia."[24]

NOTES

1. List of Emigrants on the *Marmion* assisted by the HIES
2. Cannon, M, 1971, *Who's Master? Who's Man?*, p. 132.
3. Cannon, M, 1971, *Who's Master? Who's Man?*, p. 123.
4. *Illustrated London News*, 10th July 1852.
5. Public domain, Scottish Archives Network Ltd.
6. *Illustrated London News*, 13th April 1844.
7. Charlwood, D, 1981, *The Long Farewell, Settlers Under Sail*, p. 194.
8. Cannon, M, 1971, *Who's Master? Who's Man?*, p. 126
9. Charlwood, D, 1981, *The Long Farewell, Settlers Under Sail*, p. 209.
10. Cannon, M, 1971, *Who's Master? Who's Man?*, p. 126.
11. *Illustrated London News*, 13th April 1844.
12. *Illustrated London News*, 7th July 1859.
13. *Illustrated London News*, 13th April 1844.
14. Ibid.
15. *Illustrated London News*, 17th August 1850.

16. Charlwood, D, 1981, *The Long Farewell, Settlers Under Sail*, p. 23.
17. National Library of Australia, Bibliographic ref 2100311, *Highland Emigrants in Australia, Letters from Highland Emigrants in Australia dated between September and December 1852,* letter VIII, p. 18.
18. *The Portland Guardian and Normanby Advertiser*, 10th December 1852.
19. *Illustrated London News*, 20th January 1849.
20. *Illustrated Melbourne Post*, 25th December 1865.
21. *The Portland Guardian and Normanby Advertiser*, 10th December 1852.
22. Learmonth, N F, 1960, *The Story of A Port, Portland Victoria*, p. 72.
23. *The Portland Guardian and Normanby Advertiser*, 10th December 1852.
24. National Library of Australia, Bibliographic ref 2100311, *Highland Emigrants in Australia, Letters from Highland Emigrants in Australia dated between September and December 1852,* letter IV, p. 11.

16

Life Back in the Highlands

Back in the Highlands, evictions and emigration continued, but the job of the Highland and Island Emigration Society and that of the Colonial Land and Emigration Commissioners became more challenging. Towards the end of 1852, the impact of the gold rush in Australia increased fares to the country. Rather than a fare of £14, the Colonial Land and Emigration Commissioners now had to pay £23.

To further their object of encouraging Highlanders to emigrate and raise funds, the Highland and Island Emigration Society produced a booklet in 1853 of letters written by emigrants not long after their arrival in Australia.[1] Those letters, written by former residents of the Isle of Skye, provide graphic and interesting accounts of what they experienced on their sea voyage and news of their life in Australia.

The Society's booklet also provided some interesting background information for anyone who purchased it for the sale price of one shilling: "These characteristic letters will be read with interest and satisfaction; but in order to understand their peculiarities, it must be born in mind that the writers think and ordinarily speak Gaelic, and that these letters are therefore virtually translations of Gaelic modes of speech and habits of thought. The family emigration from the pastoral districts of Scotland to Australia has, on every point, fully answered expectations which were formed of it. The change from starvation and idleness in Skye to abundance and industry in Australia, might be considered, if it were not well authenticated, to belong to romance... The emigrants are highly satisfied with their condition and prospects... and resisted the attractions of the diggings, and settled on sheep farms. But perhaps, the most interesting feature of these letters is the strong family and social affection they display. This virtue of the Celtic character has shone forth in the recent famine in Ireland and north of Scotland, and in the great migration to America and Australia consequent upon it, and establishes a strong claim upon the sympathy of those who regard the charities of domestic and social life as deserving to be cherished beyond all human treasures."[2]

Although the Highland and Island Emigration Society extended its operations to Kintyre, Islay, Colonsay, Jura and Gigha in 1853, there was a reduction in the number of emigrants who departed with their help in that year. There was a growing reluctance to emigrate as economic conditions had begun to improve. The timing for the selection of suitable emigrants for the Society was an important aspect of its work which apparently also contributed to fewer assisted passages in 1853. The selection process had begun too late in the season, when many suitable applicants had either sown a crop or dispersed to

159

seek work in the Lowlands.

Emigrant numbers sponsored by the Society picked up markedly in 1854. Colonial governments in Australia were increasingly prepared to support the Society's efforts. The Van Diemen's Land Government had requested three ships loaded with emigrants and was prepared to give the Society £3,000 towards the cost. Favourable reports from those who had gone to Australia and poorer conditions in the Highlands prompted another surge in emigration. That however was not to last.

Continuing Hardship and Ill-fated *Hercules*

Hardship and evictions continued for many who did not emigrate. As the emigration rate in the early 1850s grew, there was a growing belief by some, that emigration and the work of the Highland and Island Emigration Society was being used by landlords as a pretence to justify and facilitate clearing tenants from their estates. Those attitudes coincided with the national fervour created by the Crimean War.

Printed pamphlets brought to public attention criticism of the methods employed by factors to evict tenants and the Society's role in emigration. Pamphleteer Donald McLeod was scathing in his criticism of Sir John McNeill's emigration work, describing him as "the Chief pauper gouger of Scotland"[3] responsible for draining off the best blood of the nation.

In 1854, Donald Ross, philanthropist and prominent critic of the Clearances, published a pamphlet called "Real Scottish Grievances". In that publication, Ross documented the hardship endured by tenants when they were evicted and described the results of "a body calling itself the Highland and Island Emigration Society". The results he referred to concerned 10 families on Lord Macdonald's estate on Skye who had been issued with summonses of removal, and subsequently secured a passage to Australia in late 1852, on an emigrant ship chartered by the Society.[4] The ship was the *Hercules*.

H.M.S. Hercules was a former man-of-war which had large gun ports on her lower deck high above the water line, and a larger crew than merchant vessels. The Highland and Island Emigration Society secured its service despite numerous warnings as to the dangers of using such a ship for the conveyance of passengers.[5] The ship was sent to the port of Campbeltown at the mouth of the Firth of Clyde on the Kintyre Peninsula in Argyllshire to embark the emigrants.

The emigrants booked on the *Hercules* were from the islands of Skye, Uist and Harris. The steamer *Celt* picked them up from those islands and took them to Campbeltown. The *Celt* was hired by the Highland and Island Emigration Society because the season by then was too cold and boisterous for the emigrants to travel on the open deck of a regular steamboat that plied the waters between the islands and the mainland.[6] Certified to carry 224 passengers, the *Celt* was permitted to carry extra Society passengers (provided safety wasn't compromised) at the request of Sir John McNeill.[7] It did so on the two pick ups it made.

56. The emigrant ship *Hercules* in Campbeltown Harbour.[8]

James Chant, the Benevolent and Intelligent Officer for the Colonial Land and Emigration Commissioners travelled on the *Celt* to supervise the pick up of the emigrants from their home islands. On board the *Hercules* he would see to their well-being, check their papers and before the ship departed, complete a nominal list for each colony.

On arrival at Campbeltown, emigrants had to negotiate a gangplank to the *Hercules* from the steamer *Celt* moored alongside. A vivid description of the first batch of 350 emigrants of all ages to transfer from the *Celt* to the *Hercules* was recorded at the time. Due to storms and delays, some had spent five days and nights on the steamer: "Nearly all the females and children suffered greatly from sea-sickness; and when on the afternoon of Sunday 12th, they passed from the *Celt* to the deck of the *Hercules*... many of them were still much exhausted; but the men, accustomed to beating, seemed to have suffered little. It was curious to observe them, as they stepped over the gangway of the great ship. The young women came first - some looking cheerfully round, some sad and some in tears; but all took pains to adjust their shawls and handkerchiefs, their tresses or their capes, as they made their appearance before strangers. The married women and children followed, the latter skipping and dancing on the broad deck overjoyed at their escape from the confinement of the steamboat; the former, so completely absorbed by the care of their children, and the fear of losing them in the crowd that they did not seem to be conscious of where they were or what had brought them there. The men looked dark and stern, like men about to confront danger, and not likely to shrink from the encounter, but relaxed into a smile at the first kind word."[9]

While not his usual practice, Sir John McNeill inspected the ship to see what it was like. He made the following comments about the emigrants who were about to sail: "As regards these people whose life is passed in the open air or in houses through which the wind is continually whistling, I consider the risk from exposure to weather as nothing compared to the risk of being too much between decks... I do dread the effect of much confinement below, especially in bad weather when the ports cannot be kept open on the lower deck."[10]

With 747 emigrants on board, the *Hercules* began its ill-fated voyage on 26th December, 1852. Soon after leaving port, it had to contend with a storm and adverse winds for five days and was forced to seek shelter back in the Firth of Clyde at the Isle of Bute's Rothesay Harbour. The ship arrived there disorganised, with split sails and damaged rigging, where it remained for two weeks.[11] Four days after resuming its voyage, an outbreak of smallpox that spread rapidly among the emigrants forced the *Hercules* into the southern Irish port of Cork where there was a naval hospital.

Anchored in Cork, typhus fever spread by fleas and lice was discovered. With two potentially deadly infectious diseases among the emigrants, the local authorities refused to allow anyone to disembark. While they remained on board the *Hercules* in cramped conditions, illness continued to spread and the vessel couldn't be fumigated.

Eventually, to cope with the situation, the Haubowline Island Naval Hospital in Cork was opened for smallpox patients and others who were sick, while those with typhus fever were quarantined on board the Hulk *Duc d'Orleans* moored in the harbour. To prevent disease spreading, healthy people were separated and accommodated in the Queenstown Military Barracks where they would stay until their voyage could resume.[12]

After more than two months in Cork and contagious diseases still prevalent among many of the *Hercules* passengers, it was decided the ship should set sail with 380 emigrants who were in good health. Those who were still unwell could be sent out to Australia on other ships when they recovered. At a later date, some 305 emigrants sailed in small groups on 12 other emigrant vessels.[13] A number of children who had lost their parents were returned to their native districts.

The *Hercules* sailed from Cork on 14th April 1853 with a little over half its original complement of passengers, bound for Adelaide in South Australia, and Melbourne in Victoria. The ship's surgeon and matron were among 56 persons who died before the ship left Cork, where a further number died later in hospital. After dropping some emigrants off in Adelaide in late July, the *Hercules* arrived in Melbourne on 3rd August 1853, a little over eight months after commencing its harrowing voyage.

There was little respite for the crofting tenants back on the Macdonald estates on Skye. As an eye witness, Donald Ross described the mass eviction of tenants on Lord Macdonald's estates there during 1853. He drew attention to the incongruous position of the estates' ground officer evicting people, while also employed as the Inspector of the Poor for the parish.[14] The evictions on Skye were particularly harsh:

"The tenants of Suisinish and Boreraig were the descendants of a long line of peasantry on the Macdonald estates, and were remarkable for their patience, loyalty, and general good conduct... The only plea made at the time for evicting them was overpopulation. They were all warned out of their holdings. They petitioned and pleaded with his lordship to no purpose. They were ordered to remove their cattle from the pasture and themselves from their houses and lands... In the middle of September, following Lord Macdonald's ground officer, with a body of constables, arrived and proceeded to eject in the most heartless manner the whole population, numbering thirty-two families, and that at a period when the able-bodied male members of the families were away from home trying to earn something by which to pay their rents, and help to carry their families through the coming winter. In spite of the wailing of the helpless women and children, the cruel work was proceeded with as rapidly as possible. The furniture was thrown out... The aged and infirm, some of them so frail they could not move, were pushed or carried out of the humble dwellings. The scene was truly heart-rending... Mothers with tender infants at the breast looked helplessly on, while their effects and their aged and infirm relatives were cast out and the doors of their houses locked in their faces... No mercy was shown to age or sex, all were indiscriminately thrust out and left to perish on the hills."[15]

The Crimean War

In October 1853, the Crimean War (October 1853-February 1856) broke out. Fought mainly on the Crimean Peninsula, it was a conflict over Russia's demands for protection of Orthodox Christians in the Ottoman Empire and the rights of Russian Orthodox and Catholic Churches in Palestine. It was a conflict among the great powers of the Middle East that began with Russia going to war against Turkey. Britain and France supported the Turks, entering the war in March 1854.

The employment boom created by the Crimean War checked the activities of the Highland and Island Emigration Society and saw a decline in emigration. It also saw a marked change in the attitude of young men to their recruitment into Highland regiments for military service.

As it had done in the past during times of military conflict, the British Government sought the help of leading Scottish landowners such as the Duke of Argyll and the Duke of Sutherland, to raise recruits for Highland Regiments from the tenantry on their estates. Those landowners however were confronted with a new reality. Not only were potential recruits few and far between compared to previous times, but those who were available didn't want to enter military service like they once would have. That change was evident in a letter Trevalyan wrote to Sheriff-substitute Fraser on Skye which asked "why do not

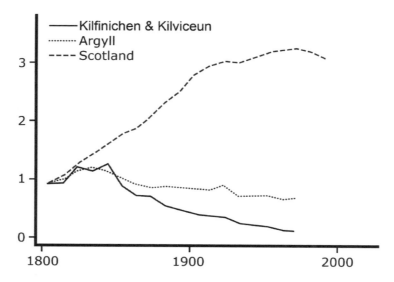

57. The relative change in population of Scotland, County of Argyll and the Parish of Kilfinichen and Kilviceuen from 1801 until 1971. While Scotland's population increased by 3 times, the Ross of Mull was only one fifth what it was in 1801. The most dramatic fall there was between 1841 and 1851 when the parish population fell from 4,113 to 3,054 due to the potato famine and the clearances.[16]

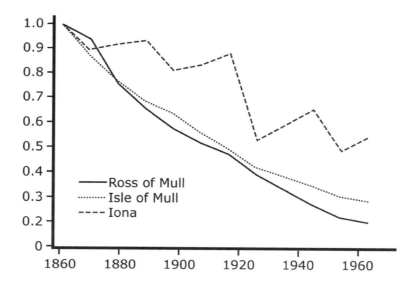

58. The relative change in population of the Isle of Mull, the Ross of Mull and the island of Iona from 1861 to 1971. Regrettably detailed figures for the famine years are unavailable. The Ross of Mull lost population at a faster rate than the rest of Mull while Iona, except for a dramatic fall between 1921 and 1931, was more stable.[17]

the young men show a disposition to enlist at the present time of National Emergency?"[18] Two possible answers to the question raised by Trevalyan were not apparently obvious to the authorities or the aristocracy.

Firstly, few joined the army as so many families had been evicted from their homes and so many had been forced to emigrate. Rather than an over-abundance of young men in the Highlands, there was an ever increasing number of sheep in their place - the lairds four footed clansmen, as those sheep were sometimes referred to.

Sutherland County was typical. The Duke of Sutherland's factor and two ministers spent days touring local parishes seeking recruits with little success. The potential recruits that were available, gave the following reason to the ministers for their refusal to sign up: "We have no country to fight for. You robbed us of our country and gave it to the sheep. Therefore, since you have preferred sheep to men, let sheep defend you."[19]

Secondly, there was widespread resentment throughout the Highlands over tenant evictions, none more so than on the Sutherland estates. Frustrated at the lack of success recruiting soldiers from his properties, the Duke of Sutherland travelled from London to Golspie in the Highlands where a meeting was convened for him to make a direct appeal to the locals. As an inducement, he offered a substantial cash incentive from his own purse to anyone who enlisted. His appeal and offer fell on deaf ears. A perplexed Duke was given the reason: "It is the opinion of this country that should the Czar of Russia take possession of Dunrobin Castle and of Stafford House next term, that we couldn't expect worse treatment at his hands than we have experienced in the hands of your family for the last fifty years..."[20]

Better employment opportunities, the depopulation of the Highlands caused by the Clearances and the bitterness felt by those who remained towards their landlords, saw only three Highland infantry battalions out of 33 deployed to the Crimea.[21]

An Eviction on the Argyll Estate

The wholesale eviction of numerous people from an estate at one time as described previously on Skye, was not a common practice on the Duke of Argyll's Estate on the Isle of Mull. Individuals, however, continued to be evicted from their premises for a variety of reasons.

The Braighcreich McPhees' eldest son Duncan, who did not emigrate with them, is a good example. He had married Ann MacLean in 1845. In 1855, Duncan, his wife and several children were living in Kintra, the village where his parents resided before going to the colony of Victoria. They may well have been living in the house vacated by his parents. Life must have still been extremely hard because Duncan and family were evicted. Information from the police archives in the form of Sheriff Courts Letters of Removal,[22] permits a fascinating insight into the ruthless way some families were evicted from their homes.

On the 1st August, 1855, "at the instance of His Grace George Douglas Campbell

Duke of Argyll", the sheriff officer removed 'Duncan MacFee', his family and his goods from the "dwelling house possessed by him" at Kintra. The sheriff officer was Alex MacDonald, the same person who five years beforehand had evicted Duncan's father. He was assisted by John MacDonald and Archibald MacDonald. The presiding officer listed the family's meagre possessions as they were put outside the home:

> "...viz: Ten pieces partition plank, three plain plates, one potatoe spade, one broken tea pot, one large jar, one small pot, one potatoe beater, one dresser top, one table, one small jar, one broad plank, one half blanket, one sheet, one pillow, three bundles of thatch straws, six small planks, one old boat keel, one close bedstead with bottom and top frame, one high post bedstead and bottom, one table, one parcel of old clothes, one square cast metal plate, one large chest, one parcel clothes, one barrel salt, one chair, one crock, one gaff, one stool, a quantity of peats, one hoist, one lot of sticks."[23]

The McPhees were not evicted without a struggle. While the eviction was in progress, Duncan's wife Ann was sitting in the corner of the house cradling a baby at the breast. A neighbour had given the baby to her for that purpose for a certain time. As she sat there, she shouted and swore that she would not move on any account from the house unless she was given another home. The sheriff officer then informed her that she was being removed for the second time as she had during the previous year broken the door to the house and re-entered it. He also said that she could expect "to receive no favours from the hands of His Grace the Duke of Argyll."[24] The sheriff officer then ordered the men to physically remove her. Ann resisted and the men found themselves unable to move her without causing harm to her and the child.

After a standoff, Duncan McPhee told the officer that though he was now out of the house with his family and goods, as soon as the men left he would break down the barrier and re-enter in defiance of the law. Both Duncan and Ann were warned that should they do so, they would incur the penalties of the law. Following the eviction, the McPhees secured a house elsewhere.

End of an Era

As economic conditions began to improve in the latter half of the 1850s, fewer people emigrated from the Highlands. The Highland and Island Emigration Society dispatched its last ship to Australia in July 1857, when the *Persian* took a full ship load of destitute emigrants from Coll and Harris to Tasmania.

On 26th April 1858, Sir Charles Trevelyan wrote to hard working Benevolent and Intelligent Officer James Chant to advise him that "the operations of the Highland and Island Emigration Society in London have been closed, and the balance of the fund (upwards of £800) have been paid over to Sir J McNeill to be employed in assisting such deserving cases of emigration as may be brought to his notice from the same districts in the discharge of his duties as Chairman of the Board of Supervision for the Relief of the Poor - and no doubt you will continue to cooperate with him until the last farthing has been expended."[25] He also mentioned to Chant the completion of a "Great Register of Emigrants"[26] which he had previously proposed be drawn up.

Despite some shortcomings, the Highland and Island Emigration Society achieved a great deal. Although a non-government organisation, it was reliant on the expertise and goodwill of public servants. Three people were central to its success; firstly, its Chairman, Sir Charles Trevelyan, secondly, the Emigration Commission Chairman, Sir Thomas Murdoch, and thirdly, the Chairman of the Board of Supervisors for the new Poor Law in Scotland, Sir John McNeill. All three bureaucrats played key roles but Sir Charles Trevelyan was the main architect and driving force behind the Society.

Trevelyan was an incisive public servant. He was resolute in his belief that relief measures were ineffective in solving the problem of destitution and overpopulation in the Highlands. He was equally resolute in his view that providing welfare to those in the affected areas only encouraged laziness and dependency.

Australia was chosen as the logical destination for the mass migration of crofters, cottars and others from the Highlands of Scotland. Charles Trevelyan reasoned correctly that their skills and experience with sheep, cattle and farming would be ideal for Australia and would be welcomed by colonial settlers. In 1852 he wrote "the transfer of thirty or forty thousand persons composing the redundant population of the Western Highlands and Islands... most suitable labour for the sheep farmers."[27]

While Trevelyan's estimated number of emigrants never eventuated, between 1852 and 1857 the Highland and Island Emigration Society was responsible for assisting nearly 5,000 Highlanders to emigrate to Australia. That figure comprised approximately 1,500 men, 1,800 women and 1,700 children.

In the early days of its operation Trevelyan wrote: "Five hundred years hence, a few of the most aristocratic families of the great Australian Republic will boast of being able to trace their ancestors in the Highland and Island Emigration Book of 1852-53".[28]

Thanks to Trevelyan's foresight the Society's activities have been preserved for historians and genealogists. Three years before the Society was wound up he wrote "The records will be deposited at the Register House in Edinburgh. They may have social and statistical interest hereafter."[29] To have the central records of a private Society saved for posterity is a remarkable achievement.

NOTES

1. National Library of Australia, Bibliographic ref 2100311, *Highland Emigrants in Australia, Letters from Highland Emigrants in Australia dated between September and December 1852.*

2. National Library of Australia, Bibliographic ref 2100311, *Highland Emigrants in Australia,*

Letters from Highland Emigrants in Australia dated between September and December 1852, Preface.

3.   RAHS, Vol 49, November 1963, Part 3, p. 180.

4.   Mackenzie, A, 1914, *The History of the Highland Clearances*, 2nd edn, p. 202.

5.   Balfour, R A C S, 1973, *Emigration from the Highlands and Western Isles of Scotland to Australia during the Nineteenth Century*, University of Edinburgh Thesis, p. 159.

6.   Clarke, W B, 1989, *H.M.S. Hercules Scottish Emigrant Ship 1853*, p. 42.

7.   Ibid, p. 29.

8.   *London Illustrated News*, 15th January 1853.

9.   Ibid.

10. Clarke, W B, 1989, *H.M.S. Hercules Scottish Emigrant Ship 1853*, p.22.

11. Ibid, p. 25.

12. Ibid, p. 64-65.

13. Ibid, p. 10.

14. Richards, E, 1982, *A History of the Highland Clearances*, p. 433.

15. Mackenzie, A, 1914, *The History of the Highland Clearances*, 2nd edn, p. 202-203.

16. ROMHC, *Population Changes in the Ross of Mull Across the Last Two Centuries*.

17. Ibid.

18. RAHS, Vol 49, November 1963, Part 3, p. 184.

19. Prebble, J, 1963, *The Highland Clearances*, p. 301.

20. Ibid.

21. Prebble, J, 1963, *The Highland Clearances*, p. 298.

22. The original record at the NRS could not be located.

23. ROMHC, Letters of Removal, Tobermory Sheriff Court Records.

24. Ibid.

25. NRS, HIES file HD4/4, Trevelyan to James Chant, 26/4/1858, p. 105.

26. NRS, HIES file HD4/5, the Great Register of Emigrants is digitised in Register House.

27. RAHS, Vol 49, November 1963, Part 3, p. 173.

28. RAHS, Vol 49, November 1963, Part 3, p. 178.

29. RAHS, Vol 49, November 1963, Part 3, p. 164.

Postscript

Crofting continued in the 1870s much as it had done in the decades preceding it. Tenant dissatisfaction however, grew, which saw the beginning of significant agitation over high rents, a lack of security of tenure over land, and lack of access to traditional areas of occupation. That agitation grew as the position of tenants became more difficult towards the end of the 1870s, following several poor harvests.

History repeated itself in the early 1880s, when bad weather devastated grain crops, blight hit potato crops, and low cattle prices combined to produce great hardship in the crofting communities. As a consequence, crofters began to take direct action by refusing to pay rent and defying the law by occupying sheep grazing areas. At this time the Highland Land Law Reform Association also agitated for change.

The prospect of unrest and lawless action spreading throughout the Highlands forced the British Government to take action. In 1883, it set up the Royal Commission of Inquiry into the Condition of Crofters and Cottars in the Highlands and Islands. Chaired by Lord Napier, it became known as the Napier Commission. The Commission's extensive and thorough report of 1884, was the most accurate and damning assessment of the inequalities and hardships endured by the Gaelic tenantry during the 1800s.

As a result of the Napier Commission's findings, a number of its recommendations were enshrined in the Crofters' Holdings (Scotland) Act of 1886. While failing to satisfy all of the crofters grievances, it provided security of tenure for larger, more viable crofts, and other legal rights. It also highlighted the fact there was insufficient land available in the Highlands to provide viable crofts for the entire crofting population. The Commission advised the Government, that in some districts, there was an urgent need for emigration just as there had been in 1851.

Appendix 1

The Campbells of Argyll, Earls and Dukes

Name	Title	Life Span	Notes
Colin	1st Earl of Argyll	d. 1493	created Earl in 1457
Archibald	2nd Earl of Argyll	d. 1513	killed with the King at Flodden
Colin	3rd Earl of Argyll	d. 1529	
Archibald	4th Earl of Argyll	d. 1558	
Archibald	5th Earl of Argyll	1532-1573	
Colin	6th Earl of Argyll	1558-1584	
Archibald	7th Earl of Argyll	1575-1638	known as 'Grim-faced Archie'
Archibald	8th Earl of Argyll	1598-1661	devoted Presbyterian, executed for treason
Archibald	9th Earl of Argyll	1629-1685	restored to Earldom also beheaded
Archibald	10th Earl & 1st Duke	1658-1703	Crown ally, raised regiment for Crown
John	2nd Duke of Argyll	1680-1743	Gov. commander at Sheriffmuir, no heir
Archibald	3rd Duke of Argyll	1682-1761	2nd Duke's younger brother, no heir
John	4th Duke of Argyll	1693-1770	3rd Duke's cousin
John	5th Duke of Argyll	1723-1806	enthusiastic 'improver'
George	6th Duke of Argyll	1768-1839	left debts, numerous illegitimate children
John	7th Duke of Argyll	1777-1847	helped restore the family's finances
George	8th Duke of Argyll	1823-1900	government cabinet minister
John	9th Duke of Argyll	1845-1914	no heir
Niall	10th Duke of Argyll	1872-1949	9th Duke's nephew, never married
Ian	11th Duke of Argyll	1903-1973	10th Duke's cousin, a socialite
Ian	12th Duke of Argyll	1937-2001	worked to restore the family name
Torquhil	13th Duke of Argyll	b 1968	June 2002 Torquhil Ian became Duke

Source: A History of Clan Campbell by Alastair Campbell of Airds, et al.

Appendix 2

The McDuffie/McPhees Recorded on the Ross of Mull

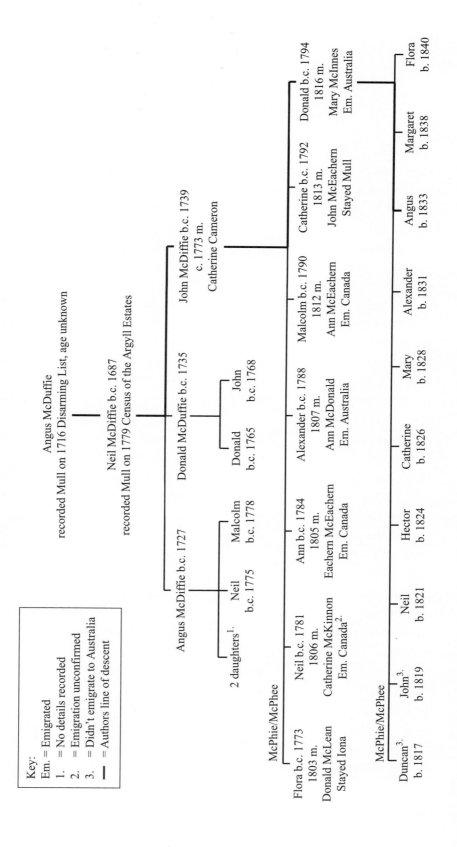

Key:
Em. = Emigrated
1. = No details recorded
2. = Emigration unconfirmed
3. = Didn't emigrate to Australia
──── = Authors line of descent

Angus McDuffie
recorded Mull on 1716 Disarming List, age unknown

Neil McDiffie b.c. 1687
recorded Mull on 1779 Census of the Argyll Estates

John McDiffie b.c. 1739
c. 1773 m.
Catherine Cameron

Donald McDuffie b.c. 1735

Angus McDiffie b.c. 1727

Donald
b.c. 1765

John
b.c. 1768

Neil
b.c. 1775

Malcolm
b.c. 1778

2 daughters[1].

Alexander b.c. 1788
1807 m.
Ann McDonald
Em. Australia

Malcolm b.c. 1790
1812 m.
Ann McEachern
Em. Canada

Catherine b.c. 1792
1813 m.
John McEachern
Stayed Mull

Donald b.c. 1794
1816 m.
Mary McInnes
Em. Australia

McPhie/McPhee

Flora b.c. 1773
1803 m.
Donald McLean
Stayed Iona

Neil b.c. 1781
1806 m.
Catherine McKinnon
Em. Canada[2].

Ann b.c. 1784
1805 m.
Eachern McEachern
Em. Canada

Hector
b. 1824

Catherine
b. 1826

Mary
b. 1828

Alexander
b. 1831

Angus
b. 1833

Margaret
b. 1838

Flora
b. 1840

McPhie/McPhee

Duncan[3].
b. 1817

John[3].
b. 1819

Neil
b. 1821

Appendix 3

Ross of Mull Men Recorded on the 1716 Disarming List

1. Ardachy		6. Assapol	
Angus McDonald	very old	John McQuarie younger, Ulva	N
Neil McDonald	N	Hugh McLean	N
Charles McLean	R	fferquhard McIlvra	N
Charles McLean	R	Neil McIlvra	N
2. Ardalanish		Archibald McArtna	R
John McDonald	at Glasgow	Mildony Mcffaden	sick
Rodger McArtna	N no arms	**7. Bunessan**	
Neil McArtna	N no arms	Hugh McLean	N
John McMillan	R	Neil Beaton	sick
Hector McLean	-	John Mcffaden	-
Donald McLean	-	Donald Mcffaden	N
John McArtna	old	John McBhodich	R
John McKenich	old, infirm	Martine McIlvra	-
Malcolm McIlvoill	-	Lachlan dou McDonald	R
3. Ardchiavaig		Archibald McMillan	R
Malcolm McEwn oige	R wounded	**8. Creich**	
Hugh McEwn oige	-	John McLean	R
John McOlonich	N	John dow McErrichir	N
Malcolm McMillan	N	Hugh fferqr McEan dui Vcffeqr	-
Donald McGillean	N	Edmun Morrison	R
Duncan Lamont	R	Dushie McInnish VcErichir	N
Malcolm Beaton	N	Rory McErichir dhui	N
Donald McLucas	N	Hector McLean	N
4. Ardfenaig		John McEoin VcIllchallum	R
Hugh McKenrig	-	Duncan Obrolochan	N
5. Ardtun		**9. Erraid**	
Donald Campbell	Ross Baillie	Hector McLean	-
Donald Mcffarlan	R	**10. Fidden**	
John McIlvra	R	Dugald McIllmichell	R
Neil McKinlay	N	Donald McIllmichel	R
John McArtna	N	Hugh McMichell	N
Donald McKinlay	very old	Roger McDonald	
		Neil McIlchrivan	N

John McRuarie	old	**15. Saorphin**	
ffinlay McInnish	sick	Dussni McIlvra	N
Duncan McInnish	old	Donald McIlvra	N
Neil McDhoil roy	-	Charles McEachern	old and sick
Donald Mcffarlan	-	John McEachern	N
Donald Mcphaden	N	Rodger McEachern	R
11. Kilviceun		Charles McInnish	N
Lachlan McLean of Gruline	R	Neil McEachern	N
Archibald Mcffarlan	R	**16. Scoor**	
Donald McEan dui	R	Donald McLean	N
Murdoch McIlvra	R	Donald McArtna	N
John McKoinich	N	Hugh McArtna	N
Donald McMillan	N	**17. Shiaba**	
Angus McDuffie	N	John McLean	R
John McLean	R	Alexander McLean	N
12. Knocknafenaig		ffinlay McEachern	N
John Cameron	-	John McIlvra	N
John Beaton	R	Charles McLean	R
John McLean	sick	Malcolm McIllinaine	N
Hector McLean	old and infirm	**18. Suidhe**	
Donald McLean	N	John Mcffarland	R
Neil McLean	N	Duncan McEachern	N
Neil Beaton	N	Hector McIlvra	-
13. Knockvalagan		Angus McIonaich	-
Donald bane McLean	N	Allan McDhoil Eachnie	R
Gilbert McEwn oig	N	**19. Tireregan**	
John McVurich	-	Archibald McInleagh	-
14. Pottie		Hector roy McLean	-
Donald bane Mcffaden	R		
Hew McLean	-		

N = not in the rebellion   R = was in the rebellion

Source: Inhabitants of the Inner Isles Morvern and Ardnamurchan 1716: Nicholas Maclean-Bristol.

Appendix 4

A Typical Crofter Removing Summons

His Grace George Douglas Campbell Duke of Argyll
Against
Arthur MacArthur & Euphemia McInnes [in] Catcheon
Archibald MacKinnon, William Beaton, Donald McPhee and Alexander Campbell in Creich

Robert Bruce Esquire Advocate Sheriff of the Sheriffdom of Argyll
To
Officers of the said Sheriffdom conjointly and severally specially constituted. Greeting.
Whereas it is Humbly Meant and Shown to me by my Lord His Grace George Douglas
Campbell Duke of Argyll

1. That the Pursuer is Heritable Proprietor of the subjects aftermentioned, with the pertinents
2. That Arthur MacArthur (No 3). Item Euphemia MacInnes possess the lands and farm of Catcheon or some part or portion thereof with the pertinents. Item Archibald McKinnon (No 9). Item William Beaton (No 14). Item Donald Macphee (No 6). Item Alexander Campbell (No 23) possess the lands and farm of Creich or some part or portion thereof with the pertinents situated in the United Parishes of Kilfinichen and Kilvickeon and Sheriffdom aforesaid under Leases Missives or Lets from the pursuer which expires the term of Whitsunday next (Old Style Eighteen hundred and forty nine); as to the houses, grass and pastureage and at the separation of the ensuing crop from the ground as to arable land under crop ~
3. That by Act of Sederunt of the Lords of Council and Session of date the fourteenth December seventeen hundred and fifty six anent removing it is inter alia provided and declared that it "shall be lawful to the Heritor or the setter of the Tack in his opinion either to use the meter prescribed by the Act of Parliament made in the year fifteen hundred & fifty six intitled 'Act anent the Warning of Tenants' and thereupon pursue a Removing and Ejection, or to bring his action of Removing against the Tenant before the Judge ordinary; and such action being called before the Judge ordinary at least forty days before the term of Whitsunday shall be held as equal to a warning" execute in terms of the foresaid Act and the Judge shall thereupon proceed to determine in the Removing in terms that Act, in the same manner as if a Warning had been executed in terms of the foresaid Act of Parliament.
4. That although the Pursuer had oft and diverse times desired and required the said Defender to flit and remove themselves their wives bairns families servants subtenants cottars dependents, Goods and Gear forth from their occupation and possessions of the subjects and others above mentioned at the expiry of their title or Right of Possession to the same as aforesaid that they refuse to so do unless compelled.

Therefore the said Defenders ought and should be dicerned and ordained by Decreet of Court to flit and remove themselves and their foresaids forth and from their occupations and possessions of the houses gardens grass and pastureage of the said lands and pertinents thereof at the said term of Whitsunday next old style Eighteen hundred and forty nine and from the said arable grounds therof at the separation of the ensuing crop in the said year and to desist and cease there from and leave the same void and red at and against the said terms or at such other time or terms as may correspond with the time of their right of Entry into possession to the Effect the pursuer or others in his name, may then enter thereto and set use and dispose therof at pleasure conform to the said Act of Sederunt and Laws and daily practices of Scotland used and observed in the like cases in all points. Therefore I command you that on sight hereof ye pass and lawfully summon declare and charge you the said Defenders personally at their respective Dwelling places to compear before me or my substitute within the ordinary Court House of Tobermory upon the seventh day next after the date of your citations if a court day, or if not on the first court day thereafter in the Hour of Cause with continuation of days to answer at the instance of the said pursuer anent the matter libelled that is to say to hear and see the premises verified and proved and sentence and Decree given and pronounced therein ut supra or close to allow a reasonable cause on the contrary with certification as… According to Justice and given under the subscription of the Clerk of Court at Tobermory the Nineteenth day of March Eighteen hundred and forty nine years.

Statement of the Sheriff Officer as to delivery of the summons.

Upon the Twenty second and Twenty fourth days of March Eighteen hundred and Forty nine years by virtue of the foregoing Summons of Removing dated at Tobermory the Nineteenth day of March abstracted thereof at the instance of his Grace George Douglas Campbell Duke of Argyll [in] presence of Alexander Mac Donald Sheriff Officer for Argyllshire passed in Her Majesty's name and authority and in name and authority of the Sheriff of the said Shire lawfully summoned warned and charged Arthur Mac Arthur (number three) Item Euphemia Mac Innes both residing at Catcheon Item Archibald Mac Kinnon (number nine) Item William Beaton (number fourteen) Item Donald MacPhee (number sixteen) Item Alexander Campbell (number twenty three) all residing in Creich, Defenders, to compear before the said Sheriff or his substitute within the ordinary Court House of Tobermory upon the seventh day next after the date of my petition if a court day or if not on the first court day thereafter in the hour of… with continuation of days to answer at the instance of the said pursuer in the matter libelled with certification conform to the said Summons of Removing in all points, a full double wherof to the will, with a first copy of citation to the effect foresaid thereto subscrived, I delivered to each of the saids Arthur Mac Arthur, William Beaton and Donald McPhee all personally apprehended and the both of all double and copy of the citation. I left for the saids Archibald McKinnon in the hands of his wife and for Alexander Campbell in the hands of his daughter within their respective dwelling houses at Creich. To be given to them as I could not find themselves personally and that upon the first date hereof also the like full double and copy of citation I delivered to the said Euphemia Mac Innes personally and upon the second and last date hereof which copies of citation were severally signed by me did bear the respective dates hereof date of such said summons with the name and designation of Alexander MacDonald Junior residing at Bunnessan witness to the premises and… with me subscribing.

Signed Alex MacDonald Sheriff Officer
Signed Alexander MacDonald Junior Witness

Source: NRS Sheriff Court Records, Tobermory. Summons of Removal, SC59/2/6/1.

Appendix 5

Highland and Island Emigration Society Ships 1852-1857

Date	Ship	Departed	Destination	Date	Places of Origin
26/1/52	*Mangerton* [1]	Liverpool	Melbourne	5/6/52	Skye
26/5/52	*Borneuf* [2]	Liverpool	Geelong	3/9/52	Skye, Raasay
20/6/52	*Araminta*	Liverpool	Geelong	4/10/52	Skye
25/6/52	*Medina*	Liverpool	Adelaide	19/10/52	Skye
13/7/52	*Georgiana*	Greenock	Port Philip	16/10/52	Skye
3/8/52	*Ontario*	Liverpool	Sydney	15/12/52	Skye
4/8/52	*Ticonderoga*	Liverpool	Port Philip	22/12/52	Skye, Raasay
5/8/52	*Blanche*	Liverpool	Port Philip	18/11/52	Skye
28/8/52	*Marmion* [3]	Liverpool	Portland Bay	4/12/52	Mull, Iona, Morv., Ard.
13/9/52	*Allison*	Liverpool	Melbourne	8/2/53	Skye, Ard., Moidart
24/9/52	*Louisa*	Plymouth	Hobart	10/1/53	Skye
13/10/52	*Priscilla*	Liverpool	Melbourne	24/2/53	Skye, St. Kilda, Kintail
27/10/52	*Arabian*	Liverpool	Melbourne	14/2/53	Skye, Kintail
3/11/52	*Thames*	Liverpool	Melbourne	10/3/53	Skye
26/12/52	*Hercules* [4]	Campbel.	Melbourne	3/8/53	Skye, N. Uist, Harris
8/1/53	*British Queen*	Liverpool	Melbourne	3/5/53	Mull
8/1/53	*Panama*	Liverpool	Hobart	27/4/53	Mull
29/3/53	*Bloomer* [5]	Liverpool	Sydney	26/7/53	Inverness
23/8/53	*New Zealander*	Liverpool	Portland Bay	30/11/53	Skye, Mull, Morv., etc
28/10/53	*Sir Allan McNab*	Liverpool	Hobart	1/2/54	Coigach, Kintyre, etc
3/11/53	*Utopia*	Liverpool	Portland Bay	25/1/54	Lochaber, Tiree
3/6/54	*Arabian*	Liverpool	Portland Bay	19/9/54	Skye
17/6/54	*Edward Johnston*	Liverpool	Portland Bay	3/9/54	Raasay, Coll, Mull, Morv.
29/7/54	*Hornet*	Liverpool	Geelong	23/10/54	Ard., Sutherland, Ross
18/8/54	*James Fernie*	Liverpool	Adelaide	17/11/54	Lewis, Lochaber
1/10/54	*Derry Castle*	Liverpool	Portland Bay	21/1/55	Lochaber
16/6/55	*Switzerland*	Liverpool	Adelaide	12/9/55	Skye
15/8/55	*Royal Albert*	Plymouth	Adelaide	2/12/55	Isle of Lewis, N. Uist
25/7/57	*Persian*	Liverpool	Hobart	31/10/57	Harris, Coll

(1) Assisted by Skye Em. Society (2) Included 32 Raasay people whose expenses paid by proprietor (3) Originally destined for Moreton Bay, Queensland (4) refer to Chapter 16 (5) Destitute Isle of Barra people who sought shelter in Inverness. NB Morv. = Morvern; Ard. = Ardnamurchan.

Source: Journal of the Royal Australian Historical Society Volume 69, June 1983, et al.

Appendix 6

Estates Providing Emigrants for the Highland and Island Emigration Society
April 1852-1853

No	Estates	No of Families	Souls	Total Amount Advanced			One-third charged to Proprietors		
				£.	s.	d	£.	s.	d
1	Lord Macdonald lands in Skye	215	1,315	3,758.	6.	1	1,252.	15.	6
2	MacLeod of MacLeod, Skye	45	277	786.	5.	1	262.	1.	8
3	Strathaird	25	148	460.	0.	10	153.	6.	11
4	Skeabost	25	130	368.	9.	3	122.	16.	5
5	Waternish	6	41	138.	2.	3	46.	0.	9
6	Lyndale	5	37	111.	4.	4	37.	1.	5
7	Dr. Martin	6	31	93.	15.	1	31.	5.	0
8	Vice-Chancellor Stewart	2	16	39.	3.	1	13.	1.	0
9	Raasay	3	24	8.	6.	9	2.	15.	7
10	Lord Dunmore in Harris	19	95	229.	11.	7	76.	10.	6
11	Sir James Riddell, Ardnamurchan	15	90	170.	6.	5	56.	15.	5
12	W. Robertson Esq.	6	46	110.	8.	1	36.	16.	0
13	Dr., Martin Moidart	4	24	74.	6.	5	24.	15.	5
14	Alex McDonald, Esq.	1	9	31.	11.	1	10.	10.	4
15	Duke of Argyll's estates	11	70	176.	16.	11	58.	18.	11
16	Lord Compton lands in Torloisk	5	34	83.	6.	8	27.	15.	6
17	Mr. McLean of Coll	3	18	50.	0.	7	19.	3.	6
18	Mr. Clark of Ulva	6	37	208.	10.	6	69.	0.	2
19	Aros	3	21	74.	1.	10	24.	13.	11
20	A. Matheson Esq. MP, Bundalloch	10	52	238.	7.	5	79.	9.	1
21	Mr. Sinclair of Lochalin	8	47		-			-	
22	Col Ross' lands in Glenmoidart	1	7		-			-	
23	J. M. MacLeod Esq., St Kilda	7	36		-			-	
	Totals	471	2,605	7,220.	0.	10	2,406.	13.	7

Source: Report of the Highland Emigration Society, from its formation in April 1852, until April 1853.

Appendix 7

Origins of Highland and Island Emigration Society Emigrants 1852-1857

Area	1852	1853	1854	1855	1857	% of Total
Skye	1,958	186	514	160	0	59
Raasay	24	0	131	0	0	3
Harris	95	21	5	184	120	6
Ardnamurchan	90	0	23	0	0	2
Moidart	77	0	7	0	0	2
Mull & Iona	168	84	43	0	0	6
Kintail & Lochalsh	52	50	10	0	0	2
Morvern	47	4	20	0	0	2
St. Kilda	36	0	0	0	0	1
Inverness	0	15	0	0	0	0.3
Sutherland	37	82	81	0	0	4
Lochiel/Ardgour	0	88	123	0	0	4
Tiree	2	13	0	0	0	0.3
Coll	10	0	32	0	81	2
Kintyre	0	41	0	0	0	0.8
Rothiemurchus	0	44	0	0	0	0.8
Torridon	0	0	49	0	0	0.9
Lewis	0	0	17	0	0	0.3
Lochaber	0	0	24	0	0	0.4
Glenelg/Knoydart	9	0	25	0	0	0.5
Arisaig	0	0	21	0	0	0.4
Others	0	0	7	0	0	0.14

Source: The Great Highland Famine, Hunger, Emigration and the Scottish Highlands in the Nineteenth Century: T. M. Devine.

Appendix 8

Departures from Principal Scottish Ports During the Famine Years 1846-1856 to USA, Canada, Australia and New Zealand

Year	USA	Canada	Australia & NZ	Total	Annual %
1846	1,157	1,903	70	3,427	3
1847	3,782	4,219	366	8,616	7
1848	7,241	3,855	282	11,505	8
1849	10,639	5,447	746	17,127	13
1850	11,488	3,025	378	15,154	11
1851	10,864	10,000	541	18,646	14
1852	9,792	5,642	5,450	21,044	15
1853	7,819	5,038	4,166	16,503	12
1854	3,534	6,941	2,699	13,307	9
1855	1,819	5,015	1,286	8,227	6
1856	2,748	0	0	2,748	2
	70,883	51,085	15,994	136,304	100
	51%	36%	13%		

Source: The Great Highland Famine, Hunger, Emigration and the Scottish Highlands in the Nineteenth Century: T. M. Devine.

Appendix 9

Government Regulations on Board the Emigrant Ship *Asia*

1. Out of bed at seven.
2. Beds to be rolled up, and, in fine weather, carried on deck.
3. Breakfast at eight.
4. Clean decks at ten.
5. Dine at one.
6. Tea at six.
7. Each mess to clean the space in front of its own sleeping places by one man appointed in rotaton for the purpose.
8. Each mess to have a Head-Man, approved by the Surgeon Superintendent, who shall settle the above rotation, and report to the Surgeon any misconduct or neglect requiring complaint.
9. On cleaning decks, the men are also to brush out or sweep their berths.
10. There is no objection to Women cleaning their side of the deck, if they prefer it; but in case of their not doing it effectually, the Men must be ready to do the whole.
11. The women are to brush out their own berths.
12. The bottom-boards of the berths to be removed, and dry scrubbed, and taken on deck once or twice a week as may be ordered by the Surgeon Superintendent. All grown people, to assist on these occassions.
13. Two men are to be taken every day, in rotation, from the whole list of the Males above 15, to be sweepers for the day. They are to sweep both sides of the deck. The deck to be swept down after every meal.
14. One man is to be taken away every day, in rotation, to be the Cook's Assistant. The Coppers should be cleaned regularly.
15. One or two men, as may be found necessary, must be taken, in rotation, to clean the Male Hospital, and any spaces of the deck that do not belong to any particular Mess.
16. One or two Women, as may be necessary, to be taken in like manner to clean the Female Hospital. Every one above 15 to take her turn.
17. For the Superintendence of duties not under the Head-Man of Messes, and for general uses, 4 Constables are to be appointed by the people, to relieve each other, and one to be constantly on duty.
18. A certain number of men to be on watch at night. One lantern is to be kept burning at each of the three hatchways, and is not to be removed.
19. On beginning to clean the Decks at Ten, everybody under 15 is to be sent on deck, weather permitting, to be inspected by the Surgeon or the Teachers, and seen to be clean.
20. After inspection, School.

21. On every Sunday, the people are expected to assemble before Divine Service, in order of their berths, the Males on one side, and the Females on the other, that the Surgeon may pass along them and see that they are clean and decent. The constables will muster them for this purpose.

22. Washing days every Monday and Thursday. When those days are not fine, others to be substituted as the Surgeon may direct.

23. No washing is on any account to be suffered between decks, and no drying of Wet Clothes there.

24. Spirits are not to be allowed.

25. The Surgeon is enjoined to refuse the Wine, when Wine is in issue, to any person who obstructs or neglects the preceding Regulations; and in case of gross misconduct or violence, he will report it to the Governor on arrival.

26. All doubtfull points to be settled by the authority of the Surgeon.

27. The Cook, and the Hospital Man, if the Surgeon appoints one, to be exempt from all other duties whatever.

28. The Constables and the Teachers to be exempt from cleaning decks.

29. The people are recommended to appoint large watches to be on decks at night in the warm latitudes.

30. They cannot be to diligent in observing the rules, to avoid wet between decks, and in attending to every sort of cleanliness of person and abode.

31. They will not fail to bear in mind that on their arrival in the Colony, their conduct during the voyage will be known; and that, therefore, not only is it essential to their health, and perhaps even safety, to attend to the Rules which have been agreed to for their well-being on the passage, but that individuals who perversely thwart them may feel the consequences seriously in their prospects afterwards.

T. Frederick Elliot,
Devonport, November 6, 1838

Source: Balfour, R A C S, 1973, *Emigration From the Highlands and Western Isles of Scotland to Australia during the Nineteenth Century*, University of Edinburgh Thesis, Appendix IV.

Appendix 10

Duties of a Schoolmaster on an Emigrant Vessel

Colonial Land & Emigration Office,
9, Park Street, Westminster,
29'. Dec 1848

Sir,

With reference to your application I am directed by the Colonial Land and Emigration Commissioners to state that they have appointed you to be Schoolmaster, on board the Emigrant Ship, Sir Geo Seymour and to transmit to you the following instructions for your guidance.

1. You will consider yourself under the Orders of the Surgeon Superintendent. J. J. McGregor Esq.
2. You will hold School daily, weather permitting, during such hours as may be settled by you, with the concurrence of the Surgeon.
3. You will give instructions not only to the children, but to such of the Adult Emigrants as may be willing to receive it, and for this purpose you will make suitable arrangements, so as not to interfere with the Childrens' classes.
4. You will give your best attention to the maintenance of good order and regularity among all the Emigrants, in the manner directed by the Surgeon Superintendent.
5. It will be your duty to inspect the Children daily to see that they are clean, before School commences.
6. A supply of Books, and other articles, of which a List is annexed has been put on Board, and are to be considered as under your charge during the Voyage. Such of the Books as are not of an educational character, are intended to be lent out to those Emigrants who may desire to read them, and will engage to take care of and return them.
7. You will keep a List of the parties to whom the Books are lent, and see that they are duly returned to you in a reasonable time, and that care be taken of what has thus been provided for the amusement and instruction of all.
8. At the conclusion of the Voyage you will deliver up all the Books &c to the Surgeon Superintendent, in order that he may distribute them to the most deserving of the Emigrants.
9. In conclusion, I am to state, that in addition to your free passage, the Commissioners will recommend you to the Local Government for a gratuity of £15, provided you discharge the duties of your Office to the satisfaction of the Colonial Authorities.

Source: Florence Chuk, The Somerset Years (Ballarat, 1987) contained in Administering emigration: Thomas Elliot and government-assisted emigration from Britain to Australia 1831-1855, Margaret Ray, Durham University Thesis 2001.

Appendix 11

Recorded Mull Clearances

Year	Landowner	Place and notes	Families Evicted
1785	Duke of Argyll	Usiken: emigrants to America	n/a
1789	Duke of Argyll	Ardnacross	n/a
1789	Allan MacLaine	Ledirkle, Garmony, Scallastle	25
1800	Allan MacLaine	Ledirkle, Garmony, Scallastle	11
1801	Ronald MacDonald	Ulva: tenants helped to emigrate	n/a
1804-8	Murdoch MacLean	Ardmeanach: tenants emigrate at own cost	n/a
1804	Charles MacQuarie	Glenforsa	n/a
1814	Duke of Argyll	Caliach	15
1814	Duke of Argyll	Mornish & Arin	11
1814	Duke of Argyll	Inivea	4
1823	J Gregorson/M MacLean	Scallastle: cottars removed	n/a
1824	Donald MacLean	Carsaig: houses demolished	n/a
1824	Donald MacLean	Kinloch: houses demolished	n/a
1829	Hugh MacCaskill	Ensay: evictions	n/a
1830	Hugh MacCaskill	Sunipol & Arin	n/a
1832	Hugh MacCaskill	Inivea	6
1832	MacLean of Coll	Quinish	5
c.1835	MacLean of Coll	Achnadrish	24
c.1835	MacLean of Coll	Ledmore	6
c.1835	MacLean of Coll	Teanga	8
c.1835	MacLean of Coll	Ardhu	6
-	Marquis of Northampton	Ensay, Kilmory, Langamull	12
-	Marquis of Northampton	Torloisk, Ballygowan, Fanmore, Kilbrennan, Kilninian, Tostary, Reudle	65
1840-50	Lord Strathallan	Killicronan, Achronich, Acarn, Killimore, Oskamull	43
1843	Hugh MacCaskill	Calgary	30-40
c.1845	Dr. MacLean	Ardhu	6
1846	Mrs. Shaw	Ardvergnish	n/a
1846-7	Murdoch MacLean	Ardmeanach: tenants emigrate at own cost	n/a

1847-51	Francis Clark	Ulva	75
1847-54	Duke of Argyll	Ross of Mull: including Shiaba, Saorphin, Kilvickeun, Knocknafennaig, Ardachy, Ardalanish, Tireregan, Knockvologan	70
1849	James Forsyth	Sorne, Penalbanach, Leiphinn, Baliachrach	44
1850's	Mr. MacArthur	Ardmanach	n/a
1850's	Andrew Mitchell	Rossal & Kinloch	15
1851	Murdoch MacLean	Ardmeanach: tenants emigrate at own cost	n/a
1856-60	Dr. MacNab	Penmore	15
1857	James Forsyth	Dervaig: tenant grazing rights removed	n/a
1858	James Forsyth	Antuim, Coriachen	4
1858	James Forsyth	Drimnacroish	4
1859	Mr. Steel	Ardmore & Rairaig	20
1862	Capt. George MacKay	Treshnish & Haunn	7
1864	Francis Clark	Gometra	17
1867	Capt. George MacKay	Crackaig & Glac Gugairidh	7

NB 1.   n/a meaning either not applicable or not available.

NB 2.   The population of Mull fell from 10,600 in 1821 to 5,229 in 1881, mainly due to the clearances. The population at the time of publication is approximately 3,000.

Source: The Mull Museum, Tobermory, Isle of Mull.

Selected Bibliography

Archives

A&BC, *Argyllshire Road Act 1843.*

A&BC, FH 65, *Rolls of the poor, parish of Kilfinichen & Kilvickeon, 1845, 1846, 1847.*

A&BC, FH 182, *Rental of the Duke of Argyll's Estates in Mull, 1744.*

A&BC, FH 213A, *Expenses of passage money, etc. to Australia... per Dunoon Castle.*

A&BC, FH 224, *List of cottars, quoad sacra Parish of Iona receiving aid from Relief Fund.*

A&BC, FH 274, *List, tenants & cottars warned on His Grace's estates Tiree & Mull 1852.*

A&BC, FH 276, *List, names of people wishing to emigrate to Upper Canada,.... 1847.*

A&BC, FH 277, *List of arrears due from the Duke of Argyll's Estates in Mull 1840.*

A&BC, FH 344, *Report, Improvements upon farms, His Grace's Estate, Mull 1802-1804.*

A&BC, FH 357, *Petitions of Crofters in the Ross of Mull for meal 1847.*

British Census, 1841, *Quoad Sacra Parish of Iona.*

British Census, 1851, *Parish Kilfinichen and Kilvickeon.*

British Census, 1871, *Parish Kilfinichen and Kilvickeon.*

Census of the Argyll Estates 1779.

NSA, Vol. vii (Edinburgh 1845), Parish of Kilfinichen and Kilviceuen, by Rev. Donald Campbell.

NLS, *Report on The Islands of Mull, Ulva, Iona, Tiree and Coll, and on Part of the Parish of Morvern, by A Deputation of the Glasgow Section of The Highland Relief Board, October, 1849.*

NLS, *Eleventh Report by the Glasgow Section of the Central Board on the Fund for Relief of Destitution in the Highlands of Scotland 30th June, 1849.*

NLS, *Slaters Directory of Scotland*, 1852.

NRS, Highland & Island Emigration Society files, Edinburgh.

NRS, *Division of Commonties Act 1695.*

NRS, HD. 7/9, Graham, R, *Report on the Highland Destitution of the Year 1837.*

NRS, HD4_6, Promissory Note Book.

NRS, *Jamieson's Scottish Dictionary*, 1880, Paisley, Vol III.

NRS, Meal Distribution Records, New Register House, Edinburgh.

NRS, Road Tax files, Edinburgh.

NRS, Sheriff Court Records, Tobermory Summons of Removal, Edinburgh.

NRS, Old Parish Registers.

OSA, Parish of Marnoch, County of Banff, 1791

OSA, Number xii (1791), Parish of Kilfinichen & Kilviceuen, by Rev. Dugald Campbell.

RAHS, Vol 49, November 1963, Part 3.

RAHS, Vol 69, June 1983.

Report to the Board of Supervision on the Western Highlands, by Sir John McNeill on the Western Highlands and Islands.

Report of the Highland Emigration Society, from its Formation in April 1852 - 1853.

Books, Articles and Theses

Anon, *The Story of St. Ernan's Church, Creich, Isle of Mull, Centenary 1899-1999.*

Argyll, Duke of, 1887, *Scotland As It Was and As It Is*, 2nd edn.

Auchindrain Museum, *Auchindrain A Historical and Traditional Farming Community.*

Balfour, R A C S, 1973, *Emigration from the Highlands and Western Isles of Scotland to Australia during the Nineteenth Century*, University of Edinburgh Thesis.

Black, G F, 2004, *The Surnames of Scotland.*

Burt, E, 1998, *Burt's Letters from the North of Scotland.*

Cameron, J S, 2013, *Stewart: A History of the Ross of Mull.*

Campbell, Alastair of Airds, 2002, *A History of Clan Campbells*, Vol 1.

Campbell, Alastair of Airds, 2002, *A History of Clan Campbell*, Vol 3.

Cannon, M, 1971, *Who's Master? Who's Man?.*

Charlwood, D, 1981, *The Long Farewell: Settlers Under Sail.*

Clarke, W B, 1989, *H.M.S. Hercules Scottish Emigrant Ship 1853.*

Cregeen, E R, 1998, *Argyll Estate Instructions Mull, Morvern and Tiree 1771-1805.*

Cregeen, E R, 1963, *Inhabitants of the Argyll Estate 1779.*

Cullen, K J, 2010, *Famine in Scotland: The 'Ill Years' of the 1690s.*

Currie, J, 2001, *Mull The Island and its People.*

Davies, N, 2000, *The Isles A History.*

Devine, T M, 1994, *Clanship to Crofters' War.*

Devine, T M, 1994, *Scottish Elites.*

Devine, T M, 2004, *The Great Highland Famine.*

Donnachie, I, and Hewitt, G, 2003, *Dictionary of Scottish History.*

Douglas, M, 2003 *Lost Townships, Silent Voices.*

Faithfull, J, 1994, *The Ross of Mull Granite Quarries*, 2nd edn.

Fenton, A, 1978, *The Island Blackhouse and a Guide to the Blackhouse No. 42 Arnol.*

Garnett, T, 1911, *Observations on a Tour Through the Higlands and Part of the Western Isles of Scotland*, 2 volumes.

Gilchrist, A, and Powell, G, 1998, *John Dunmore Lang Australia's Pioneer Republican.*

Grant, I F, 2003, *Highland Folk Ways.*

Grant, N, 1987, *Scottish Clans and Tartans.*

Harrington, P, 1991, *Culloden 1746 the Highland Clans' Last Charge.*

Hume Brown, P, 1995, *Scotland A Concise History.*

Johnson, S, and Boswel, J, 1984, *A Journey to the Western Islands of Scotland and the Journal of a Tour to the Hebrides.*

Jonas, L, and Milner, P, 2002, *A Genealogist's Guide to Discovering Your Scottish Ancestors.*

Keay, J & J, 1994, *Encyclopaedia of Scotland.*

Lang, Rev. J D, 1978, *The Fatal Mistake.*

Learmonth, N F, 1960, *The Story of a Port, Portland Victoria.*

Loder, J De Vere, 1935, *Colonsay and Oronsay in the Isles of Argyll.*

Lynch, M, 2001, *Oxford Companion to Scottish History.*

MacArthur, E M, 2002, *Iona the Living Memory of a Crofting Community,* 2nd edn.

MacCormick, J, 1923, *The Island of Mull its History, Scenes and Legends.*

Mackenzie, A, 1914, *The History of the Highland Clearances,* 2nd edn.

Maclean, C, 1997, *The Isle of Mull Placenames, Meanings and Stories.*

Maclean-Bristol, N, 1998, *Inhabitants of the Inner Isles Morvern and Arnamurchan 1716.*

MacLeod, J L, 2000, *The Second Disruption, The Free Church in Victorian Scotland and the Origins of the Free Presbyterian Church.*

Macmillan, D S, 1967, *Scotland and Australia, 1788-1850: emigration, commerce and investment.*

MacPhee, E D, 1972, *The Mythology, Traditions & History of MacDhubhsith-MacDuffie Clan,* vol 1.

Madwick, R B, 1969, *Immigration into Eastern Australia 1788-1851,* 2nd edn.

Martin, M, 1976, *A Description of the Western Islands of Scotland,* 2nd edn 1716.

McDonald, R A, 2002, *The Kingdom of the Isles, Scotland's Western Seaboard c.1100 - c.1336.*

McGeachy, R A A, 2005, *Argyll 1750-1850.*

McIan, R R, 1983, *The Clans of the Scottish Highlands.*

Pennant, T, 1998, *A Tour in Scotland and Voyage to the Hebrides 1772.*

Perrott, D, 2001, *The Western Islands Handbook.*

Prebble, J, 1963, *The Highland Clearances.*

Ray, M, 2001, *Administering emigration: Thomas Elliot and government-assisted emigration from Britain to Australia 1831-1855*, Durham University Thesis.

Report of the Highland Emigration Society, from its formation in 1852, until April 1853.

Riddell, C, 1996, *The History of 'Tireragan' Township, Ross of Mull. A Study in Local History.*

Richards, E, 1982, *A History of the Highland Clearances.*

Ritchie, G, and Harman, M, 1996, *Argyll and the Western Isles.*

Ross of Mull Historical Centre, 2004, *Discover the Ross.*

Rothney, S J, 2011, *The Presbyterian response to the famine years 1845-1855 within Ireland and in the Highlands of Scotland*, University of Glasgow Thesis.

Sadler, J, 1996, *Scottish Battles.*

Skene, W F, 1886, *Celtic Scotland,* 2nd edn, vol. III.

Smout, T C, 1969, *A History of the Scottish People 1560-1830.*

Stewart, J, 1974, *The Camerons A History of Clan Cameron.*

Sutherland, R, 1877, *The History of the Presbyterian Church of Victoria.*

Walker, J, and McKay, M M, 1980, *The Rev. Dr. John Walker's Report on the Hebrides of 1764 and 1771,* Edinburgh, J. Donald.

Watson, D, 1984, *Caledonia Australis.*

Whittaker, J, 2004, *Mull Monuments and History.*

Willis, D, 2001, *Crofting.*

Index